MINZO
PASS

Pass Your Washington, DC Life Insurance Exam

Your Complete District of Columbia Life Insurance Pre-Licensing Guide with Four Simulated Exams, Study Guide and State Law Supplement, Test Taking Strategies, Plus More

1st Edition

Dr. Beko Saye Mantein

Pass Your Washington DC Life Insurance Exam:

Your Complete District of Columbia Life Insurance Pre-Licensing Guide with Four Simulated Exams, Study Guide and State Law Supplement, Test Taking Strategies, Plus More

First Edition

Published by: Minzo Pass
1420 N St NW, Ste 102
Washington, DC 20005
Email: MinzoPass@MinzoPass.Com
Website: www.MinzoPass.com

ISBN: 979-8-9902168-0-8

Table of Contents

DEDICATION

I dedicate this book to my late grandmother, Yah Wonlea Mantein, affectionately referred to as Ma Gohmah, for her unending love and helping to mold me into the man I am. Although God took you away from me before I could give you the life you deserved, I promise to continue to make you proud.

Helpful Resources

1. Email us at MinzoPass@MinzoPass.com

2. Subscribe to our email list

3. Join our private Facebook group
   https://www.facebook.com/groups/1513896509443066/

4. Visit our website www.MinzoPass.com

5. Our Instagram https://www.instagram.com/minzopass/

6. Become an affiliate and earn up to $3,000 every month
   https://www.minzopass.com/affiliate_users/sign_up

7. Listen to our Pass Your Life and Health Insurance Exam Podcast
   https://minzopass.podbean.com/

8. Our Youtube Channel https://www.youtube.com/@minzopass3325

9. Our TikTok Page https://www.tiktok.com/@minzopass_lifeinsurance

10. Washington DC Life Insurance Exam Content Outline
    https://tinyurl.com/DCExamOutline

Thank You for Making a Difference

Imagine a country that experienced 14 years of brutal civil war where an estimated 250,000 people were killed. The healthcare and educational systems and infrastructure are almost nonexistent. "85% of the youth (age 15 -35) are unemployed"[1], 93% live on US $5.50 a day[2], and 44% live on US $1.90 a day[3].

Due to the massive youth unemployment, most young people who graduate college cannot find any gainful employment. Sadly, this leads some of these young people to resort to crime or prostitution.

Dear reader, this is the disheartening story of my beloved homeland, Liberia, on the West Coast of Africa. I agonized over the plight of my fellow Liberian youth for years and decided to help in my little way. Hence, in 2021, I launched Minzo, an organization I established to provide in-demand job training skills to Liberian youths in their 20s and 30s. I fund this organization entirely, and I have only been able to help a handful of Liberian youths thus far. However, I aim to provide in-demand job training skills like website development, insurance, database, cloud computing, video and audio editing, and mobile app development, to name a few—to 150,000 Liberian Youths and provide subsequent employment for them in the next ten years. After training, I will hire them or find them remote jobs overseas.

From my experience growing up in West Africa, every good paying job—meaning a job that pays at least USD 500 monthly—has a direct economic impact in lifting ten people out of abject poverty. For example, a person who is earning a decent wage can afford to send his children to school, take care of his parents and siblings, and even help extended relatives from his village.

One income earner can provide a direct financial lifeline to at least ten people.

With this in mind, if we could provide good-paying jobs to 150,000 Liberian youths, we would have lifted at least 1.5 million Liberians out of crushing poverty.

You come in here because I cannot achieve this goal alone. Part of the proceeds from this book and all of our insurance pre-licensing courses and products will go towards making this goal a reality. However, I would highly appreciate it if you could please go further and donate to this worthy cause. Any amount, even as low as $10, will go a long way in helping to lift Liberian

1

2 https://www.macrotrends.net/countries/LBR/liberia/poverty-rate

3 https://knoema.com/atlas/Liberia/Poverty-rate-at-dollar19-a-day

youths out of poverty. You can donate at https://linktr.ee/minzoliberia, www.MinzoLiberia.com, Paypal at info@MinzoAcademy.com, or CashApp at $MinzoCash.

Some people close to me have ridiculed this idea. They have flat-out told me that it is impossible and that I should limit my help to just a few dozen individuals instead of trying to help that many people. One person, a loved one, told me on October 4, 2022, that I was "delusional" for attempting to waste my time trying to do something this big. This person went further, stating, "If this was possible, don't you think the Liberian Government or another NGO would have done it by now? You are wasting your time on something destined to fail, but if you want to waste your life, go ahead." Her statement hit me like a hundred-pound brick because part of me felt that this person was right, and maybe I was just wasting my time and that this whole project would fail. After a few days of contemplating whether this entire project was worth my sacrifice, I started to think about the impact it had already had on the few people enrolled.

For example, 26-year-old Ezekiel Sesay dropped out of college after his father passed away because his mother could not afford his tuition.

Thanks to Minzo, he re-enrolled in college full-time and is working part-time. Ezekiel could not only afford his tuition, but he now helps his siblings and mother financially.

Ezekiel Sesay,

another example, was in February 2022, when 625 young Liberians applied for the Minzo Training Program. Sadly, I could only afford to accept 20 of them into the program due to insufficient funds. In addition to free training, they receive a weekly stipend and free food. I want to extend this to at least 150,000 young people by 2034. However, I cannot do it alone. For this reason, I am asking you to please donate in addition to purchasing this training manual. Every dollar counts. Even a donation of as little as $10 helps. Any amount you can contribute will go a long way in helping to lift young people out of poverty in Liberia. You can donate at https://linktr.ee/minzoliberia, www.MinzoLiberia.com, Paypal at info@MinzoAcademy.com, or CashApp at $MinzoCash.

Below are pictures of some of the young people at our office

Words of Encouragement

Congratulations on taking the first step to obtain your life insurance license. From my experience, people tend to thumb their noses at insurance agents. They may wrongly assume that insurance agents don't make enough money or that being an insurance agent is somehow something only people who have no options do.

I remember about a decade ago, when I started in the insurance industry, friends and family would look down on me. "Beko, but you are a pharmacist, for Heaven's sake. Why are you doing this? This is beneath you. This is only for people who have no options, not you." Some people would tell me that what I was doing was a scam.

In the coming months and years, the people who mean the most to you—like your romantic partner, siblings, parents, and close friends—will discourage you from pursuing this path. They will tell you the same things they told me and countless others before you. Things like *it's a waste of time, a scam, beneath you,* etc. I must admit that if you choose to become an employee, the compensation is not that great. It is only slightly higher than the national average income. For example, the average annual salary for life insurance agents in Washington, DC, is $59,000. However, if you choose to own a financial agency instead of being an employee, you can turn your yearly income into your monthly income. You, my friend, have the potential to create generational wealth beyond your wildest dreams. For more information on how to create your financial agency, you can contact us at MINZOPASS@MINZOPASS.COM.

Although you will obtain a life insurance license, your license will enable you to sell more than just life insurance. With just a life insurance license, you will be able to help clients with:

- 401(k)s, IRAs, and other retirement accounts rollover
- College Savings Plans
- Fixed Index Annuities
- Wills and Trusts
- Funeral Concierge Plans
- Debt Consolidation Services
- Back Tax Support Referrals
- Executive Bonus Plans
- Personal Financial Analysis
- Life Insurance
- Creating Their Own Family Bank
- Higher Education Guidance Referrals

As you can see, contrary to what your friends and family may think, you are not just an insurance agent—You are a full-fledged financial professional. You would agree that it would be unfair to call a mechanic an 'oil changer.' Can a mechanic change your vehicle's engine oil? Absolutely. However, a mechanic can do more than just change your engine oil. He can repair your engine and brakes and even do body work. Therefore, it'd be unfair and inaccurate to limit a mechanic to being just an "oil changer."

The same applies to being reduced to an "insurance agent" because your life insurance license allows you to do more than "just sell life insurance." Never let anyone, including your clients or loved ones, reduce you to *just being a life insurance agent* because you are more than that—-YOU ARE A LICENSED FINANCIAL PROFESSIONAL.

This license you are about to obtain is more valuable than a pharmacist, nursing, or medical doctor license. It is not an exaggeration. With this license, you *could* earn hundreds of thousands or millions of dollars annually if you decide to own your financial agency. So, please do yourself a favor and not allow others to talk you out of this great opportunity. Again, if you want to learn how to start your nationwide financial agency that will enable you to live the WFA (work from anywhere) lifestyle, please contact us at minzopass@minzopass.com.

Getting into the financial industry was by far one of the best financial decisions of my life. I hope that you can say the same thing soon.

Wishing you the best,

Dr. Beko Saye Mantein
Lead Instructor, Minzo Pass

Advantages of Our Training

Welcome to Minzo Pass' District of Columbia (DC) Life Insurance Exam Pre-licensing Training Manual. We are thrilled you selected our book to help you pass your exam. Trust us, you made the right decision. At Minzo Pass, we take pride in educating people and changing lives. We hope we can help transform your life by helping you pass your District of Columbia Life Insurance Exam.

Although this textbook alone is a good resource for preparing for your District of Columbia Life Insurance Exam, for the best result, we recommend that you supplement it with our self-study online course for The District of Columbia. You can purchase that course at www.MinzoPass.Com or www.PassYourLifeAndHealthInsuranceExam.com.

Many Life Insurance Exam Prep courses are on the market, so you may be wondering what makes us better than the rest. Below are the unique advantages of using Minzo Pass:

1. **We Used DC's Life Insurance Exam Content Outline to Create Our Course**
   Our course content is limited to only the content most likely to be tested on your exam. We organized our course according to the District of Columbia's exam outline. Please review the District of Columbia Life Insurance Exam Outline at **https://tinyurl.com/DCLifeExamOutline**. Unfortunately, students using other exam prep providers study general insurance topics that will not appear on their exams. Why, you may ask? Because they create one general study material for all 50 states. Not Minzo Pass because our practice questions and course content are only developed using your state's exam outline. There is no need to study material that will not appear on your exam.

2. **Innovative T80 S20 Approach to Exam Preparation**
   The exam preparation model used by all the big-named course providers relies on an outdated approach to studying for public exams. What is the approach, you may ask? Well, they give you a book that is a few hundred pages long or an online course material to study. Then, while studying, they sprinkle a few practice questions in between and a final exam at the end to test your knowledge. Most students spend approximately 80% of their study time ***reading*** and only 20% of that time ***testing*** themselves.

   Here at Minzo Pass, we flipped that upside down. In our course, 80% of your study time will be spent actively testing your knowledge, and you will spend 20% studying *only* the materials you just can't understand.

   This approach works because research has proven that students who spend more time ***actively*** studying perform better, retain the information for a more extended period, and take less time to remember what they studied than students who ***passively*** study. Reading is ***passive,*** and testing yourself is ***active.***

3. **Active Recall Studying**
   What is an active recall? Active recall means ***actively*** stimulating your memory to retrieve a piece of information. An example of active recall would be when you try to remember the answer to a question on a flashcard without looking at any answer choices. Active recall stimulates your brain to retrieve the information, and you are more likely to remember it the next time you encounter it.

   A significant portion of this course requires you to actively recall information. Active recall will significantly increase your chance of passing your exam. Why? When you actively recall the exam content and not rely on just *recognition,* you are more likely to get the exam questions right, no matter how tricky.

   Below are helpful resources to learn more about the science behind active recall
   i. Science Magazine
      1. THE CRITICAL IMPORTANCE OF RETRIEVAL FOR LEARNING, vol 319 No. 5865, pp. 966-968
      2. https://www.science.org/doi/full/10.1126/science.1152408
   ii. Brainscape.com
      1. https://www.brainscape.com/academy/active-recall-definition-studying/
   iii. Wikepedia
      1. https://en.wikipedia.org/wiki/Testing_effect
   iv. Youtube
      1. How my friend ranked 1st at Medical School: The Active Recall Framework
         a. Creator: Ali Abdaal
         b. https://www.youtube.com/watch?v=fDbxPVn02VU

4. **Course Created By An Experienced Life and Health Insurance Expert**
   This course was created by Dr. Beko Mantein, a licensed Life and Health Insurance professional in many states with almost two decades of insurance industry experience. He is also the host of the *Pass Your Life and Health Insurance Exam Podcast*, the most popular free life insurance prelicensing podcast in the country.

5. **Private Facebook Study Group**
   You can join our student community, join study groups, and get your questions answered. We want you to know that you are not alone on this journey. We are here for you every step of the way.

6. **YouTube**

You can also watch our YouTube videos to help with your studies.

7. **Podcast**
   For those who prefer to learn while on the go, we have you covered. You can listen to our exam prep podcast while exercising, cooking, working, driving, or doing daily activities.

8. **Post-Exam Help**
   Unlike our competitors, we will still help you after you pass your exam. Whether you need help applying for your license, looking for your first insurance job, or starting your own financial services agency (yes, you are not just an insurance agent——---you are a financial professional), we will help you along this journey in your new career.

9. **One-on-One Tutorial**
   One-on-one tutoring is available for an extra fee. 98% of our one-on-one training students pass their exam. Please inform us if you are available and one of our experienced life insurance instructors will tutor you.

DC Life Insurance Producer License Requirements

Description	Requirement	Comment
Pre-licensing required?	No.	This means you are not required to take any exam prep course before being allowed to sit for your exam.
How to register for your exam?	Online or by phone	Register online at https://home.pearsonvue.com/dc/insurance or call (800) 274-0610.
Exam fee	$75.00	This is a non-refundable fee, even if you do not show up to take your exam.
Can you take both your life and health insurance exams on the same day?	Yes,	You'll just have to take one exam first, then go back to the test center to take the other one.
Does DC offer the Life and Health Combo Exam?	No	DC administers the Life exam alone and the Health Insurance Exam separately. There is no combination exam.
Maximum exam retakes allowed	Unlimited	You can take the exam as often as you like until you pass. Remember that you must pay the $75 exam fee each time you take the exam.
Total number of exam questions	95	15 of the 95 questions are pretest questions and will not affect your exam score.
Passing score	70%	Means you can get 24 questions wrong and still pass your exam.
Duration of the exam	2 hours.	This equates to approximately 1 minute 20 seconds per question.
When should you arrive at the testing center?	At least 30 minutes before your exam.	Failure to do so may result in your exam being delayed or rescheduled.
Identification required to take the exam	2 valid forms of government-issued ID	One of the IDs must be a photo ID with your signature (Ex, driver's license, passport, green card, military ID, etc.).
How will you be	Either PASS or	At the end of your exam, you will receive a

graded?	FAIL	printed piece of paper stating whether or not you passed. If you pass, it will have instructions on how to apply for your license.
After You Pass your exam, what should you do?	Fingerprints background check, and apply for your license	Contact Sheila Johnson-Parker, the licensing specialist manager, at sheila.parker@dc.gov to schedule your fingerprint appointment. You can also contact her at Insurance Bureau District of Columbia Department of Insurance, Securities and Banking 1050 First Street, NE, Suite 801 Washington, DC 20002 P: (202) 442-7795 Fingerprints and background checks are performed by the DC Metropolitan Police Department Apply for your license at www.nipr.com or www.sircon.com
License Application Fee	$100	
What is the average processing time for the license application?	2 weeks	This is the average length of time it takes to process life insurance producer license applications after ALL requirements are received by The DC Department Of Insurance
After you receive your license, what should you do?	Maintain it	Maintain your license by completing the required 24 hours of continuing education (CE) training and renewing your license every 2 years.
Is the general exam combined with the State Law Exam?	No	The state law exam is administered as a separate 35-question exam, and the general portion is a separate 60-question exam. A test taker is required to pass both exams in order to be eligible to apply for a license.

Helpful Study Tips

Below are valuable tips to increase your chance of passing your exam. One hundred percent (100%) of our former students who followed ALL these tips passed their exam on their first attempt.

1. **Schedule your exam before you start studying**

   a. From our experience, procrastination is one of the major problems most students face. To avoid this problem, we recommend scheduling your exam by 21 days in advance, preferably within seven days. Scheduling your exam before you begin studying helps to motivate you to start studying immediately and consistently to be prepared for your exam before you take it. Most people would not want their hard-earned money wasted, so they would be incentivized not to delay their studies. In addition to scheduling your exam before you start studying, we recommend scheduling your exam 21 days in advance. Sometimes, when students schedule their exam longer than 21 days in advance, life happens—things come up that require them to abandon their studies or significantly delay their studies. Scheduling your exam before you start studying can help you prepare for and take it. It will more likely help you avoid significant delays due to unexpected events. If you have the available time to study, taking your exam within one week is preferred because you decrease the chance of forgetting the material you learned and also avoid unexpected events delaying you.

2. **Commit to a fixed study schedule**

   a. A fixed study schedule helps you stay organized, prevents distractions, and helps keep you on track to be prepared to take your exam as scheduled. Block out specific times on your calendar to study—for example, Monday, Wednesday, and Friday, 6 PM - 9 PM. The average study time for the Life Insurance Exam is 20 hours. With this in mind, you can predict how long it'll take you to prepare for your exam. For example, if you plan to study for five hours on Saturdays and Sundays, that's ten hours a week. It will take you two weeks to prepare for your exam. Contrast that with another student who studies for four hours on Monday, Tuesday, Wednesday, Thursday, and Friday. That student will need only five days to prepare for their exam.

   b. A great planning tool is a calendar, like a Google Calendar if you have a Gmail account. You could also use the calendar app on your smartphone to block out study time and send you automatic text message reminders.

3. **Get an accountability partner**

    a. Join our Facebook group and find an accountability partner. An accountability partner could be a fellow student to whom you will be accountable for staying on track with your studies. Think of an accountability partner as a workout buddy.

4. **Follow our active study strategy.**

    a. Trust us, it's a much more challenging method than passive studying, but it works. Unlike traditional exam prep providers, you will spend 80% of your time doing practice questions after practice questions. No more than 20% of your time should be spent *passively* studying.

5. **Study in a quiet environment (e.g., a library, your room, etc.)**

    a. Studying in a quiet environment maximizes your studying time because your brain can focus 100% on the material without any distractions. To increase your concentration even more, we recommend playing baroque classical music at a moderate volume while you study. Research has proven that baroque classical music helps increase concentration and memorization.

6. **Score at least 90% on three simulated exams**

    a. We have provided you with simulated exams to simulate the types of questions most likely to appear on your exam. Please take as many of them as possible.

7. **Take your state exam within 72 hours of scoring 90% on your simulated exams.**

    a. Take your exam as soon as possible while the material is still fresh in your memory. By doing this, you significantly increase your chance of passing the exam.

8. **Get at least seven hours of sleep the day before your exam**

    a. Unfortunately, depriving your body of much-needed rest could cause you to fail. We recommend at least seven hours of sleep to be fully alert and retrieve most of the information you studied. We have heard many stories from students about "brain freeze" during exams because they only got 2 or 3 hours of sleep the night before. Although these students studied the material very well, unfortunately, they failed their exams due to lack of sleep.

9. **Time yourself when you take the simulated exams**

    a. Time management is very important during the state licensing exam. Use your simulated exams to practice your time management skills because you will have about one minute and 20 seconds per question. Please pace yourself. Only spend up to 1-minute on any question. If, by the 1-minute mark, you still don't know the answer, guess the answer and mark that question for review. If you have time, you will be allowed to review the questions you marked for review at the end of your exam.

10. **During your state exam, do not change your answers**

    a. More often than not, your first answer is correct. Please refrain from changing your answers unless you are confident that the initial answer you selected is wrong. Many students fail because they change from correct to incorrect answers. Please do not make the same mistake. Trust us, your first answer is usually correct.

Study Roadmap

Please take each simulated exam *FIRST* before studying the answers. We know this is counterintuitive because we have been trained throughout our lives to study first before testing. However, we *intentionally* flipped that concept upside down. We want you to please follow this strategy: test–study explanations—read the national study guide and state law supplement—test again. Trust us, this is how you'll increase your retention and reduce your study time—IT WORKS.

We divided this course into four simulated exams. Please study them in order. Remember, the goal is not to become an expert. The goal is JUST to pass your exam. Please review and study the result of each simulated exam at least once after taking it before proceeding to the next simulated exam.

A cautionary note: The goal of this training manual is **not** to make you a life insurance expert. We created this course just to help you pass your exam. You will learn a thousand percent more about life insurance from your regular company training than you would ever learn from studying any insurance exam prep course or book. Our course is *intentionally* structured to provide the bare minimum information you need to pass your exam. If it wouldn't help you pass your exam, it is not in this book.

Some students who study just to pass their exam pass after three days of study. Contrast that with students who study for one or two months because they want to master every sentence before moving on. Which student would you like to be? The choice is yours.

Good luck with your exam,
Dr. Beko Saye Mantein

District of Columbia Simulated Exam 1 Questions

ID: MINZOPASSEMADC361C1A1040222Q1DC

1. Roland owns a whole life insurance policy, what should he expect when his policy endows?

A. The death benefit is reduced by the cash value, and the balance is paid to the policy owner
B. Whole life policies do not have cash value
C. The policyowner receives the face amount of the policy
D. The insurer gets to keep the cash value

ID: MINZOPASSEMADC3Q65C1A2040222Q3DC

2. A producer educates a client on the concept of limited-pay life insurance. Which of the following statements is **NOT** true?

A. Limited-pay life insurance has a higher premium
B. The premium payments will be lower
C. Limited-pay life is a type of whole life policy
D. The policy will be fully paid up before age 100

ID: MINZOPASSBMXCC3Q25C1B04022022Q1DC

3. Kebbeh is 40 years old. She is looking for a life insurance policy that will allow her to be flexible and change her coverage as her requirements do. What policy would you recommend to her?

A. Variable life
B. Universal Life
C. Variable Universal life
D. Modified Endowment Contract

ID: MINZOPASSEMADC3Q67C1B2040222Q12DC

4. A __________ insurance has a guaranteed minimum death benefit. The face amount can increase or decrease based on how well the stock market performs. It also affords the policyowner the choice of sub-accounts to which cash value can be assigned and a fixed premium.

A. Equity Indexed Universal Life
B. Variable Life
C. Graded Whole Life
D. Variable Universal Life

ID: MINZOPASSBMXCC3Q27C1B04022022Q3DC
5. Which statement is true about a Variable Universal Life policy?

A. Policyowner cannot select the premium mode. However, the policyholder directs investment
B. The policy owner has control over where the investment goes and chooses the amount of the premium payment
C. ALL of the policyholder's premiums go into the insurer's general account
D. The policyowner has no control over where their premium is invested

ID: MINZOPASSESKAC4Q23C1A1041322Q27DC
6. What happens with interest-sensitive whole life insurance policies?

A. The cash value fluctuates according to interest rates
B. The policy pays guaranteed quarterly dividends
C. Guaranteed 5% interest rate
D. The policyowner bears the investment risk

ID: MINZOPASSBMC1B5061422Q2DC
7. Which life insurance policy offers a minimum guaranteed interest rate, guarantees the principal amount and its cash value performance is tied to a linked stock-market index?

A. Variable life
B. Variable Universal life
C. Indexed universal life insurance
D. Level Term insurance

ID: MINZOPASSEMADC3Q63C1C1040222Q2DC
8. A "level term" insurance means ______ remain(s) the same during the policy's tenure.

A. Cash account
B. Cost of insurance
C. Premium
D. Policy proceeds

ID: MINZOPASSESKAC4Q13C1C041122Q24DC
9. Decreasing term policy could be used in all of the following scenarios, EXCEPT

A. Coverage for outstanding business loan
B. Mortgage protection
C. To save for retirement
D. To protect a family with young kids

ID: MINZOPASSBMC1C3ID060922Q1DC
10. All the following are true about the Return of Premium Term, Except

A. It is a type of increasing term policy
B. If the insured lives out the term policy or passes away within the time frame specified, the full premium is paid in addition to the death benefit.
C. It is more expensive than a regular level term policy
D. It is cheaper than a regular level term policy

ID: MINZOPASSESEXC2Q27C2B7040422Q10DC
11. Which policy contains the LEAST expensive premium during its first year?

A. Variable life Term
B. Decreasing term
C. Increasing Term
D. Annually Renewable Term

ID: MINZOPASSESXCC3Q37C1C040522Q13DC
12. A term policy that continues its coverage even after the expiration of the initial policy period is known as what type of term policy?

A. Increasing
B. Continuable
C. Renewable
D. Decreasing

ID: MINZOPASSESXCC471C2B6040622Q16DC
13. What factor should the policy owner expect to be primarily affected when determining whether to use his original age or attained age in converting his convertible term life insurance policy to a whole life insurance policy?

A. The beneficiaries
B. The cost
C. The settlement options
D. The Nonforfeiture options

ID: MINZOPASSESXCC7Q10C1D040622Q42DC

14. Chris has been paid a $200,000 lump sum retirement bonus by his former employer and intends to buy an annuity that will pay a guaranteed income for life immediately. Which of the following annuities should Chris buy?

A. Periodic Premium
B. Single Premium
C. 403(b) Plan
D. Deferred Premium

ID: MINZOPASSJDADC5Q6C1D04032022Q5DC

15. Which one of the following statements is **NOT** accurate about a flexible premium deferred annuity?

A. Before annuitization, you can make scheduled and unscheduled principal payments anytime.
B. Annuitization is possible at any time. A delayed annuity cannot be annuitized if the principal value is subject to a surrender charge.
C. Payments to the annuitant begin within 30 days of the contract's issue.
D. Each year, a few partial surrenders are allowed without paying a surrender fee

ID: MINZOPASSESXCC7Q3C1D040622Q35DC

16. Which of the following is not an acceptable annuity choice if a person, age 49, buys an annuity to receive income for life beginning at age 60?

A. Straight Life annuity
B. Immediate annuity
C. Deferred annuity
D. Fixed annuity

ID: MINZOPASSTAXCC9Q27C1D204092022Q66DC

17. Which annuity allows the owner to contribute to an Individual Retirement Account?

A. Fixed Immediate Annuity
B. MEC
C. Period certain
D. A Deferred annuity

ID: MINZOPASSJDADC5Q10C1D04032022Q9DC
18. What is "fixed" in a fixed annuity?

A. The number of annuitants and the number of beneficiaries
B. The number of annuitants
C. The interest rate
D. The number of beneficiaries

ID: MINZOPASSJDADC5Q11C1D04032022Q10DC
19. What qualification(s) does an insurance producer need to sell variable annuities?

A. In addition to a life insurance producer license, a securities license is also required
B. At least five years of licensed insurance producer experience
C. A written petition letter from his insurer
D. An insurance license only

ID: MINZOPASSESXCC7Q1C1D040622Q33DC
20. Which of the following differentiates an indexed annuity from a fixed annuity?

A. Indexed annuity owners receive quarterly dividends
B. Fixed annuity owners must have a separate investment account
C. Owners of index-linked annuities may get awarded interest based on changes in the linked index
D. Fixed annuity owners receive credited interest linked to the fluctuations of the linked index

ID: MINZOPASSTAXCC9Q24C1D204092022Q59DC
21. The accumulation period of an annuity may continue after the

A. Benefit payments begin
B. The purchase payments cease
C. Annuity is surrendered or the annuitant dies, whichever occurs first
D. Annuitant dies, or the purchase payments cease, whichever occurs first

ID: MINZOPASSPCXC9Q38C1D304092022Q56DC

22. John recently bought a straight-life fixed immediate annuity. He is both the annuitant and the owner. His benefits will be distributed as follows

A. Pays a lump sum death benefit if John dies
B. Payment amount will depend on the S&P 500 performance, and payments will cease after a particular number of years
C. He will receive the same benefit payment amount for the annuity period
D. None of the above

ID: MINZOPASSESEXC2Q16C1D040422Q19DC

23. Princess won a $20,000,000 Jackpot and was told she would receive a monthly check each month for the next 20 years. What type of annuity product will make this possible?

A. Immediate annuity
B. Deferred interest annuity
C. Variable annuity
D. Deferred annuity

ID: MINZOPASSJDEXGEXQ12C1E104052022Q3DC

24. A life insurance policy that is designed for two people and pays a face amount upon the death of the first death is known as what?

A. Joint Life
B. Survivorship Life
C. Non-revocable Beneficiary
D. Second-to-Die

ID: MINZOPASSEMEXSEXQ2C1E2204052022Q5DC

25. When is death benefit paid in a survivorship life policy?

A. When the last insured dies
B. When the beneficiary dies
C. When the last insured dies
D. 50% of the death benefit when the first insured dies and another 50% when the second insured dies

ID: MINZOPASSEMADC3Q75C2A1040222Q2DC
26. In terms of the premium waiver rider, after a disability, a policyholder typically:

A. Reapplies for the insurance because the insurance contract must be ended before disability benefit payments begin
B. Is not required to repay the premiums during the time of disability
C. Shall reimburse the insurer for a minimum of 25% of the premiums paid during the disability period
D. Must show proof of insurability to continue the policy after the disability

ID: MINZOPASSEMADC3Q84C2A204042022Q1DC
27. What is the guaranteed insurability rider?

A. Allows one to have additional coverages in the future at specified dates without having to prove insurability
B. Allows one to have additional coverages in the future at specified dates with Proof of insurability
C. Comes standard on all permanent policies
D. Decreases an insured's premium when added to a life insurance policy

ID: MINZOPASSESEXC3Q39C2A3040522Q1DC
28. The rider that would NOT cause the Death Benefit to increase is known as what?

A. Cost of Living Rider
B. Payor Benefit Rider
C. Guaranteed Insurability Rider
D. Accidental death & dismemberment

ID: MINZOPASSJDADC14Q1C2A404052022Q1DC
29. Which of the following assertions about an accidental death and dismemberment policy for a group is correct?

A. The employer's premiums are considered part of the employee's income
B. The beneficiary is not liable to pay taxes on any benefits received
C. The premiums covered by the employer are not deductible by the employer as a business expenditure
D. Accidental Death and Dismemberment Insurance is only accessible on an individual basis, not for groups

ID: MINZOPASSESEXC3Q45C2A5040522Q1DC

30. Which rider allows the policyholder to customize the policy to provide more temporary insurance on the insured, or allows other family members to be covered by an amount of temporary insurance?

A. Accidental death and dismemberment rider
B. Term rider
C. Guaranteed insurability rider
D. Insured rider

ID: MINZOPASSEMADC3Q68C2A6040222Q1DC

31. As a producer, your client wants to know what jumps in a jumping juvenile policy. What should you tell your client?

A. The gross premium increases by a multiple of five on the child's 21st or 25th birthday
B. The net premium increases by a multiple of five on the child's 21st or 25th birthday
C. The death benefit, at age 21 or 25, jumps up to five times the face amount ONLY once
D. The face amount and the premium jump up to five times the face value once, at age 21 or 25

ID: MINZOPASSEMADC3Q71C2A7040222Q1DC

32. What advantage(s) does a long-term care rider have over a living needs rider?

A. Only pays benefits if a licensed medical provider certifies that an insured is expected to die within 24 months

B. Pays a monthly income based on a proportion of the death benefit to an insured who is unable to do any of the six activities of daily living (ADL)

C. Allows a chronically ill person who is unable to do any four of the six activities of daily living (eating, bathing, walking, toileting, etc) to receive up to 100% of the death benefit to be distributed daily or monthly for non-hospital expenses

D. Allows a chronically ill person who is unable to do two of the six (6) activities of daily living (eating, bathing, walking, toileting, etc) to receive up to 100% of the death benefit for non-hospital costs, paid out either daily or monthly.

ID: MINZOPASSEMADC3Q73C2A8040222Q1
33. When an insured person dies when an increasing term rider is still in force, the beneficiary will receive the death benefit amount plus the total premiums paid. Your client wants to know the name of this rider attached to their policy. What should you tell your client?

A. Guarantee Cash Addition Rider
B. Increasing Term Rider
C. Return of Premium Rider
D. Waiver of Premium Rider

ID: MINZOPASSBMC2A9061922Q1DC
34. All of the following are disability riders, except

A. Waiver of Premium
B. Disability Income Benefit
C. Payor Benefit
D. Accelerated Death Benefit

ID: MINZOPASSESXCC3Q54C2A2040622Q6DC
35. What provision does the cost-of-living rider make to the insured?

A. Monthly income
B. Additional death benefits
C. Decreasing premiums
D. Tax incentives

ID: MINZOPASSESEXC3Q31C2B1040422Q4DC
36. What policy provision states that the contract is the delivered policy, the application, and any riders/amendments?

A. Unilateral contract
B. Entire contract
C. Complete contract
D. Insuring Clause

ID: MINZOPASSJDADC4Q1C2B204022022Q1DC
37. Which of the following is stated in the insuring agreement of a life insurance policy?

A. Should an error be found in the original application for coverage at the time of the insured's passing, the insurance provider can decline to pay a death benefit.

B. Unless all premiums are paid in advance, the insurance company will not cover death claims in the event of suicide or other policy exclusions

C. If the beneficiary is not named in the application, the policyowner will reimburse the insurer for the proceeds of the policy

D. The insurance company must pay the policy proceeds upon presentation of valid proof of the insured's death that occurred while the policy was in effect

ID: MINNZOPASSJDEXGEXQ13C2B304052022Q1DC
38. A period of time, usually ten days or more from the Date Of Delivery of The Policy, given to an applicant to decide whether or not to accept insurance coverage from an insurance company is known as what?

A. Endowment period
B. Elimination period
C. Free look period
D. Delivery of the policy

ID: MINZOPASSESXCC3Q57C2B4040622Q1DC
39. What relevant detail is included in the Consideration Clause of a life insurance contract?

A. The offer and acceptance
B. The policyowner must complete the application and pay the initial premium
C. The absolute assignment
D. The frequency of application

ID: MINZOPASSJDADC4Q11C2B50402022Q1DC
40. In a policy, the____________enables the owner to designate a beneficiary, select a payout or settlement alternative, and borrow from the contract.

A. Incontestable Clause
B. Insuring Clause
C. Assignment Clause
D. Ownership Provision

ID: MINZOPASSJDADC4Q14C2B604022022Q3DC
41. Chris is the covered party. Brita, his spouse, is the primary beneficiary. Their three kids are the contingent beneficiaries. In a common accident, Chris and Brita are killed. Chris's insurance proceeds would be distributed to

A. Brita's estate
B. Chris's estate
C. Chris's parents
D. The children

ID: MINZOPASSJDEXGEXQ39C2B604052022Q8DC
42. What type of beneficiary designation allows the beneficiary to be changed at any time?

A. Revocable
B. Primary
C. Irrevocable
D. Contingent

ID: MINZOPASSESEXC3Q37C2B6040522Q5DC
43. Under which circumstance can an irrevocable beneficiary be changed?

A. With written permission from the beneficiary
B. The owner can change the beneficiary anytime they please
C. The beneficiary can NEVER be changed under any circumstance
D. The beneficiary cannot be changed for at least five years

ID: MINZOPASSJDADC4Q7C2B604022022Q2DC
44. Which of the following is why beneficiary "class" designations could be problematic?

A. They are meant to make it possible for people who are not identified to share the proceeds of insurance policies
B. They are ambiguous beneficiary designations that could lead to a court having to decide who will or will not receive the policy benefit
C. They indicate who can claim the proceeds of the policy
D. They make it impossible to name contingent beneficiaries.

ID: MINZOPASSESEXC3Q43C2B6040522Q6DC
45. Upon the death of Kiesha, the insured, which of the following beneficiaries named in the policy would NOT directly receive death benefits?

A. Keisha's former husband
B. Keisha's estate
C. Keisha's business partner
D. Keisha's 14-year-old daughter

ID: MINZOPASSJDADC2Q44C2B704022022Q2DC
46. Which of these premium payment modes will result in Roberto paying the least for his life insurance every year?

A. Quarterly
B. Annual
C. Monthly
D. Semi-annually

ID: MINZOPASSJDADC4Q3C2B704022022Q3DC
47. A life insurance policy's grace period is usually 31 days long and covers the following:

A. Payment of the premium after the due date is subject to a maximum penalty of 5%.
B. The application period
C. Payment of a premium after the due date without incurring a penalty or causing coverage to lapse
D. The time before getting coverage

ID: MINZOPASSJDADC4Q21C2B704022022Q8DC
48. If the policyowner forgets to pay the premium by the end of the grace period, which provision keeps the policy from lapsing as long as there is sufficient cash value

A. Grace period
B. Automatic Premium Loan
C. Assignment
D. Reinstatement

ID: MINZOPASSBMC2B7E072122Q12DC
49. Most life insurance premiums are flexible

A. True
B. False

ID: MINZOPASSJDADC4Q22C2B804022022Q1DC
50. If a life insurance policy expires due to nonpayment of premiums, it may be reinstated by doing which one of the following?

A. Only providing evidence of insurability
B. Only repaying overdue premiums
C. A & B only
D. Paying overdue premiums (plus interest), submitting proof of insurability, and submitting a new application

ID: MINZOPASSJDADC4C5C2B904022022Q1DC
51. All of the following are included in policy loan provisions, with the exception of:

A. Annual interest is charged
B. The loan's value is increased by the amount of unpaid interest
C. At the time of claim, outstanding loans will be subtracted from the face amount
D. When a loan is sought, the death benefit of a policy is automatically lowered

ID: MINZOPASSEMADC2Q56C2B10040122Q1DC
52. A ____________ account is an amount held by an insurance company to cover current or potential liabilities owed to policyholders.

A. Separate
B. General
C. Premium
D. Reserve

ID: MINZOPASSJDADC4Q10C2B1104022022Q1DC
53. Which of the following options is not available as a dividend option?

A. Refund in cash
B. Paid-up option
C. Lifetime income
D. Reduce premiums due

ID: MINZOPASSJDADC4Q2C2B1204022022Q1DC
54. What does it mean when a life insurance policy is declared incontestable?

A. After two years, the insurer cannot deny a claim based on false information in the primary insurance application
B. The policyowner cannot sue the insurer for mistakes made by the producer during the policy's sale after two years
C. The insurance will only pay for suicide after two years if the insured was suffering from mental illness at the time of death
D. Following two years, the insurer will not contest who is the primary or contingent beneficiary

ID: MINZOPASSJDEXGEXQ11C2B1304052022Q1DC
55. Using one's life insurance policy as collateral for a loan is known as what?

A. Absolute assignment
B. A unilateral agreement
C. A collateral assignment
D. Aleatory contract

ID: MINZOPASSESXCC3Q50C2B14040522Q1DC
56. What does the insurer do to resolve a case where the insured takes his own life during the policy's contestability period?

A. Pays twice the face amount under the double indemnity clause
B. Pays only 50% of the death benefit
C. Denies claims under the Suicide Clause of the policy
D. Pays only 25% of the death benefit

ID: MINZOPASSESXCC3Q53C2B15040622Q1DC
57. Serina misstates her age on her life insurance application. How is the Misstatement of Age Provision in life insurance handled?

A. Requires that a replacement policy should be applied for if a misstatement of age is found on the current policy
B. The Insurer may void the contract if a misstatement of age is discovered
C. The Misstatement of Age provision is valid only during the contestability period
D. Coverage will be adjusted to reflect the insured's *true* age if an incorrect age is discovered

ID: MINZOPASSEMKAC6Q7C2B1604122022Q1DC
58. Jametta's spouse was the primary beneficiary of her $200,000 life insurance policy. He received payments of approximately $600 every month while he was alive. When he died, their two kids received a single large payment of $100,000 each. What settlement option was in effect on Jametta's policy?

A. Reduced Paid-up
B. Interest-only
C. Extended Term
D. None of the above

ID: MINZOPASSEMADC3Q77C2B1704042022Q1DC
59. What happens to amounts paid out under the accelerated death benefit rider?

A. Subtracted from the contract's death benefit before paying it out to the beneficiary
B. Same as accidental death and dismemberment(AD&D)
C. Must be repaid
D. Must be taxed on both the federal and state levels

ID: MINZOPASSESEXC3Q36C2C040522Q2DC
60. The clause that denies death benefit if death was caused by war is the _________.

A. Result or war clause
B. Aviation clause
C. Hazardous occupation clause
D. Exclusions clause

ID: MINZOPASSBMC2C207262022Q8DC

61. If an insured dies while flying a plane as a pilot or working as a crew member on a flight, the insurer will

A. Pay claims only after the contestability period
B. Pay claims
C. Not pay claims
D. Pay claims only if the policy had a double indemnity rider

ID: MINZOPASSBMC2C307262022Q7DC

62. If an insured dies due to a hazardous occupation or hobby, the insurer will

A. Not pay claims
B. Pay claims
C. Pay claims only after the contestability period
D. Pay claims only if the policy had a double indemnity rider

ID: MINZOPASSEMADC2Q52C3A1040122Q1DC

63. On a life insurance application for an adult, all of the following signatures are required, with the exception of the:

I. Insured
II. Producer
III. Applicant
IV. Beneficiary

A. Only III
B. II & IV
C. I, II, III
D. IV

ID: MINZOPASSJDEXGEXQ29C3A204052022Q1DC

64. What must the producer do if he notices that a mistake has been made on an application by an applicant?

A. Make the necessary changes upon receiving the application
B. Inform the insurer
C. Hide it from the insurance company and push policy delivery
D. Apply only after correctly filling out the application for the applicant

ID: MINZOPASSJDEXGEXQ3C3A304052022Q1DC
65. Some questions were unanswered on an application for insurance, but the policy was still issued. Can the insurer get the answers to the unanswered questions? If yes, when?

A. Yes, the insurer can obtain the answers during the elimination period
B. Yes, at any time during the 10-day grace period
C. Yes, the insurer will have to wait until assignment
D. No, the insurer has waived all rights of getting answers when it issued the policy

ID: MINZOPASSESADC1Q13C3A4033122Q1DC
66. What is a warranty?

A. A statement on an insurance application guaranteed to be true
B. A statement considered true to the best of the applicant's ability
C. A notarized insurance application
D. An intentionally false statement on an insurance application

ID: MINZOPASSJDADC1Q24C3A504012022Q1DC
67. An applicant fills out the application and sends it with the insurance company's initial premium. When is the offer of the applicant considered accepted by the insurance company?

A. When the applicant signs the policy's delivery receipt
B. Upon completing any required medical exams
C. When the insurer issues the policy
D. Upon receiving the premium check

ID: MINZOPASSEMADC7Q93C3A604042022Q1DC
68. The following are permitted transactions in Section 1035 Exchange transactions, Except:

A. An annuity is exchanged for an equity-indexed annuity
B. An annuity contract is traded in for a different one
C. A Universal Life Policy is traded for a Whole Life Policy
D. A Variable Universal Life Policy is exchanged for an Equity-Indexed Annuity

ID: MINZOPASSEMADC2Q3C3A7040122Q1DC
69. Which statement is correct about HIV-related issues and point-of-sale disclosures?

A. Insurers may refuse to issue policies to those who have tested positive for HIV
B. Personal information gathered during testing must be kept confidential by the insurers.
C. For the risks of AIDS, insurers must prevent unjust discrimination among persons in the same underwriting class
D. All of the above

ID: MINZOPASSESXCC5Q79C3A8040622Q1DC
70. The anti-money laundering compliance program insurers must establish and maintain is regulated under which federal act?

A. National Association of Insurance Act (NAIA)
B. Federal Regulatory Act
C. Fair Credit Reporting Act
D. USA Patriot Act

ID: MINZOPASSBMC3A907282022Q1DC
71. Which of the following is false about the 1999 Gramm-Leach-Bliley Act?

A. Repealed parts of the Glass-Steagall Act of 1933. This law made it legal for insurers, banks, and securities companies to merge
B. Established the Financial Privacy Rule and The Safeguards Rules. These two rules Protect the privacy of consumer information
C. The Financial Privacy Rule requires insurers to provide consumers with a privacy notice at the time the policy is issued and annually thereafter
D. On the first page of the privacy notice, the following line must be included in bold 12-point font: **"During the first six months of receiving this notice, you are not entitled to opt out of the information being shared with unaffiliated parties."**

ID: MINZOPASSJDADC2Q37C3B104012022Q1DC
72. All of the following people could apply for life insurance on Toyin's life, Except

A. Toyin
B. Toyin's husband
C. Toyin's neighbor
D. Toyin's adult daughter

ID: MINZOPASSESXCC5Q78C3B2040622Q1DC
73. The ______________ is a corporation that was established to purposely share medical data with its member companies.

A. Attending Physician Corporation
B. Medical Information Bureau (MIB)
C. Lloyds of London
D. National Association of Underwriters (NAOU)

ID: MINZOPASSJDADC1Q36C3B204012022Q1DC
74. Which of the following assertions is true under the FCRA?

A. Shield reporting agencies from public disclosures
B. If a person is denied coverage, they have the right to obtain a copy of the report
C. The reporting agency can decide to correct incorrect information at their discretion
D. Anyone with a FCRA account has the right to access a consumer's report

ID: MINZOPASSBMADC1Q4C3B4033122Q1DC
75. Which department of an insurer accepts and either declines or accepts insurance risk?

A. Underwriting
B. Actuarial
C. New Client Department
D. Both A & B

ID: MINZOPASSEMADC2Q51C3B5040122Q1DC
76. What exactly is the insured doing in a STOLI/IOLI transaction?

A. They are transferring ownership of their life insurance to their estate
B. Selling their mortality to a third party for a lump sum payment
C. Taking a loan from a third party in order to obtain the required level of insurance
D. They are transferring ownership of their life insurance to their children

ID: MINZOPASSJDADC2Q50C3C104022022Q1DC
77. When is a formal request for the insurer to issue a policy submitted?

A. At policy delivery
B. During the underwriting process
C. Upon completing the application
D. None of the above

ID: MMINZOPASSJDADC1Q28C3C204012022Q1DC
78. Which of the following is not a producer's responsibility to an applicant?

A. Taking a look at the applicant's present insurance coverage and hazards
B. Offering the cheapest policy
C. Evaluating and determining the applicant's need for insurance
D. Getting premiums to the insurer as soon as possible

ID: MINZOPASSBMXCC2Q18C3D104012022Q6DC
79. What does the Consideration clause of an insurance contract include?

A. The schedule and amount of premium payments
B. The buyer's guide
C. A summary of the coverage provided
D. The statement guaranteed to be true

ID: MINZOPASSJDADC1Q23C3D104012022Q4DC
80. Which of the following is NOT a required component of any legal contract?

A. Offer and Acceptance
B. Indemnity
C. Competent Parties
D. Legal Purpose

ID: MINZOPASSESEXC1Q9C3D1040422Q8DC
81. Which of the following does not represent a competent party to a contract?

A. Jeremiah, who is not under the influence of alcohol or drugs
B. David, because he is under the influence of drugs or alcohol
C. Sarah, because she is mentally competent to understand the contract
D. Jessica, because she is not a minor

ID: MINZOPASSEMEXSEXQ8C3D104052022Q9DC
82. Which of the following does NOT constitute an essential element of an insurance contract?

A. Consideration
B. Legal purpose
C. Counteroffer
D. Agreement

ID: MINZOPASSJDADC1Q18C3D204012022Q3DC
83. What is a conditional contract?

A. A false statement on an insurance application
B. Only one party, the insurance company, is legally bound to the contract
C. Both parties must do certain things in order to make the contract legally binding
D. None of the above

ID: MINZOPASSBMXCC2Q13C3D204012022Q7DC
84. In what type of contract is the insurer the only party making a legally enforceable promise?

A. One-Sided Contract
B. Unilateral Contract
C. Contract of Adhesion
D. Unenforceable Contract

ID: MINZOPASSBMXCC2Q12C3D204012022Q6DC
85. A contract written by one party and presented to the other on a "take-it or-leave-it" basis is called a(an):

A. Contract of adhesion
B. Estoppel
C. Aleatory
D. Unilateral

ID: MINZOPASSEMEXSEXQ1C3D204052022Q13DC
86. Adenike, the insured, pays $100 every month for her insurance coverage. The insurer promises to pay Adenike $10,000 if a loss occurs. Which feature(element) of insurance contracts makes this possible?

A. Statement of good health
B. Unilateral
C. Aleatory
D. Conditional

ID: MINZOPASSBMXCC2Q1604022022Q2DC
87. Third-party ownership provides that policy owners who are named as beneficiaries must have:

A. All their family members involved
B. The agent finishes a third-party application
C. Insurable interest in the insured
D. Strangers or investors

ID: MINZOPASSEMADC3Q76C4C040422Q2DC
88. The similarity between a life settlement transaction and a viatical settlement transaction is that

A. The insured is about to die
B. The policy is about to end
C. A third party pays less than the face value of a life insurance policy
D. The policy is old

ID: MINZOPASSEMADC7Q95C4D104052022Q1DC
89. Which of the following is false about the transactions that qualify as 1035 exchange?

A. Converting a variable annuity into an equity-indexed annuity
B. A variable universal life insurance policy with an equity-indexed annuity
C. A fixed annuity into a variable annuity
D. A whole life policy into a universal life policy

ID: MINZOPASSEMADC6Q56C4D204042022Q1DC
90. A contributory plan has which of the following features?

A. Only employees who have been with the employer for more than 2 years are eligible
B. Dependents of eligible employees are not covered
C. A portion of the premium is paid by qualified employees
D. Employers must enroll 100% of eligible employees

ID: MINZOPASSEMADC6Q86C4E104042022Q1DC
91. All of the following are features of a qualified retirement plan, EXCEPT:

A. Employee contributions are either tax-deductible or pre-tax
B. For death, incapacity, eligible education expenditures, medical expenses, and first-time homeowners, the penalty for premature distributions may be waived
C. Employers in the private sector must establish pension schemes
D. The employer's contributions are instantly tax deductible

ID: MINZOPASSJDADC5Q2C4E204032022Q1DC
92. Although life insurance may help save money for retirement, a non-qualified annuity in the long term is better because

A. It provides income payments that are tax-free for the rest of the beneficiary's life
B. Principal growth is tax-deferred
C. It provides regular income payments that the annuitant will not be able to outlive
D. Principle that is tax-deferred and interest that is tax-free

ID: MINZOPASSJDADC2Q45C4F104022022Q1DC
93. Which of the following best describes a personal use of a life insurance?

A. Buy-sell agreements
B. Conserving an estate
C. Key person insurance
D. Executive bonus plans

ID: MINZOPASSEMADC6Q69C4F204042022Q1DC
94. Which of the following describes a Key Employee?

A. A chief financial officer
B. The company's cashier
C. A rank-and-file employee
D. The company's bus driver

ID: MINZOPASSEMADC6Q61C4F2B04042022Q1DC
95. A Buy-Sell Agreement

A. Ensures the survival of the firm by enabling the remaining business partner(s) to acquire the interest of a deceased business partner
B. Is the same as an Executive Bonus Plan
C. Specifies which relatives of a business owner have the right to buy that person's share of the company
D. If a business owner dies unexpectedly, this clause specifies the circumstances and procedures that must be met before the business can be sold to a third party

ID: MINZOPASSEMADC7Q99C4H104052022Q1
96. Premiums on life insurance policies create a _____________ in the policy for tax reasons.

A. Dividend
B. Cash value
C. Cost basis
D. Loan

ID: MINNZOPASSJDADC2Q47C4H204022022Q1DC
97. Which statement best sums up group life insurance?

A. The employees are issued the master policy
B. A single policy provided to a firm that covers the lives of employees
C. A group can be formed specifically for the purpose of obtaining coverage
D. Cannot be converted to an individual policy if the employee voluntarily quits

ID: MINZOPASSEMADC7Q98C4H304052022Q1DC
98. Tax penalties do not apply to distributions from a Modified Endowment Contract (MEC) made on or after age ___________

A. 70 ½
B. 59 ½
C. 65
D. 64

ID: MINZOPASSJDEXGEXQ67C5A104052022Q1DC
99. All of the following are authorities bestowed on the Insurance Commissioner, EXCEPT

A. At any time, rewrite or make alterations to the insurance law
B. Examine books and records of companies and individuals
C. Issue cease and desist orders and licenses
D. Issue certificate of authority

ID: MINZOPASSEMADC3Q54C5A2040122Q1DC
100. When an insurance company factors in mortality and interest, and adds more charges to cover all contract costs, what is this called?

A. The gross premium
B. The net premium
C. The cost of insurance
D. Cumulative Premium

ID: MINZOPASSESXCSEQ25C5A3040622Q3DC
101. When a producer is found guilty of a felony, within how many days must he/she notify the Commissioner?

A. 45
B. 60
C. 31
D. 30

ID: MINZOPASSJDXCSEXQ13C5B104072022Q6DC
102. An insurer licensed to operate business in Washington D.C, but domiciled in Maryland, would be considered a ___________ insurer in Washington DC.

A. Foreign
B. Non-Admitted
C. Alien
D. Domestic

ID: MINZOPASSBMXCC1Q5C5B204012022Q8DC
103. A mutual insurer issues a participating insurance policy. This means policy owners

A. Are allowed to share benefits with another policyholder
B. Pay assessments for company losses
C. Are entitled to receive dividends
D. Are not entitled to vote for members of the board of directors

ID: MINZOPASSESXCSEQ42C5B3040722Q10DC
104. What document, when obtained, permits an insurance company to transact business in the District of Columbia?

A. License
B. Business permit
C. Certificate of authority
D. Certificate of admittance

ID: MINZOPASSJDADC14Q33C5C104052022Q5DC
105. A producer license requires all of the following, with the exception of

A. Be eighteen (18) years of age or older
B. Pass a licensing examination
C. Pay the license fee
D. Be twenty-one (21) years of age or older

ID: MINZOPASSESXCSEQ47C5C2040722Q5DC
106. Under what circumstance may a producer's license be rejected, revoked, or suspended in the District of Columbia?

A. Engaging in replacement of an existing policy
B. Declaring personal bankruptcy
C. Declaring business bankruptcy
D. Making false statements in order to obtain the license

ID: MINZOPASSJDKAC23Q37C5C304122022Q10DC
107. What role does the mayor play in insurance regulations?

A. Appoints the commissioner of insurance
B. Sign insurance laws created by the state legislature
C. Issue and revoke licenses
D. Both A & B

ID: MINZOPASSJDADC14Q16C5C404052022Q1DC
108. How is the Commissioner appointed in Washington, DC?

A. By the Governor
B. The Mayor appoints the commissioner with the advice and consent of the City Council
C. The City Council, with the advice and consent of the Mayor
D. Through an election

ID: MINZOPASSJDADC14Q23C5C104052022Q2DC
109. Which of the following is a legal requirement for keeping an insurance license active?

A. Any change in address must be reported to the Commissioner within 10 days
B. Any change in address must be reported to the Commissioner within 90 days
C. Any change in address must be reported to the Commissioner within 40 days
D. Any change in address must be reported to the Commissioner within 30 days

ID: MINZOPASSESXCSEQ30C5C6040722Q4DC
110. Every 24 months, an insurance agent in The District of Columbia is required to complete _______ hours of continuing education.

A. 12
B. 24
C. 20
D. 21

ID: MINZOPASSJDXCSEXQ30C5D104072022Q5DC
111. Which of the following is an example of false advertising?

A. An insurer exaggerating its dividends in an advertisement
B. Paid testimonials from celebrity endorsements
C. Very detailed policy information in client brochures
D. A producer spending more than $10 on marketing gifts for a client

ID: MINZOPASSJDXCSEXQ18C5D204072022Q12DC
112. Which of the following statements best describes rebating?

A. Receiving policy dividends
B. Receiving stock dividends
C. Issuing false advertising brochures to clients
D. Offering a prospective client something of value not specified in the contract in exchange for their business

ID: MINZOPASSESXCSEQ44C5D3040722Q11DC
113. Comparing two insurance policies in an unfair way is defined as

A. Defamation
B. Misrepresentation
C. Coercion
D. Twisting

ID: MINZOPASSESXCSEQ16C5D4040622Q6DC

114. A booklet that contains an inaccurate statement about a competitor's ability to settle claims illustrates what unfair trade practice?

A. Slander
B. Coercion
C. Rebating
D. Defamation

ID: MINZOPASSEMEXSEXQ92C5D504072022Q6DC

115. Which of the following is NOT considered unfair discrimination by an insurance company?

A. Charging the premiums for applicants with similar health histories based on their ethnicity
B. Discriminating in coverages and benefits due to the insured's habits and lifestyle
C. Terminating coverage based on marital status
D. Charging people different rates based on sexual orientation

ID: MINZOPASSJDEXGEEXQ80C5D604052022Q1DC

116. John, an insured person, is informed by an agent that his dividends will increase by 50% and his premiums will decrease by 50% if he replaces his current insurance policy with a newer one. This is untrue, as the agent is aware. What kind of misrepresentation is this?

A. Twisting
B. Replacement
C. Distortion
D. Rebating

ID: MINZOPASSBMC5D708052022Q1DC

117. Which one of the following is not a penalty for engaging in unfair trade practice(s) in The District of Columbia?

A. Cease and Desist order
B. Civil penalty of up to $1,000 for each violation
C. The producer's license may be suspended, revoked, or not renewed by the commissioner
D. In addition to suspending, cancelling, or declining to renew a producer's license, the commissioner may also impose a civil penalty of up to $20,000.

ID: MINZOPASSJDXCC8Q55C5D804112022Q13DC
118. According to The District of Columbia law, no legal action can be taken against an insurance company for failing to pay a valid claim after _____years have passed since proof of loss has been provided.

A. 3 years
B. 2 years
C. 5 years
D. 4 years

ID: MINZOPASSBMADC1Q7C5E033122Q2DC
119. What are some responsibilities a producer has?

I. Fiduciary responsibility
II. Sending premiums to the insurer on time
III. Writing and attaching an agent's report to each insurance application
IV. Recommending only low premium policies

A. I & IV
B. II
C. III & IV
D. I, II, & III

ID: MINZOPASSBMC5F08052022Q6DC
120. Insurance companies are prohibited from deciding to test a proposed insured for HIV/AIDs based on

I. Gender and beneficiary designations
II. Occupation and lifestyle
III. Sexual orientation, sexual expression, and sexual identity
IV. Living arrangements

A. I only
B. III & IV
C. I & II only
D. I, II, III, & IV

ID: MINZOPASSJDEXGEXQ65C5G04052022Q4DC
121. The Life and Health Insurance Guaranty Association serves which purpose?

A. Protect insurance companies from legal liability against illegal acts
B. Provide benefits to insureds whose insurers have become Insolvent
C. To issue licenses
D. To regulate premium rates

ID: MINZOPASSESXCSEQ45C6A1040722Q9DC
122. Individual life insurance policies in The District of Columbia have a _______ day grace period.

A. 30
B. 45
C. 60
D. 31

ID: MINZOPASSJDEXGEXQ75C6A20405202Q2DC
123. All of the following must be done by the insured when reinstating a life insurance policy, EXCEPT

A. Repay any outstanding loans and interest
B. Pay next year's premium in advance
C. Pay back premiums
D. Pay any interest owed on overdue premiums

ID: MINZOPASSEMEXSEXQ77C6B104052022Q10DC
124. What is the maximum annual loan interest rate insurers may charge for Life insurance policies that have been in force for three years?

A. 7.5%
B. 5%
C. 6%
D. 8%

ID: MINGOPASSEMEXC6Q84C6B204052022Q4DC
125. Chan and Hung are married. Hung is the beneficiary of Chan's $500,000 life insurance policy. Chan is accidentally killed in a car crash. Six months later, Hung is notified by John, Chan's best friend, that he owes him $50,000 in personal loan, for which he has a notarized loan document as evidence. John wants Hung to repay him the $50,000 out of the $500,000 death benefit. Can Hung LEGALLY deny payment of Chan's debt? If yes, which insurance provision gives her that right to do so?

A. No, revocable beneficiary clause
B. Yes, legal protection clause
C. Yes, spendthrift clause
D. No, irrevocable beneficiary designation

ID: MINZOPASSESXCSEQ29C6C1040722Q9DC
126. Lisa is a worker who is insured by a group life insurance policy. Lisa's conversion privilege allows her to convert to_______ if her employment is terminated.

A. An individual policy without submitting evidence of insurability
B. An individual policy with a larger coverage limit
C. An individual policy with proof of insurability
D. An individual policy without proof of insurability only if the employer pays for it

ID: MINZOPASSJDEXGEXQ60C6D104052022Q6DC
127. Which one of the following regulates variable insurance and variable annuities?

A. Department of Insurance only
B. NAIC only
C. Department of Insurance, FINRA and SEC
D. SEC only

ID: MINZOPASSTAXCC10Q39C6E104112022Q49DC
128. Steve is a retired man who recently divorced his wife. His old employer provides him with benefits from a qualified retirement plan. Steve's benefit payments will be shared between him and his ex-wife, according to the plan's trustee. Which IRS rule is likely to be broken by this decision?

A. Benefits Sharing or Separation Exception
B. Separation Exception
C. Alienation of Benefits
D. Benefits Sharing

ID: MINZOPASSJDXCSEXQ22C6F04062022Q15DC

129. In the case of the borrower's death, a life insurance policy owned by and only benefiting the creditor is known as __________.

A. Credit life
B. Lender's life
C. Decreasing term life
D. None of the above

ID: MINZOPASSJDEXGEXQ95C6F04062022QDC

130. The type of life insurance policy designed to pay off any outstanding credit or loan debt upon the death of the borrower is known as what?

A. Debtor life
B. Credit death insurance
C. Borrower's limit of liability
D. Credit life

District of Columbia Simulated Exam 1 Answers

ID: MINZOPASSEMADC361C1A1040222Q1DC

1. Correct answer: C

Because the insured has not yet died, the cash value of a whole life policy will equal the face amount of insurance at the endowment. The policy expires, and the policyowner receives the cash value.

- Term Life Insurance has no Cash Value
- Cash value can only be found in whole/Traditional Life Insurance policy
- Cash value is the portion of your insurance that earns interest and can be withdrawn or borrowed in specific circumstances, like an emergency.
- The face amount is the amount included in the policy as the benefit after death of the insured and it is the limit of liability for the insurer.

ID: MINZOPASSEMADC3Q65C1A2040222Q3

2. Correct answer: B

The underlying premise behind insurance premiums is that paying less frequently results in a lower *total* premium. Because payments fund the cash value in cash value plans, the real amount per payment in a limited payment policy will be larger when the number of payments is reduced. Premiums for a 20-pay insurance are greater than for a 30-pay policy, but the total of the 20 payments is substantially less than the total of the 30 payments.

Definition of Limited Pay Life:

Limited pay life is a form of traditional whole life insurance that gives the policyowner the chance to pay a premium for a specific period of time, but the coverage of the policy continues for a lifetime or endows at age 100, like any other traditional/whole life policy.

ID: MINZOPASSBMXCC3Q25C1B04022022Q1DC

3. Correct Answer: B

Flexible premiums and an adjustable death benefit are distinguishing features of universal life insurance policies. Universal life policies offer flexibility.

ID: MINZOPASSEMADC3Q67C1B2040222Q12DC

4. Correct answer: B

These characteristics are exclusive to Variable Whole Life, commonly referred to as Variable Life. The death benefit of Variable Universal Life is not adjusted in proportion to stock market performance. Cash value cannot be invested in stock-based funds with Equity Indexed Universal Life. Investment Grade Whole Life Insurance does not exist.

Variable Life Insurance has two accounts: the General Account and the Separate Account.

The General Account - The general account is fixed and guaranteed, with a minimum death benefit guaranteed until age 100. The general account can be used to fund policy loans.

Separate Account - The separate account is invested in the insurance company's equity securities. The owner has the option of investing the premium in one of several separate accounts. The value of the cash in the separate account will change depending on market conditions and the separate account's performance, which is comparable to that of a mutual fund.

In Variable Life Insurance, the premium is fixed, the insurer determines the premium, which remains constant and level throughout the contract.

In a Variable Life Insurance policy, there's a guaranteed minimum death benefit.
Note: To sell Variable Life INSURANCE, an individual will need two licenses: a *life insurance license* and a *security license*.

ID: MINZOPASSBMXCC3Q27C1B04022022Q3DC
5. Correct Answer: B
The policy owner of a variable universal life insurance policy can control the premium paying schedule, the premium amounts, and where to invest cash values.

ID: MINZOPASSESKAC4Q23C1A1041322Q27DC
6. Correct Answer: A
Whole-life contracts that are Interest-sensitive do not pay dividends. Remember that dividends are never guaranteed. The cash value rises and falls in accordance with interest rates.

ID: MINZOPASSBMCQB5061422Q2DC
7. Correct answer: C
Indexed life insurance, of which universal life is the only kind, is an insurance policy that offers a minimum guaranteed interest rate, guarantees the principal amount, and its cash value performance is tied to a linked stock-market index. This is similar to *indexed* annuities because indexed annuities offer a minimum guaranteed interest rate, but the credited interest rate may be higher depending on the interest rate of the linked stock market index like the S & P 500. Indexed insurance products are better than regular insurance products at protecting against inflation, with the exception of variable products, because they provide relatively higher interest rates.

ID: MINZOPASSEMADC3Q63C1C1040222Q2DC

8. Correct answer: D

The death benefit or face amount is another name for the policy proceeds. Depending on the policy name (level, declining, or growing term), the face amount or proceeds will be handled differently. A level term insurance means that the proceeds of the policy remain the same throughout the policy's duration.

Decreasing Term

- is when the death benefit/policy proceeds decrease, but the premium remains the same.

Growing/Increasing Term

- Is when the premium stays level, but the death benefit increases or grows.

ID: MINZOPASSESKAC4Q13C1C041122Q24DC

9. Correct Answer: C

Decreasing term insurance is ideal for insurance needs that decrease over time. For example, a family's insurance needs are assumed to decrease each year because the kids get older. The same can be said of mortgage protection and business loan balance because as the loan balance decreases, so does the amount of insurance coverage need. Term insurance cannot be used to save for retirement because it does not have any attached savings or investment account.

ID: MINZOBMC1C3ID060922Q1DC

10. Correct Answer: D

Retun of premium term is more expensive than a standardized level term policy. All of the other options are true for Return of Premium Term Policies. Return of Premium Term can be attached as a rider to a level term policy or it can be issued as a standard stand-alone term policy.

ID: MINZOPASSESEXC2Q27C2B7040422Q10DC

11. Correct answer: D

For annually renewable term insurance, the death benefit is level all throughout, but the premium increases each year as the insured's attained age increases.

The annually renewable term (ART) is the most basic type of term insurance. Most group life insurance is written as an annually renewal term.

More on Types of Term Insurance:

Note: Only the face amount is subject to change during the term, not the premium. The premium only changes when renewing or converting the term policy based on the ATTAINED age. Attained age is the applicant's age at the time of application.

Decreasing Term

- death benefit decreases

- The premium doesn't change over the course of the policy's duration

Level term

- The death benefit and premium remain level

Increasing term

- The death benefit increases
- Premium remains the same

ID: MINZOPASSESXCC3Q37C1C040522Q13DC

12. Correct Answer: C

Renewable term policy guarantees the insured the right to continuous insurance coverage even when the initial policy period comes to an end.

ID: MINZOPASSESXCC471C2B6040622Q16DC

13. Correct Answer: B

It is generally accepted that the cost of insurance is the most significant consideration for policyowners deciding whether to convert term insurance at the insured's entry age (original age) or the insured's current age (attained age).

ID: MINZOPASSESXCC7Q9C1D040622Q41DC

14. Correct Answer: B

Single premium annuity is an annuity that is bought with only one premium. It is usually ideal for people who have a lump sum amount of money. In this case, a Single Premium Annuity would be ideal for Chris.

ID: MINZOPASSJDADC5Q6C1D04032022Q5DC

15. CORRECT ANSWER: C

By definition, a flexible premium annuity permits the addition of more principal value at any point before the annuitization of the contract. Within a month of the policy's issuance, payments to the annuitant begin for a Single Premium Immediate Annuity ("SPIA"). Payments for SPIAs must start within a year (12 months) after the policy's release.

.

ID: MINZOPASSESXCC7Q3C1D040622Q35DC

16. Correct Answer: B

Within a year of the issuance date, immediate annuities begin to pay out immediately and do not have an accumulating term. Nonetheless, annuity payments often begin to be made within 30 days of the purchase.

ID: MINZOPASSTAXCC9Q27C1D204092022Q66DC

17. Correct answer: D

In the accumulation phase, a qualified deferred annuity can be utilized to finance an IRA and allow for continuous contributions up to the IRS's maximum limits. Contributions are no longer allowed to annuitized IRA funds.

ID: MINZOPASSJDADC5Q10C1D04032022Q9DC

18. CORRECT ANSWER: C

The interest rate is the "fixed" part of a fixed annuity. When the contract is annuitized, a fixed annuity also offers a fixed payout to the annuitant.

ID: MINZOPASSJDADC5Q11C1D04032022Q10DC

19. CORRECT ANSWER: A

To sell variable life or annuity contracts, a licensed life agent must also have a securities license. The characteristics of variable annuities are as follows:

- Separate account
- No guarantees by the insurance company
    - Owner bears all the investment risk and has the right to determine how money is invested
    - Benefit payment amount not guaranteed
- Premium buys accumulation units
    - Accumulation units are the accumulated values of variable annuities. This is similar to shares purchased in a stock. The value of the accumulation unit is determined by dividing the total value of the separate account by the number of existing accumulation units
    - The accumulation units are converted to annuity units when the annuity contract is annuitized
    - Annuity units stay constant, but the annuity value varies depending on investment performance
    - Accumulated funds, if annuitized, purchase annuity units.
- A producer must be licensed by the state and security regulators (SEC & FINRA) to sell
- The two primary advantages are the high rate of return and the capacity to act as a hedge against inflation.

ID: MINZOPASSESXCC7Q1C1D040622Q33DC

20. Correct Answer: C

Owners of index-linked annuities might get credited interest based on changes in the linked index, but owners of fixed annuities wouldn't.

ID: MINZOPASSTAXCC9Q24C1D204092022Q59DC

21. Correct answer: B

After the purchase payments stop, the annuity's accumulation term normally continues until the annuitant begins receiving regular benefit payments.

Remember that an annuity is either in the accumulation phase or the annuitization phase. Even when payments stop, as long as the annuitant has not begun taking money out, the money is still there, *accumulating or accruing interest.*

ID: MINZOPASSPCXC9Q38C1D304092022Q56DC

22. Correct answer: C

For the length of the annuity period, a straight life fixed immediate annuity pays the same benefit amount. This is a straight life annuity, sometimes referred to as a pure life annuity or a life-no-refund annuity, which implies that the annuitant will get benefit payments for the duration of their life. However, the annuity contract will be void and payments will cease upon the annuitant's death.

ID: MINZOPASSESEXC2Q16C1D040422Q19DC

23. Correct answer: A

For this arrangement, a 20-year fixed period distribution, annuities purchased with a single lump sum payment will do just fine.

ANNUITY:

- insurance product that provides income for a fixed number of years or for life.
- protects against outliving your money
- opposite of life insurance
- liquidates an estate

Parties to an annuity contract:

- Owner
    - can be a corporation, trust, or natural person
    - Has all ownership rights
- Annuitant
    - First in line to receive benefits, the insured
    - must be a natural person. CANNOT be a corporation or trust
- Owner & annuitant may be different.
- Beneficiary
    - receives benefits if the annuitant dies.

Premium Payment options

- Single premium Vs periodic(flexible) premium

Benefit Payout options

- Immediate vs. deferred

Interest Rate Options

- Fixed vs. variable vs. indexed

Settle Options

- Life Income (Pure, Life with No Refund, or Straight Life)
- Life Income with Refund (Cash Refund or Installment)
- Joint Life Annuity
- Joint & Survivor Annuity

ID: MINZOPASSJDEXGEXQ12C1E104052022Q3DC

24. Correct answer: A

A joint life insurance policy provides coverage for two people, typically spouses or domestic partners, but it only pays out in the event that one of them dies. There is only one premium due and the insureds' ages are AVERAGED. Consider combined bank accounts when considering joint life insurance.

ID: MINZOPASSEMEXSEXQ2C1E2204052022Q5DC

25. Correct answer: A

In a survivorship insurance policy, death benefits are paid upon the death of the last insured.
Special Life Insurance Policies:

i) Juvenile

- ➔ policy written on the life of a minor
- ➔ The most common type is JUMPING Juvenile Policy.
    - ◆ allows an automatic increase of 5X death benefit between the ages of 21 and 25 without proof of insurability.
- ➔ For the term of the insurance contract, the premium stays the same.

ii) Joint Life (First to Die)

- ➔ whole life policy that covers 2 or more insureds
- ➔ Upon the death of the first insured, the death benefit is paid.
- ➔ Policy is automatically canceled when the death benefit is paid
- ➔ Premium is based on the average age of both insureds
- ➔ Premium is usually lower than two separate policies
- ➔ Provides income protection for the surviving spouse

iii) Joint Survivorship Life (Last to Die)

- ➔ whole life policy that covers 2 or more lives and the death benefit is ONLY paid when the last insured dies
- ➔ premiums are based on the average age of both insured
- ➔ lower premium than 2 separate policies
- ➔ usually used to provide a lump sum death benefit to pay estate taxes when the second insured dies

iv) Return of Premium Term

- ➔ Provides a complete premium refund in the event that the insured survives to the conclusion of the term.
- ➔ Premiums are higher than regular term insurance policies.

ID: MINZOPASSEMADC3Q75C2A1040222Q2DC
26. Correct answer: B
The waiver of premium rider exempts the disabled policy owner from paying premiums for the duration of his or her disability, therefore the premiums do not have to be repaid.

Waiver of Premium

- If an insured person becomes totally handicapped, the insurer will waive premiums for the period of the disability or until the policy expires, whichever comes first. The insured must be disabled for a minimum of 3-6 months to be eligible for the waiver (90 days - 6 months).
- During the waiting time, the policyowner must continue to pay premiums, but once eligible, the waiver is retroactively applied from the beginning of the disability.

ID: MINZOPASSEMADC3Q84C2A204042022Q1DC
27. Correct answer: A
With a guaranteed insurability rider, one can obtain additional coverage at predetermined future periods without having to prove insurability. Riders, by their nature, never come standard because they are add-ons(attachments) to a life insurance policy. Adding rider(s) to a life insurance policy will usually increase the premium.

ID: MINZOPASSESEXC3Q39C2A3040522Q1DC
28. Correct answer: B
If the payor is deceased or disabled, the payor benefit rider covers the premiums. That has no effect on the death benefit.

The death benefit is increased by each of the following riders:

- Guaranteed Insurability Rider

    - at specific ages or events, the death benefit can be increased by the policyholder (ex. new baby, adoption, etc)
- Cost of Living Rider
    - automatically raises the death benefit in order to keep up with inflation
- Accidental Death Benefit Rider
    - if the insured dies from an accident, the beneficiary receives a specified amount more than the policy's death benefit. The accidental death benefit rider usually pays two or three times the death benefit when the insured dies.

ID: MINZOPASSJDADC14Q1C2A404052022Q1DC

29. Correct Answer: B

The benefits are not subject to taxation for the receiver. All the other choices are false.

Accidental Death and Dismemberment

- Employer-paid premiums are tax deductible
- The benefits are not taxable
- Usually pays 2 to 3 times the death benefit when attached as a rider to a life insurance policy

ID: MINZOPASSESEXC3Q45C2A5040522Q1DC

30. Correct Answer: B

When a policyowner wants to customize a permanent life insurance policy to their liking, they may go for a term rider. This rider is also called the base insured rider.

ID: MINZOPASSEMADC3Q68C2A604022022Q1DC

31. Correct answer: C

A "jumping juvenile" policy will often increase the face amount of insurance by a multiple of five at the next anniversary anywhere between 21 and 25 years old, with no change in price (depending on the policy). At that point, the policy is transferred to the child, who is now an adult.

Jumping Juvenile Insurance is the term for life insurance for minors that the death benefit increases automatically at age 21 without the need for an additional premium or proof of insurability. When a parent or guardian buys the policy on behalf of the child, they sign on behalf of the child because a minor cannot sign a policy.

ID: MINZOPASSEMADC3Q71C2A7040222Q1DC

32. Correct answer: D

A long-term care rider allows a chronically ill person to receive an advance payment of the death benefit for covered long-term care expenses.

More on Long-Term Care (LTC):

- LTC—The rider may pay up to 100% of the policy benefits if the insured meets the specified requirements for long-term care benefits, such as being unable to carry out two of the six activities of daily living.

ID: MINZOPASSEMADC3Q73C2A8040222Q1DC
33. Correct answer: C
If the insured dies during the term, the beneficiary receives the death benefit of the insurance policy and the total premiums paid.

More on Riders:
Return of Cash Value (The Early Cash Value Rider)

- Added to IUL (index universal life) to eliminate or reduce the policy's surrender charge in the first 1 to 5 years. This allows the policyowner to obtain higher cash liquidity in the first five years.

Waiver of Premium

- If an insured person becomes totally handicapped/disabled, the insurer will waive premiums for the period of the disability, or until the policy expires, whichever comes first. For eligibility to receive the waiver, the insured must have been disabled for a minimum of three to six months (90 days - 6 months). During the waiting time, the policyowner must continue to pay premiums, but once eligible, the waiver is retroactive to the beginning of the disability.

ID: MINZOPASSBMC2A9061922Q1DC
34. Correct Answer: D
All of the other riders are disability riders except accelerated death benefit rider.

ID: MINZOPASSESXCC3Q54C2A2040622Q6DC
35. Correct Answer: B
The cost-of-living rider automatically increases monthly benefits after the onset of a disability (therefore giving additional death benefits) as the consumer price index (PCI) increases. It protects the insured against inflation.

ID: MINZOPASSESEXC3Q31C2B1040422Q4DC
36. Correct answer: B
The ENTIRE CONTRACT is the delivered policy, copy of the application, and any attached riders/amendments. This is a requirement found in all life insurance policies.

THE STANDARD LIFE INSURANCE POLICY PROVISIONS developed by the National Association of Insurance Commissioners (NAIC) are:

1. Entire Contract

2. Insuring Clause
3. Free Look
4. Consideration
5. Owner's Rights
6. Assignments
7. Beneficiary Designations
8. Premium Payment
9. Reinstatement
10. Incontestability
11. Misstatement of Age and Gender
12. Policy Loans, Withdrawals and Partial Surrenders
13. Exclusions
14. Suicide

ID: MINZOPASSJDADC4Q1C2B204022022Q1DC

37. CORRECT ANSWER: D

When a claim is proven, the insuring agreement is the basic guarantee to pay the benefit provided in the policy. A real certified copy of the death certificate is an acceptable proof of death for life insurance purposes.

ID: MINNZOPASSJDEXGEXQ13C2B304052022Q1DC

38. Correct answer: C

A life insurance policy's free look period, which typically lasts 10 days and starts when you receive your policy, allows a new owner to terminate the policy. During this time, there are no penalties, such as surrender charges.

ID: MINZOPASSESXCC3Q57C2B4040622Q1DC

39. Correct answer: B

According to the consideration clause, in order for the insurance company to consider the applicant for the policy, they must submit an application and pay the first premium.

More on Consideration Clause:

- The amount and premium payment mode(frequency) are included in the consideration clause
- The definition of consideration is the exchange of something valuable.
- It is one of the four elements of a LEGAL contract
- The insurer's consideration is approving and issuing the policy and agreeing to pay future claims

ID: MINZOPASSJDADC4Q11C2B50402022Q1DC

40. CORRECT ANSWER: D

The policy owner's ownership rights are a standard contract provision that permits them to do all these and more.

Ownership provision

- The policyowner has complete control over the policy, including the ability to identify or replace revocable beneficiaries, assign the policy, and make any policy-related changes
- It is also the responsibility of the owner to pay the premiums
- All rights in the policy are retained by the policy owner

ID: MINZOPASSJDADC4Q14C2B604022022Q3DC

41. CORRECT ANSWER: D

In the event that the primary beneficiary is not available, the policy funds are distributed to the contingent beneficiaries. If the primary beneficiary and the insured are killed in the same accident or due to the same accident within 90 days, then the *common disaster clause* states that the primary beneficiary perished before the insured. Therefore, since Chris(insured) and Brita (primary beneficiary) died in the same accident, their children (contingent beneficiaries) will receive the death benefit.

ID: MINZOPASSJDEXGEXQ39C2B604052022Q8DC

42. Correct answer: A

A revocable beneficiary named in a policy can be changed at the will of the policy owner. An irrevocable beneficiary can only be changed with the written consent from the beneficiary.

ID: MINZOPASSESEXC3Q37C2B6040522Q5DC

43. Correct answer: A

A policy with an irrevocable beneficiary needs written permission from the beneficiary to change and name a new beneficiary.

ID: MINZOPASSJDADC4Q7C2B604022022Q2DC

44. CORRECT ANSWER: B

Beneficiary class designations are intended to provide benefits to a class of nameless individuals; nonetheless, they may cause issues if it is unclear exactly who is being designated as a beneficiary. "All my children". Does not specify which children are included, whether they are from the current marriage, the previous marriage, or both. Likewise, "My Minor Children" fails to recognise that children become adults and may inadvertently overlook a child.

Beneficiary Designation

- A beneficiary designation is usually chosen at the time of application. Whether or not the insured is alive when the insurer receives the notice, a change of beneficiary takes effect on the day the request was signed by the owner.
- Individual/Named — This is a fairly common designation. The beneficiary is identified by name, such as Susan Myers (sister) or Jesse Preston (wife).

More examples:

- Per Capita
    - If a named beneficiary predeceases the insured, this designation will pay all surviving beneficiaries equally.
    - If an insured chooses their three children as beneficiaries and one dies before the insured, the payout will be split equally among the remaining specified beneficiaries.
- Per Stirpes
    - This provision will give a deceased beneficiary's portion to the beneficiary's heirs if the insured passes away before the beneficiary.
    - If the insured outlives all other beneficiaries, the estate may be the third beneficiary.
    - A trust is used when the funds are to be transmitted in accordance with the insured's specified wishes and a recipient, such as minor children, does not have direct access to the death benefits.
- Minors
    - If minors are specified as beneficiaries without trust, the assets are deposited in a settlement option (held with interest) with the insurer acting as trustee.
- To cover an obligation, a creditor is designated via assignment or specified on an application. The creditor can be the named beneficiary or the assignee for a collateral assignment

ID: MINZOPASSESEXC3Q43C2B6040522Q6DC

45. Correct answer: D

A trustee or legal guardian receives the benefit on behalf of the minor. A minor does not have the legal capacity to release the insurer from further obligation.

ID: MINZOPASSJDADC2Q44C2B704022022Q2DC

46. Correct answer: B

The most expensive payment mode is monthly. The least costly premium mode is always annual. It is the least expensive because the insurer has fewer overhead expenses handling a once-yearly premium payment than a monthly premium payment.

These are the four Premium Payment Modes:

- 1. Quarterly
- 2. Monthly
- 3. Semi-Annually
- 4. Annually

ID: MINZOPASSJDADC4Q3C2B704022022Q3DC

47. CORRECT ANSWER: C

The grace period allows a policyowner to pay past due premium(s) without incurring any penalties or losing their coverage. Any claim that arises within the grace period must be paid, but any unpaid premiums will be subtracted from the claim when it is paid.
Unless state law states differently, the customary grace period is 30 or 31 days.

ID: MINZOPASSJDADC4Q21C2B704022022Q8DC

48. CORRECT ANSWER: B

The Automatic Premium Loan Provision allows the insurer to borrow enough money from the cash value to keep the policy from lapsing. This only works if sufficient cash value is available. A policy loan may include annual prepayment interest, depending on the arrangement.

ID: MINZOPASSBMC2B7E072122Q12DC

49. Correct Answer: B

False. Most life insurance premium payments are fixed. This means that the policyowner pays a fixed premium for the duration of the policy until the insured's death, the expiration of the term(for term policies), or the endowment(for permanent policies) of the policy. The few exceptions to this are adjustable whole life and universal life insurance policies.

ID: MINZOPASSJDADC4Q22C2B804022022Q1DC

50. CORRECT ANSWER: D

The insured must submit proof of insurability and pay all past premiums plus interest to restore a lapsed policy. In addition to that, they must submit a new application.

After reinstatement, a new incontestability period will begin from the date of reinstatement. However, the policy owner will maintain all rights that they had in the original policy.

ID: MINZOPASSJDADC4C5C2B904022022Q1DC

51. CORRECT ANSWER: D

Policy loans would not automatically affect a policy's death benefit. However, if there is an existing loan at the time of death, the loan amount will be deducted from the beneficiary's payout. All of the other options are correct regarding policy loans.

Policy Loan Provisions

- The amount of the insurance loan cannot exceed the cash surrender value
- Once there is enough cash value to borrow against, a policy loan can be arranged under a cash value policy
- Refusal to repay a loan or interest will not result in the policy being voided until the total amount of the outstanding loan and unpaid interest equals or surpasses the entire cash surrender value of the insurance
- Up to six months may pass before the insurer grants a loan, unless it was intended to cover any premiums (such as in the case of an automatic premium loan).
- As specified in the policy, policy loans with fixed rates usually have a maximum fixed interest rate of 8% or less.

ID: MINZOPASSEMADC2Q56C2B10040122Q1DC

52. Correct Answer: D

A reserve is an amount an insurer holds to cover potential or actual liabilities owed to policyholders. In most cases, a reserve is considered a liability.

ID: MINZOPASSJDADC4Q10C2B1104022022Q1DC

53. CORRECT ANSWER: C

Income for life is a death benefit settlement option structured like an annuity.

Dividend options

- Dividends reflect the insurer's good fortune derived from extra investment earnings, favorable mortality, and cost savings
- Mutual carriers' participating policies pay dividends. If declared, they are usually paid once a year but are not guaranteed.

The policyowner chooses which dividend option to use and can change their selection at any time

The DIVIDEND Options are (Acronym: CARPPO)

- Cash
    - On or near each policy anniversary, the policyowner receives a check for the declared dividends
- Reduction of Premium
    - Dividends are applied to the next premium due, thereby reducing the amount of money that the policyowner has to pay
- Accumulation at Interest
    - Dividends are kept by the insurer to accrue interest
- Paid-up Additions
    - Buys additional permanent benefits with a single premium when the insured reaches a certain age
    - It generates cash value and dividends as though the paid-up supplemental benefit was part of the original policy while the insured is alive

- One Year Term
    - Purchases a one-year term insurance with a single premium. Premiums are determined by the insured's current age (attained age)
- Paid-up Option
    - Pays off the policy sooner than scheduled.

ID: MINZOPASSJDADC4Q2C2B1204022022Q1DC

54. CORRECT ANSWER: A

According to the concept of incontestability, an insurance provider cannot deny payment for a death claim on the basis of the information provided in the original application. In most states, the policy becomes incontestable after two years.

The Incontestability Clause states:

- The insurer has the right to fight a claim and terminate the contract if there is proof of a *material* misrepresentation or fraud within the first two years of the policy
- Except in cases of fraud and nonpayment of premiums, the insurance will no longer be contestable after it has been in force for at least two years from the date of issuance.

ID: MINZOPASSJDEXGEXQ11C2B1304052022Q1DC

55. Correct answer: C

Collateral assignment temporarily transfers ownership of one's life insurance policy. This is mostly done with credits and loans.

ID: MINZOPASSESXCC3Q50C2B14040522Q1DC

56. Correct Answer: C

Under the Suicide Clause, an insurer will NOT pay claims if an insured commits suicide during the period of contestability, which is two years from the date of policy issue. However, all premiums paid will be returned to the beneficiary.

ID: MINZOPASSESXCC3Q53C2B15040622Q1DC

57. Correct Answer: D

If the insured's age is misstated, the insurer must adjust the amount of the insurance death benefit.

ID: MINZOPASSEMKAC6Q7C2B1604122022Q1DC

58. Correct Answer: B

Since the policy's face amount of $200,000 was still available for payout after Jametta's spouse's death, even after her spouse received regular monthly payments, it shows that it had been saved. In contrast, her deceased spouse received payments from the income the insurer earned on interest.

ID: MINZOPASSEMADC3Q77C2B1704042022Q1DC

59. Correct Answer: A

Accelerated death benefits paid out will be subtracted from the policy's death benefit before paying it to the beneficiary. Accelerated death benefits are not taxed and do not have to be repaid.

ID: MINZOPASSESEXC3Q36C2C040522Q2DC

60. Correct answer: D

Exclusions are risking an insurance policy will not cover. Aviation, dangerous occupations, war and military duty are the most common exclusions in life insurance contracts.

- Aviation
    - Excludes coverage only for test pilots, military pilots and crew, and private pilots
    - This exclusion does not apply to insureds who are fare-paying airline passengers on a regularly scheduled commercial airline or commercial airline pilots or crew.
- Hazardous Occupation/Hobbies
    - A particular occupation or interest may not be covered, or the insured may have to pay a higher premium.
- War or Military Service
    - STATUS Clause
        - covers NOTHING in the event that the insured dies while on active-duty military service
    - RESULTS Clause
        - ONLY excludes death when the insured is killed as a result of war

ID: MINZOPASSBMC2C207262022Q8DC

61. Correct Answer: C

Exclusions are a common feature of life insurance policies where the insurer explicitly states certain risks that will not be covered. Aviation is one of the exclusions in life insurance policies. The aviation exclusion excludes coverage only for test pilots, military pilots and crew, and private pilots. **Note: This exclusion does not apply to insureds who are fare-paying passengers on a regularly scheduled commercial airline or commercial airline pilots or crew.**

Note: If an insurer covers a pilot, the pilot's premium will usually be much higher than the standard premium charged for the same risk.

ID: MINZOPASSBMC2C307262022Q7DC

62. Correct Answer: A

If an insured dies due to a hazardous occupation or hobby, the insurer will not pay claims because this is a common exclusion on life insurance policies. The other two other common exclusions are war and aviation. Exclusions are a common feature of life insurance policies where the insurer explicitly states certain risks that will not be covered.

ID: MINZOPASSEMADC2Q52C3A1040122Q1DC

63. Correct answer: D

The application must be signed by both the producer and the applicant(and insured if different from the applicant). A guardian must sign the application if the insured is a minor.

Required Signatures

The Producer/ Agent:

- The producer is the agent who represents the insurance company. The producer serves as the middle man between the applicant and the insurance company

The Applicant/policy owner/policyholder

- The applicant is the one applying for the policy, pays the premium, owns the policy, and is entitled to make changes to the policy

The Insured

- The insured is the person whose life the life insurance policy is based upon
- Note: The insured's signature is needed in the case where they are different from the policyowner

ID: MINZOPASSJDEXGEXQ29C3A204052022Q1DC

64. Correct answer: B

The Producer is to alert or inform the insurer of missing information on the application form because when the policy is issued based on missing information, the company has waived the right to contest future claims.

ID: MINZOPASSJDEXGEXQ3C3A304052022Q1DC

65. Correct answer: D

Once the insurer issues a policy, the contract starts. Therefore, any information left out of the application does not affect the contract. The insurer must ensure that the application is fully completed before issuing it. Once the policy is issued, the insurer has waived its right to contest it unless for fraud or material concealment.

ID: MINZOPASSESADC1Q13C3A403312022Q1DC

66. Correct Answer: A

A warranty is a statement on an insurance application that is guaranteed to be true. The insurer may cancel the policy if a warranty is later found false.

ID: MINZOPASSJDADC1Q24C3A504012022Q1DC

67. Correct answer: C

A legal offer is accompanied by a premium check. The act of issuing a policy is considered legal acceptance. The offer is deemed accepted when the insurer issues the policy.

ID: MINZOPASSEMADC7Q93C3A604042022Q1DC

68. CORRECT ANSWER: A

The exchange of an annuity policy for any type of life insurance policy is prohibited by IRC section 1035.

ID: MINZOPASSEMADC2Q3C3A7040122Q1DC

69. Correct answer: D

All of the above are correct.

More on HIV & POS(Point-of-Sale) disclosures:

- Before testing for HIV, insurers must obtain written consent
- Under this act, the insurer needs the written consent of the applicant before testing for HIV and before disclosing the test results to an outside party

ID: MINZOPASSESXCC5Q79C3A8040622Q1DC

70. Correct Answer: D

The USA PATRIOT Act was adapted to prevent the insurance sector specifically as well as the financial services sector from being used to finance terrorists and launder money.

ID: MINZOPASSBMC3A907282022Q1DC

71. Correct answer: D

The insured can opt out of the insurer or financial institution sharing their information with third parties at any time. If the insurer or the financial institution changes its privacy policy at any time, the Gramm-Leach-Bliley Act (GLBA) mandates that the consumer must be notified again and given another consent before the insurer or financial institution shares their information with a third party. Every time the privacy notice is altered, the consumer can opt-out again.

The privacy notice must explain the following:

- The manner in which customer data is utilised
- What data is gathered regarding the customer
- How customer information is safe guarded
- Where and how that data is disseminated

ID: MINZOPASSJDADC2Q37C3B104012022Q1DC

72. Correct answer: A

Toyin's next-door neighbor does not have an insurable interest in her; therefore, she cannot apply for life insurance on Toyin's life.

ID: MINZOPASSESXCC5Q78C3B2040622Q1DC

73. Correct Answer: B

The Medical Information Bureau's (MIB) main goal is to gather and share medical information regarding an applicant's health to its members.

ID: MINZOPASSJDADC1Q36C3B204012022Q1DC

74. Correct answer: B

The Fair Credit Reporting Act (FCRA) was enacted to protect the public and requires reporting agencies to investigate disputed information and correct it if there's a mistake. Correcting incorrect information is MANDATED by law; therefore, it is NOT at the reporting agency's discretion. Only those with a legitimate and specific use for an individual's consumer report can receive it.

ID: MINZOPASSBMADC1Q4C3B4033122Q1DC

75. Correct answer: A

The Underwriting Department is in charge of determining if a risk is acceptable and if the risk is accepted, it will decide what premium to charge.

Factors affecting underwriting

- Age
- Gender
- Use of Tobacco
- Medical history and pre-existing conditions
- Hazardous hobbies and occupations

Underwriter

The underwriter's main responsibilities include risk selection and insurability determination. At that moment, insurable interest is also established.

If a risk is accepted by the insurer, the underwriter also determines the category, kind of risk and premium rating.

Underwriting protects the insurer from risks that are more likely than average to result in losses and from unfavourable risk selection. Selecting risks that are within the expected loss range is the goal. Producers are considered field underwriters.

ID: MINZOPASSEMADC2Q51C3B5040122Q1DC

76. Correct answer: B

The insureds are selling their mortality to a third party(the investor/stranger) for a lump sum payment.

These two terms describe the act of strangers (e.g., agents, brokers) and investors with no insurable interest in the insured purchasing life insurance from the insured/policyowner with the main purpose of "cashing in" when the insured dies. Because there is no insurable interest, most states have outlawed this practice.

The third party, who is usually an investor, will take over premium payment and will be named the beneficiary. Then, when the insured dies, they will receive the death benefit.

Typically, investors pay more for the insurance than it is worth in the cash value, but less than its face value. They can profit from the insured's death in this way.

ID: MINZOPASSJDADC2Q50C3C104022022Q1DC
77. Correct Answer: C
Upon completing the application is the correct answer.

ID:MMINZOPASSJDADC1Q28C3C204012022Q1DC
78. Correct answer: B
Offering the cheapest policy is NOT an agent's responsibility.

ID: MINZOPASSBMXCC2Q18C3D104012022Q6DC
79. Correct Answer: A
The Consideration clause of an insurance contract includes the schedule and amount of premium payments.

ID: MINZOPASSJDADC1Q23C3D104012022Q4DC
80. Correct answer: B
Consideration, Agreement (offer and acceptance), legal purpose, and competent parties are the four essential parts of a valid legal contract. A legal contract DOES NOT contain an indemnity clause.

ID: MINZOPASSESEXC1Q9C3D1040422Q8DC
81. Correct answer: B
Parties to a contract must be of legal age, mentally competent, and not under the influence of illicit substances or alcohol.
The Four (4) Elements of A Legal Contract [test alert] are:

- Consideration
- Legal purpose
- Agreement (offer and acceptance)
- Competent parties

ID: MINZOPASSEMEXSEXQ8C3D104052022Q9DC

82. Correct answer: C

An insurance contract consists of a *legal purpose*, *competent parties*, *consideration,* and *agreement (offer and acceptance)*. These are the four elements of any LEGAL contract, NOT just insurance.

Note, the UNIQUE features of insurance contracts are:

- Adhesion
- Aleatory
- Unilateral
- Conditional
- Personal (not for life insurance, but insurance in general)

ID: MINZOPASSJDADC1Q18C3D204012022Q3DC

83. Correct Answer: C

Both parties must perform specific duties to make the contract legally enforceable.

ID: MINZOPASSBMXCC2Q13C3D204012022Q7DC

84. Correct Answer: B

In a unilateral contract, only one party (the insurer) makes an enforceable promise.

ID: MINZOPASSBMXCC2Q12C3D204012022Q6DC

85. Correct Answer: A

A contract of adhesion is written by one party and presented to the other party with no room for negotiation. This type of contract is usually on a 'take-it-or-leave-it' basis. Insurance contracts are contracts of adhesion because the insurer writes the contract, and the applicant cannot negotiate the terms. However, the applicant can either accept or reject it.

ID: MINZOPASSEMEXSEXQ1C3D204052022Q13DC

86. Correct answer: C

Aleatory Contract is a contract with an UNEQUAL exchange of value. For just a $100 monthly premium, Adeneki's insurer agreed to pay $10,000 in the event of a loss. This is an UNEQUAL exchange of value and is unique to insurance contracts.

The other unique characteristics of insurance contracts are:

- Adhesion
- Unilateral
- Personal (Does NOT apply to life insurance)
- Conditional

ID: MINZOPASSBMXCC2Q1604022022Q2DC

87. Correct Answer: C

In third-party ownership, designated primary beneficiaries who are also the policy owners must have an insurable interest in the proposed insured.

ID: MINZOPASSEMADC3Q76C4C04042022Q2DC

88. Correct answer: C

In life settlements, an existing life insurance policy is sold to a third party for a sum more than the surrender cash value, but not as much as the death benefit. This makes them comparable to viatical settlements. One distinction between the two is that a life settlement does NOT require the insured to be terminally ill. A policyowner might sell their policy because they cannot afford their premium due to a job loss or they just want to obtain a different policy. Unlike a life settlement, a viatical settlement can only be made for terminally ill clients.

ID: MINZOPASSEMADC7Q95C4D104052022Q1DC

89. CORRECT ANSWER: B

Annuities cannot be converted into a life insurance policy under Internal Revenue Code(IRC) Section 1035.

ID: MINZOPASSEMADC6Q56C4D204042022Q1DC

90. CORRECT ANSWER: C

A contributory plan mandates that at least 75% of eligible employees participate. Non-contributory group plans require 100% participation. Employees who are eligible pay a percentage of the premium in a contributory group insurance plan. Employees that work part-time are frequently ineligible. Dependents of an eligible employee are covered and are expected to pay a percentage of the premium, which varies according to the employer.

ID: MINZOPASSEMADC6Q86C4E104042022Q1DC

91. CORRECT ANSWER: C

Qualified retirement plans usually enjoy favorable tax treatment, such as deductible employer premiums, pretax or deductible employee premiums, and penalties waived in the instances indicated. ERISA, the Employee Retirement Income Security Act, is a federal act that provides basic guidelines, but does not mandate, for private-sector enterprises to set up pension systems.

ID: MINZOPASSJDADC5Q2C4E204032022Q1DC

92. CORRECT ANSWER: C

Both annuities and life insurance are advantageous because they provide tax-deferred growth of the principal. However, in the long-term, an annuity is better because it provides income for life that the annuitant cannot outlive

ID: MINZOPASSJDADC2Q45C4F104022022Q1DC

93. Correct answer: B

A personal use of life insurance is to conserve an estate. The insurance policy's death benefit is used to settle estate taxes, allowing the estate to remain intact rather than being liquidated.

ID: MINZOPASSEMADC6Q69C4F204042022Q1DC

94. CORRECT ANSWER: A

The key person in a key person insurance plan is a member of the management team who receives pay that is much higher than that of other employees and who performs direct service, production, or sales activities. The Chief Financial Officer (CFO) is the only one on the list that meets this definition.

ID: MINZOPASSEMADC6Q61C4F2B04042022Q1DC

95. CORRECT ANSWER: A

Life insurance is used to fund a buy-sell arrangement. It is also known as a "business continuation agreement" and its objective is to ensure that the ownership of the business is transferred appropriately in the case of the death or disability of an owner or partner.

In business insurance and estate planning contexts, third-party ownership of life insurance policies is common.

ID: MINZOPASSEMADC7Q99C4H104052022Q1DC

96. CORRECT ANSWER: C

The cost basis of a policy is determined primarily by totaling the premiums put into the policy. The cost basis simply means the amount of money that a policyowner pays into an insurance product (ex: life insurance and annuity) and is used to calculate a policy owner's tax liability in the event of a taxable event like withdrawal or surrendering the policy.

ID: MINNZOPASSJDADC2Q47C4H204022022Q1DC

97. Correct answer: B

Group insurance is written as a single policy that covers a large number of people. An individual policy that covers all family members is still considered an individual policy. Under state insurance requirements, a group created only for the purpose of getting insurance is NOT a valid organization.

Group Insurance Plans

Contributory

- At least 75% of the employees are expected to participate in premium payment

Non-Contributory

- This usually requires ALL (100%) eligible employees to participate in a group plan without contributing to premium payment.

In Group Insurance, the employer or sponsor holds the Master Policy and the employees receive a Certificate of Insurance.

ID: MINZOPASSEMADC7Q98C4H304052022Q1DC

98. CORRECT ANSWER: B

There is a 10% tax penalty if a policy owner withdraws gains(profits) from a MEC before he/she reaches the age of 59 1/2. **Test Alert:** All withdrawals made from qualified retirement plans before age 59 ½ will incur a 10% tax penalty. The only exception to this is the ROTH IRA. **Know all the qualified retirement plans because they are likely to appear on your exam.**

ID: MINZOPASSJDEXGEXQ67C5A104052022Q1DC

99. Correct answer: A

- The insurance Commissioner
    - can at any time call an insurance company to order inspection of books and records
    - Issue, suspend, or revoke licenses
    - Issue certificate of authority, etc
    - But CAN NOT make alterations to the state insurance law.
        - State insurance laws can only be altered or amended by the state legislature

ID: MINZOPASSEMADC3Q54C5A2040122Q1DC

100. Correct answer: A

Insurance company expenses are called loading. Loading is added to the net premium rate and this allows an insurance company to cover all contract costs.

Examples of contract costs are:

- commissions
- Medical examination fees
- operating costs

More on Premiums:

- Net Premium = Premium - expenses(loading)
- Gross Premium = Net Premium + Expenses
- Mortality(death)
    - Insurers use it to determine LIFE insurance premium rates
- Morbidity(sickness)
    - Insurers use it to determine HEALTH insurance premium rates

- Interest (insurer profit on premium payments)
    - Interest is the amount of money an insurer earns on premium payments it receives

ID: MINZOPASSESXCSEQ25C5A3040622Q3DC

101. Correct Answer: D

A producer must notify the Commissioner of any felony conviction or administrative action taken against them within **30 days**. Remember it's NOT 31 days because 31 days and 30 days will likely be in the answer options to trick you.

ID: MINZOPASSJDXCSEXQ13C5B104072022Q6DC

102. Correct Answer: A

Foreign Insurers are insurers that are doing business in the District of Columbia but was organized or incorporated under the laws of another state.

ID: MINZOPASSBMXCC1Q5C5B204012022Q8DC

103. Correct Answer: C

A participating life policy means the policyowner (policyholder) will receive dividends deriving from the company's divisible surplus when and if declared by the directors.

Note: Another name for participating companies is a mutual insurance company. Participating company dividends are called POLICY Dividends.

ID: MINZOPASSESXCSEQ42C5B3040722Q10DC

104. Correct Answer: C

An insurance company can only conduct business in DC with a certificate of authority.

ID: MINZOPASSJDADC14Q33C5C104052022Q5DC

105. Correct Answer: D

Washington DC requires that an applicant be at least 18 years of age, not 21.

ID: MINZOPASSESXCSEQ47C5C2040722Q5DC

106. Correct Answer: D

If a producer is found guilty of misrepresentation or fraud in acquiring a license, the Commissioner of Insurance may suspend, cancel, or refuse to renew the license.

ID: MINZOPASSJDKAC23Q37C5C304122022Q10DC

107. Correct Answer: D

The mayor appoints the insurance commissioner and signs laws(in this case insurance laws) written by the DC legislature. The mayor is not involved in the day-to-day regulation of insurance in this state. That is the job of the insurance commissioner.

ID: MINZOPASSJDADC14Q16C5C404052022Q1DC

108. Correct Answer: B

In Washington, DC, the Mayor appoints the commissioner with the City Council's advice and approval. The governor of Washington, DC, is nonexistent because Washington DC does not have a governor.

ID: MINZOPASSJDADC14Q23C5C104052022Q2DC

109. Correct Answer: D

If a producer's address changes, he or she must notify the Commissioner within **30** days.

ID: MINZOPASSESXCSEQ30C5C6040722Q4DC

110. Correct Answer: B

Insurance agents with significant lines of authority like Life and Accident/Health must complete 24 credit hours every 24 months (2 years). Three of the 24 credit hours must be in ethics, while the remaining 21 credit hours may be general. In The District, extra CE credit hours are not carried over to the next year, in contrast to other states.

ID: MINZOPASSJDXCSEXQ30C5D104072022Q5DC

111. Correct Answer: A

False advertising is advertising that is false and meant to mislead customers. It is illegal. An insurer exaggerating its dividends in an online advertisement is an example of false advertising.

ID: MINZOPASSJDXCSEXQ18C5D204072022Q12DC

112. Correct Answer: D

Rebating is the illegal act of offering "something of value" that is not specifically stated in the policy as an inducement to purchase insurance. In The District, something of value is considered anything worth greater than $10(ten dollars). This does not include brochures, educational or promotional materials that cost less than $10. An example of rebating would be a producer sharing his/her commission with an applicant as an incentive to purchase insurance.

ID: MINZOPASSESXCSEQ44C5D3040722Q11DC

113. Correct Answer: B

Making an unfair comparison of two insurance policies is an example of Misrepresentation. However, if that unfair comparison included intentionally derogatory or disparaging statements meant to harm an insurer, then it would be considered *defamation*. Remember that misrepresentation is illegal and that it is one of the unfair trade practices.

ID: MINZOPASSESXCSEQ16C5D4040622Q6DC

114. Correct Answer: D

A brochure that contains false statements about a competitor's ability to settle claims is an example of defamation.

ID: MINZOPASSEMEXSEXQ92C5D504072022Q6DC

115. Correct Answer: B

Charging different rates based on the insured's habits and lifestyle is not an unfair trade practice. In fact, this is a part of the normal underwriting process.

ID: MINZOPASSJDEXGEEXQ80C5D604052022Q1DC

116. Correct answer: A

Twisting is the act of using false information or unfair comparisons of the benefits and drawbacks of two life insurance plans to persuade a policyholder to cancel an existing policy and take out a new one that is essentially of the same type.

ID: MINZOPASSBMC5D708052022Q1DC

117. Correct answer: D

Engaging in an unfair trade practice is illegal in The District of Columbia.

The penalty for engaging in unfair trade practices are:

- A cease-and-desist order could be issued by the commissioner.
- The commissioner may issue a fine of up to $1,000 for each violation if the producer does not comply with the *cease-and-desist* order
- The producer's licence may be suspended, revoked, or not renewed by the commissioner.
- The violator may be prosecuted in the Superior Court of The District of Columbia
- The commissioner has the authority to suspend, revoke, or decline to renew a producer's licence in addition to imposing a $5,000 maximum civil penalty.

ID: MINZOPASSJDXCC8Q55C5D804112022Q13DC

118. Correct answer: C

After the insured files a claim for loss, there is a 60-day waiting period before filing a lawsuit. After **five (5)** years have passed since the claim was filed, no lawsuit can be initiated against the insurance company. This, in essence, is a statute of limitation. Insureds or policyowners have **5** years from the date of submitting a claim to file a lawsuit against the insurer. The insured or policy owner forfeits their ability to sue the insurer in the District of Columbia after five years.

ID: MINZOPASSBMADC1Q7C5E033122Q2DC

119. Correct answer: D

The producer is responsible for immediately forwarding premiums to the insurer on time, recommending policies that are in the client's best interest and confidentially communicating his/her assessments of the insured in the agent's report.

ID: MINZOPASSBMC5F08052022Q6DC

120. Correct answer: D

In The District of Columbia, insurance companies are prohibited from deciding to test a proposed insured for HIV/AIDs based on

- Gender
- Occupation
- Beneficiary designations
- Sexual orientation
- Sexual expression
- Sexual identity
- Lifestyle
- Living arrangements

ID: MINZOPASSJDEXGEXQ65C5G04052022Q4DC

121. Correct answer: B

A safety net for policyholders in their state is provided by life and health insurance guaranty associations, which guarantee that they will continue to receive coverage (up to the limitations specified by state law) in the event that their insurer declares bankruptcy.

ID: MINZOPASSESXCSEQ45C6A1040722Q9DC

122. Correct Answer: A

A 30-day grace period for premium payment is required for an individual life insurance policy issued in the District of Columbia.

ID: MINZOPASSJDEXGEXQ75C6A20405202Q2DC

123. Correct answer: B

When reinstating a life insurance policy, an insured must pay back premiums with interest, if applicable, pay all credits or loans with interest, and show evidence of insurability.

ID: MINZOPASSEMEXSEXQ77C6B104052022Q11DC

124. Correct Answer: D

The maximum interest rate insurers may charge for policy loans in Washington DC is 8% per annum

ID: MINGOPASSEMEXC6Q84C6B204052022Q4DC
125. Correct answer: C
Yes, Hung can LEGALLY deny paying John because of The Spendthrift Clause. According to The Spendthrift clause, the death benefit paid to the beneficiary is protected from the insured's creditors. However, it is not protected from the beneficiary's creditors.

More on Spendthrift Clause:

Note: The spendthrift clause in a life insurance contract can be used to require that the death benefit be paid in a fixed amount or a fixed period of time. Unfortunately for the beneficiary, he/she doesn't have the right to select a different settlement option. The beneficiary also cannot borrow from the death benefit or assign the proceeds as collateral.

The spendthrift clause is meant to protect beneficiaries from their reckless spending and also from the insured's creditors.

ID: MINZOPASSESXCSEQ29C6C1040722Q9DC
126. Correct Answer: A
The conversion privilege under a group life insurance policy permits an employee to switch to an individual insurance policy upon leaving the company without having to provide proof of insurability. The individual policy must offer the same coverage, nothing less or nothing more, as the group policy. The individual will usually pay more for the individual policy than the group policy because coverage will be based on *attained* age and the individual policy is usually a permanent policy.
Remember that per Washington DC laws, the conversion must be done within **31 days,** not 30 days. This is usually a trick question that students fail on the licensing exam. ***It's 31 days for conversion.***

ID: MINZOPASSJDEXGEXQ60C6D104052022Q6DC
127. Correct Answer: C
The Department of insurance, SEC, and FINRA are tasked with regulating variable insurance and variable annuities within each state.

ID: MINZOPASSTAXCC10Q39C6E104112022Q49DC
128. Correct answer: C
Alienation of benefits occurs when a pension or retirement plan member benefits are assigned to a different person. According to IRS guidelines, it is only permissible in rare instances. Those rare instances include using the plan's participant account as collateral for a loan and certain domestic relations orders. This trustee is most certainly in breach of this provision because there is no domestic relations order in place and could be legally liable for this violation

ID: MINZOPASSJDXCSEXQ22C6F04062022Q15DC
129. Correct Answer: A
A credit life policy is a life insurance policy that is owned by the creditor and provides benefits only to the creditor in the case of the borrower's death.

Credit Life Insurance:

- Can be used by both individualsl and groups
- Usually issued as DECREASING Term
- Debtor pays the premium. The creditor is usually the beneficiary and the policyholder
- Coverage usually ends when the loan is paid off

ID: MINZOPASSJDEXGEXQ95C6F04062022Q2D
130. Correct Answer: D
In the event of a borrower's death, credit life insurance is a form of life insurance coverage intended to settle the borrower's outstanding debts. As the loan is paid off over time, a credit life insurance policy's face value decreases in direct proportion to the remaining balance until they both equal zero.

District of Columbia Simulated Exam 2 Questions

ID: MINZOPASSBMXCC3Q23C1A104022022Q2DC
1. All of the following statements are contrary to the features of a whole life policy, EXCEPT:

A. There are flexible premiums
B. There is adjustability in death benefits
C. You can borrow money against the cash value
D. Beneficiary may be changed only with the consent of the premium payor

ID: MINZOPASSEMADC3Q78C1A104042022Q3DC
2.__________ premium payments are required for a set number of years or until a certain age is achieved.

A. A limited pay
B. A maximum pay
C. A minimum pay
D. None of the above

ID: MINZOPASSBMXCC3Q26C1B04022022Q2DC
3. Another term used to refer to a universal life policy is unbundled life policy. This is because the policyholder has access to information on the premiums, interest, and

A. Insurer profits on the policy
B. Expense charges
C. Inflation factor
D. Agent Commission

ID: MINZOPASSESEXC2Q17C1B040422Q4DC
4. An agent must be in possession of all of the following when selling a variable life insurance policy, EXCEPT:

A. FINRA and SEC registration
B. A life insurance license
C. A securities license
D. None of the above

ID: MINZOPASSEMEXSEXQ56C1B104072022Q21DC
5. What kind of premium does Universal Life and Variable Universal Life have in common?

I. Flexible
II. Level and fixed
III. Decreasing
IV. Increasing

A. I
B. II
C. III & IV
D. None of the above

ID: MINZOPASSBMC1B4061422Q2
6. What is another name for Current Assumption Whole Life?

A) Straight whole life
B) Index whole life
C) Variable whole life
D) Interest-sensitive whole life

ID: MINZOPASSESXCC3Q39C1B040522Q17DC
7. These statements are true about equity Indexed Life Insurance Policies, EXCEPT:

A. The premiums can be lowered or raised according to the performance of the selected investment portfolio
B. A minimum interest rate is guaranteed.
C. Cash value performance is based on equity indexes such as the S&P 500 or Dow Jones
D. The cash value will match the index if the gain exceeds the minimum rate of return specified in the policy.

ID: MINZOPASSESKAC4Q2C1C041122Q20DC
8. Clara, who works as a civil engineer with Bold Face Construction Consortium, wants financial protection for her family for the next 10 years because all her assets are tied up in an investment for the next 10 years. What type of life insurance coverage among the following categories will give her that financial security at the lowest cost?

A) 10-year level term
B) Whole life
C) Index Universal Life
D) Single premium deferred annuity

ID: MINZOPASSESKAC4Q34C2A4041322Q29DC
9. Gertrude is 35 years old and is married. She has an 18-year-old daughter who is in her first year of college. She also has a 12-year-old son. A decreasing term policy may be recommended for Gertrude for which one of the following reasons?

A) To save for retirement
B) To ensure that her son's college tuition coverage will be paid
C) To provide a future college education for her daughter
D) To establish an emergency fund

ID: MINZOBMC1C3ID060922Q2DC
10. Regarding the Return of Premium Term, which of the following is accurate?

A. It is cheaper than regular level term insurance
B. It has been banned in most states
C. It is a type of increasing term policy
D. The full premium is paid in addition to the death benefit only if the beneficiary dies within 90 days of an accident

ID: MINZOPASSESEXC2Q30C1C040422Q7DC
11. Which option can best be associated with an annually renewable term?

A. It requires proof of insurability with each renewal
B. The premium and death benefit are not affected by the insured's age
C. It's a level term policy
D. It provides an annually decreasing death benefit

ID: MINZOPASSEMEXSEXQ25C1C104052022Q11DC
12. All of the following are types of coverages based on how the death benefit changes during the term of a life insurance policy, EXCEPT:

A. Convertible
B. Increasing
C. Level
D. Decreasing

ID: MINZOPASSESKAC4Q35C2A4041322Q30DC
13. Which one of the following assertions best describes a 5-year renewable term life insurance contract?

A) The death benefit and premium increase every 5 years
B) Provides a fixed death benefit and a premium that increases every 5 years
C) The premium remains constant and the death benefit increases every 5 years
D) The death benefit and premium decrease every 5 years

ID: MINZOPASSPCXCC9Q49C1D104092022Q68DC
14. All of these are permissible for the owner of a single premium deferred annuity, EXCEPT

A. Choose the person who will receive the annuity payments
B. Surrender the contract for cash
C. Make additional contributions to the annuity at anytime
D. Select duration of the payout/Annuitization

ID: MINZOPASSTAXCC9Q30C1D204092022Q71DC
15. _____________are usually associated with immediate annuities.

A. Tax-free benefit payments
B. No accumulation period
C. Premium paid by Installment
D. Lump-sum benefit

ID: MINZOPASSTAXCC9Q54C1D304112022Q74DC
16. Fixed annuities protect policy owners from ________________.

A. Inflation
B. Longevity that causes savings to deplete
C. Early Retirement
D. Untimely Death

ID: MINZOPASSADXCC9Q20C1D404092022Q20DC
17. Which benefit does an equity-indexed annuity offer that a fixed annuity does not?

A. Inflation protection
B. Equity loans from the separate account
C. Guaranteed interest rate
D. Retirement income

ID: MINNZOPASSJDADC5Q15C1D104042022Q12DC
18. What happens if the annuitant dies during the accumulation phase and the annuity policy owner and annuitant are the same person, and the named beneficiary is the annuitant's spouse?

I. The death benefit is paid to the spouse, who is taxed on the deferred earnings
II. If the annuitant dies before reaching the age of 59 1/2, the spouse must pay tax on all of the proceeds plus an additional 10% tax
III. The surviving spouse can become the new owner under the IRS code and the tax deferral remains
IV. If the annuitant dies after reaching the age of 70 1/2, the payout becomes tax-free

A. II. Only
B. I & III
C. IV
D. III

ID: MINZOPASSPCXCC9Q37C1D304092022Q54DC
19. During the liquidation phase of an annuity, the annuitant is usually

A. Receives nothing
B. Can increase the premium payout time
C. Continues making regular premium payments
D. Receives benefit payments at usual intervals

ID: MINZOPASSEMEXSEXQ49C1E104072022Q8DC
20. Mr. and Mrs. Smith own a permanent life insurance policy. This policy covers both of them and will pay the death benefit only when the first insured dies. What is the policy's name?

A. Family Policy
B. Family Income Policy
C. Survivorship Life Insurance Policy.
D. Joint Life Policy

ID: MINZOPASSBMXCC3Q22C4C04022022Q1DC

21. A ______________ life insurance policy covers two individuals and provides a benefits payment upon the death of the last insured.

A. Shared
B. Joint
C. Family Life
D. Survivorship

ID: MINZOPASSESEXC3Q41C2A1040522Q3DC

22. A whole life policy rider that waives premiums due to disability of the insured is known as what?

A. Status clause
B. Waiver of cost of insurance
C. Waiver of premium
D. Payor premium

ID: MINZOPASSEMADC3Q91C2A204042022Q1DC

23. The premium payable for new policies obtained through the Guaranteed Insurability Rider is calculated using what age?

A. Attained age
B. Age at the time of original application
C. Specified policy age
D. None of the above

ID: MINZOPASSESXCC3Q59C2A3040622Q2DC

24. The ______________ ensures that payments of policy premiums will be waived in the event the owner of a Juvenile Life policy becomes disabled.

A. Family Protection provision
B. Family Maintenance clause
C. Settlement provision
D. Payor clause

ID: MINZOPASSJDEXGEXQ4C2A404052022Q2DC

25. The rider that normally pays double or triple the face amount upon the death of the insured by accident is known as what?

A. Accidental death rider
B. A covered peril Rider
C. Accidental death & dismemberment rider
D. A double indemnity death rider

ID: MINZOPASSJDEXGEXQ38C2A504052022Q2DC

26. Using term insurance with a base policy to provide added benefits or modifications makes term insurance a

A. Family rider
B. Spouse rider
C. Nonforfeiture option
D. Term rider

ID: MINZOPASSJDEXGEXQ10C2A504052022Q2DC

27.Which rider will enable John Brooks and his spouse to add all members of the family to their whole life insurance?

A. Spouse rider
B. Inclusive term
C. Entire Family Rider
D. Family term

ID: MINZOPASSJDEXGEXQ2C2A704052022Q2DC

28. How does the long-term care (LTC) rider affect the death benefits of a life insurance policy after LTC benefits have been paid to the insured?

A. Triple the death benefit
B. The death benefit is reduced
C. Death benefit is not affected
D. Grow the death benefit by the LTC payment amount

ID: MINZOPASSEMKAC5Q1C2A804122022Q2DC
29. Which of the following policies, upon the insured's death, will pay the death benefit in addition to a sum equal to all or part of the paid premiums?

A) Fixed dividend policy
B) Return-of-premium policy
C) Mortgage and debt payout policy
D) Cost-of-living policy

ID: MINZOPASSBMC2A9061922Q1DC
30. All of the following are disability riders, except

A. Waiver of Premium
B. Disability Income Benefit
C. Payor Benefit
D. Accelerated Death Benefit

ID: MINZOPASSEMKAC5Q6C2A204122022Q10DC
31. Which one of the following statements about the cost-of-living rider on a life insurance contract is INACCURATE?

A) The cost-of-living rider is tied to the S&P 500 Index
B) Uses an inflation index to provide an automatic increase in the death benefit
C) Automatically increases the death benefit based on an inflation index without the insured Having to prove insurability
D) It protects the policy's death benefit against inflation

ID: MINZOPASSESXCC3Q46C2B1040522Q5DC
32. The life insurance policy provision that states that the application makes up a part of the contract is called the _______________.

A. Buyer's Guide
B. Exclusion Provision
C. Partial Contract provision
D. Entire contract provision

ID: MINZOPASSJDEXGEXQ51C2B204052022Q2DC
33. The provision that describes the scope of the policy, its coverage, and details exactly the risk that the insurer is liable for paying is known as what?

A. Entire contract clause
B. Insuring clause
C. Payment of premium
D. Status clause

ID: MINZOPASSESXCC5Q81C2B3040622Q2DC
34. For a life Insurance policy to take effect, an application submitted without an initial premium must go through all of the following, except

A. Free-look period has expired
B. The initial premium is collected
C. Policy is delivered
D. Insurance company issues policy

ID: MINZOPASSESXCC3Q57C2B4040622Q1DC
35. What relevant detail is included in the Consideration Clause of a life insurance contract?

A. The offer and acceptance
B. The policyowner must complete the application and pay the initial premium
C. The absolute assignment
D. The frequency of application

ID: MINZOPASSJDEXGEXQ54C2B504052022Q2DC
36. The authority and right to alter premium payment modes, death benefits, receive loans, and policy statements is the responsibility of the ______________.

A. Agent
B. Insured
C. Revocable beneficiary
D. Policyowner

ID: MINZOPASSJDADC4Q6C2B604022022Q1DC

37. Which of the following does a contingent beneficiary have the right to?

A. Prevent the policyholder from borrowing against the cash value of the insurance
B. If the principal beneficiary is a minor child, receive the death benefit
C. The death benefit when the primary beneficiary is not available
D. The primary beneficiary will get a portion of the death benefit

ID: MINZOPASSJDADC4Q23C2B604022022Q4DC

38. Which statement is most accurate about changing an irrevocable beneficiary?

A. It is impossible to change the beneficiary.
B. Beneficiary can be changed at any time by the policyholder
C. The beneficiary can only be changed if they give written consent or dies
D. The beneficiary can only be changed if they give oral consent or dies

ID: MINZOPASSJDADC4Q14C2B604022022Q3DC

39. Chris is the covered party. Brita, his spouse, is the primary beneficiary. The contingent beneficiaries are their three kids. In a common accident, Chris and Brita are killed. Chris's insurance proceeds would be distributed to:

A. Brita's estate
B. Chris's estate
C. Chris's parents
D. The children

ID: MINZOPASSEMEXSEXQ57C2B604072022Q20DC

40. A life insurance policy was acquired by an insured. She named her husband the primary beneficiary and her son the contingent beneficiary. When could the insured's son receive the death benefit?

A. When the insured dies, the primary beneficiary is convicted of a felony
B. When the primary beneficiary is unavailable
C. Both A & B
D. If the primary beneficiary dies before the insured

ID: MINZOPASSESXCC466C2B6040622Q13DC
41. Jeremy, a policyowner of a $1,000,000 life insurance policy, wants to change the designated beneficiary in a life insurance policy. He would like to make the beneficiary change permanent. What type of beneficiary designation should he select?

A. Revocable Beneficiary
B. Irrevocable Beneficiary
C. Secondary Beneficiary
D. Primary Beneficiary

ID: MINZOPASSESXCC4Q65C2B7040622Q13DC
42. Which provision allows a policyowner to pay premiums multiple times in a year?

A. Consideration
B. Mode of Premium
C. Payment of claims
D. Payor

ID: MINZOPASSEMEXSEXQ54C2B704072022Q17DC
43. When is the automatic premium loan provision activated?

A. 30 days before policy surrender
B. When the grace period expires
C. 7 days before the dividend period
D. 30 days before selecting a nonforfeiture option

ID: MINZOPASSEMKAC6Q21C2B1004122022Q16DC
44. Which one of the following options protects a permanent life insurance policyholder against the policy lapse for nonpayment of premium after the grace period ends?

A. Conversion Provision
B. Guaranteed Insurability
C. Automatic Premium Loan
D. Payor Benefit

ID: MINZOPASSESEXC2Q27C2B7040422Q10DC
45. Which policy contains the LEAST expensive premium during its first year?

A. Variable life Term
B. Decreasing term
C. Increasing Term
D. Annually Renewable Term

ID: MINZOPASSJDEXGEXQ20C2B804052022Q3DC
46. For an insurance policy to be reinstated, all of the following must be done, EXCEPT

A. Outstanding loans and interest, if any, must be paid
B. Prepay the premium for the following year
C. Pay lapsed premiums
D. Pay interests on back premiums

ID: MINZOPASSESXCC3Q52C2B9040522Q4DC
47. Mohammed, a policyowner of a Whole Life Insurance policy, decides to take a policy loan against the policy's cash value. The interest rate applied to the loan may vary over time. What interest rate was applied?

A. Fixed interest rate
B. Variable interest rate
C. Fluctuating interest rate
D. Increasing interest rate

ID: MINZOPASSJDADC4Q13C2B1004022022Q2DC
48. Regarding nonforfeiture options, which of the following claims is false?

A. They give a cash value policy more flexibility
B. Cash Surrender, Reduced Paid-Up, and Extended Term are the three nonforfeiture choices
C. They are employed when the insured survives until the policyholder dies
D. They safeguard the policyholder from losing all benefits if the policy is lapsed or surrendered

ID: MINZOPASSJDADC4Q24C2B1104022022Q2DC
49. Which statement about policy dividends is correct?

A. Dividends can only be received biennially
B. Dividends are guaranteed for mutual insurance policyholders
C. Dividends are paid on non-participating insurance policies
D. There are many different dividend options

ID: MINZOPASSJDADC4Q4C2B1204022022Q2DC
50. What is the principal benefit of reinstating a life insurance policy to the policyholder?

A. A new term of contestability cannot be started by the insurance provider.
B. The benefits of the original policy, including the original premium, are still available to the policy owner.
C. All outstanding policy loans are forgiven, and the entire cash value of the policy is reinstated.
D. No proof of insurability is necessary if the insured is under 40.

ID: MINZOPASSESXCPC11Q29C2B13040822Q2DC
51. What is the highest percentage of ownership for an individual life insurance policy that an insured can assign?

A. 100%
B. 80%
C. 50%
D. 20%

ID: MINZOPASSESXCC3Q55C2B14040522Q2DC
52. What is the purpose of the Suicide Clause in life insurance?

A. Discourages applicants from purchasing a policy while contemplating suicide
B. Declines applicants contemplating suicide
C. Prevents the insurance company from ever paying a claim as a result of suicide
D. Mandate that the insurers ALWAYS pay death benefit in cases of the insured's suicide

ID: MINZOPASSJDXCSEXQ29C2B1504062022Q2DC

53. Weah stated his age as 40 when he purchased a life insurance policy. Ten years after Weah's death, the carrier discovered that Weah's true age at the time of the policy issue was 47. What would the normal process be under the misstatement of age provision in reference to paying the death benefit?

A. The death benefit plus 20% interest will be paid
B. There would be no death proceeds paid out by the insurer
C. The proceeds would be reduced based on whatever the premium would have been if purchased at age 47
D. The insurer is only required to refund all premiums paid

ID: MINNZOPASSJDADC4Q12C2B1604022022Q2DC

54. Mark has a 20-pay life insurance policy. Harriet, his wife, was named as the primary beneficiary. Harriet receives a certain amount for the rest of her life if Mark dies. Which Settlement Option did Mark choose?

A. Life Income Only
B. Survivorship option
C. Joint Life
D. Fixed Period

ID: MINZOPASSEMADC7Q80C2B1704042022Q2DC

55. To be considered terminally ill, the illness must be expected to result in the person's death within _________months.

A. 6
B. 24
C.12
D.18

ID: MINZOPASSBMC2C207262022Q9DC

56. Military service is a common exclusion in life insurance policies, and it has two clauses: STATUS and RESULTS. What is the difference between the STATUS and RESULTS Clauses?

A. With the Status Clause, any death that occurs during active-duty military service is not covered, and with the Results Clause, ONLY death that occurs due to war is not covered
B. With the Status Clause, ONLY death that occurs as a result of war is not covered, and with the Results Clause, any death that occurs during the course of active duty is not covered
C. With the Status Clause, any death that occurs during active-duty military service is not covered, and with the Results Clause, any death that occurs during the course of active duty military service is not covered
D. None of the above

ID: MINZOPASSJDEXGEXQ8C2C04052022Q4DC

57. When dealing with life insurance policies, which of these options is NOT a standard Exclusion?

A. Aviation
B. War and military service
C. Disability
D. Hazardous Occupation

ID: MINZOPASSBMC2C307262022Q7

58. If an insured dies due to a hazardous occupation or hobby, the insurer will

A. Not pay claims
B. Pay claims
C. Pay claims only after the contestability period
D. Pay claims only if the policy had a double indemnity ride

ID: MINZOPASSJDADC2Q39C3A104012022Q2DC

59. All of the following are required to sign an insurance application, except?

A. Beneficiary
B. Applicant
C. Producer
D. Insured and applicant (if different from insured)

ID: MINZOPASSJDEXGEXQ48C3A204052022Q2DC
60. What should an agent do if they realize the applicant corrected specific information on the application?

A. Make the necessary correction(s) in the applicant's absence and tell the insurer
B. The agent does nothing, and changes will be made by the insurer
C. Cross out the incorrect information, write in the correct answer, and have the applicant initial the change
D. White out the information, make the necessary changes, and get the applicant to initial the change

ID: MINZOPASSJDEXGEXQ57C3A304052022Q2DC
61. All this information is needed when applying for life insurance, EXCEPT

A. Any existing life insurance with other insurers
B. All medical information
C. Health insurance policies that are in force
D. If applicable, the producer's statement

ID:MINZOPASSJDADC1Q17C3A404012022Q2DC
62. What is a representation?

A. Unequal exchange of value
B. Only one party, the insurance company, is legally bound to the contract
C. Statements on an insurance application that are believed to be true to the best of the applicant's knowledge
D. One party, the insurer, prepares the contract. The contract is not negotiable

ID: MINZOPASSJDADC2Q48C3A504022022Q2DC
63. When may a conditional receipt be issued?

A. At policy delivery
B. During the underwriting process
C. Upon completing the application
D. None of the above

ID: MINZOPASSEMADC7Q93C3A604042022Q1DC
64. All of the following are permitted transactions in Section 1035 Exchange transactions, Except

A. An annuity contract is traded for a Whole Life Policy
B. An annuity contract is traded for another annuity contract
C. A Whole Life Policy is traded for a Universal Life Policy
D. A Variable Universal Life Policy is traded for an Equity-Indexed Annuity

ID: MINZOPASSJDADC2Q38C3A704012022Q2DC
65. The following is a general summary of the basic types of life insurance that are used to assist prospective buyers when deciding what kind of insurance coverage to purchase:

A. Brochure
B. Policy summary
C. Illustration
D. Buyer's guide

ID: MINZOPASSESXCC5Q86C3A8040622Q2DC
66. What is the primary purpose of the U.S.A Patriot Act?

A. Prevent insurance fraud
B. Prevent terrorism and money laundering
C. Prevent misrepresentations
D. Prevent Insurer insolvency

ID: MINZOPASSBMC3A907282022Q2DC
67. Which law mandates financial institutions, including insurers, to provide each consumer with a privacy notice when the consumer relationship is established and annually after that?

A. Fair Credit Reporting Act
B. Gramm-Leach-Bliley Act (GLBA)
C. The Patriot Act
D. Consumer Privacy Protection Act of 2015

ID: MINZOPASSBMXCC2Q6C3B104012022Q2DC

68. Elvis and Frank entered into a partnership and took out $350,000 life insurance on each other, naming himself as the primary beneficiary. They eventually agreed to terminate their business. Subsequently, Elvis dies after a short period of sickness. Frank is still the primary beneficiary, even though Elvis was married with three children at the time of death. Nonetheless, an insurable interest no longer exists. Proceeds from Elvis' life insurance policy will be directed to:

A. Elvis' family, they are suffering financial hardship
B. None, the partnership no longer exists
C. Frank, the primary beneficiary
D. Elvis' estate, this is safe for his family

ID: MINZOPASSEMEXSEXQ560C3C204072022Q2DC

69. The applicant may receive the Buyer's Guide no later than

A. Upon delivering the policy
B. 10 days after the policy is delivered
C. Before filling out the application
D. When the policy is issued

ID: MINZOPASSBMXCC1Q1C3B304012022Q2DC

70. The producer informs a life insurance applicant of their rights under the Fair Credit Reporting Act

A. When the policy is delivered
B. Before scheduling the appointment
C. Upon completion of the application
D. After the insurer receives the MIB report

ID: MINZOPASSJDADC1Q9C3B4033122Q2DC

71. What types of hazards are dishonest inclinations that increase the risk of loss?

A. Dishonest
B. Moral
C. Legal
D. Morale

ID: MINZOPASSBMXCC2Q8C3B504012022Q2DC

72. __________ is a(an) life insurance agreement that bypasses state laws about insurable interest.

A. Investor-Originated Life Insurance
B. Indemnity Contract Insurance
C. Non-Statutory Life Insurance
D. Key Person Insurance

ID: MINZOPASSEMEXSEXQ12C3C104052022Q2DC

73. Priya paid the initial premium when she submitted her life insurance application on May 15th. The policy was issued one month later, on June 15th, as requested, with no changes. What is the effective date of Priya's policy?

A. July 1st
B. June 15th
C. May 15th
D. July 15th

ID: MMINZOPASSJDADC1Q30C3C204012022Q2 DC

74. ABC insurer issues coverage that is different from what the insured applied for. The insurer requires an additional $25 premium because it discovered some medical conditions from the medical exam. When will the contract be approved by the insurer?

A. When the applicant accepts the policy by signing the amendment and paying the additional premium
B. Only when the applicant signs the amendment
C. Only when the client pays the premium
D. None of the above

ID: MINZOPASSESEXC1Q7C3D2040422Q12DC

75.___________is NOT an essential element of an insurance contract

A. Counteroffer
B. Agreement
C. Consideration
D. Legal Purpose

ID: MINZOPASSBMXCC2Q10C3D104012022Q5DC
76. An offer, an acceptance, and consideration make up a(an)_______________.

A. Estoppel
B. Legal Contract
C. Warranty
D. Representations

ID: MINZOPASSESADC1Q12C3D1033122Q2DC
77. The following are elements of a legal contract, except

I. Indemnity
II. Legal Purpose
III. Competent Parties
IV. Consideration

A. I & IV
B. I
C. III & I
D. II, III, IV

ID: MINZOPASSEMEXSEXQ8C3D104052022Q9DC
78. Which of the following does NOT constitute an essential element of an insurance contract?

A. Consideration
B. Legal purpose
C. Counteroffer
D. Agreement

ID: MINZOPASSESEXC1Q5C3D2040422Q11DC
79. Which contract enables claims to be paid if a proposed insured makes premium payments on a new policy but dies and the policy is approved?

A. Unilateral
B. Adhesion
C. Personal
D. Conditional

ID: MINZOPASSEMADC1Q16C3D2033122Q2DC
80. What is a unilateral contract?

A. Unequal exchange of value
B. Only one party, the insurance company, is legally bound to the contract
C. Both parties must do certain things to make the contract legally binding
D. False statement on an insurance application

ID: MINZOPASSJDADC1Q19C3D204012022Q4DC
81. What is a contract of adhesion

A. The insurer is the only party legally bound to the insurance contract
B. Both parties must do certain things to make the contract legally binding
C. False statement on an insurance application
D. One party, the insurer, prepares the contract. The contract is not negotiable

ID: MINZOPASSEMEXSEXQ10C3D204052022Q14DC
82. What does the aleatory feature in life insurance mean?

A. Take-it-or-leave-it contract
B. Exchange of unequal values
C. Only one of the parties is legally bound by the contract
D. Ambiguities in the contract are interpreted in favor of the insured

ID: MINZOPASSEMADC6Q68C4A04042022Q3DC
83. An example of third-party ownership is all of the following except

A. A life settlement
B. A viatical settlement
C. A buy-sell agreement
D. A universal life insurance policy for which David is both the owner and the insured

ID: MINZOPASSEMADC3Q76C4C040422Q2DC
84. The similarity between a life settlement transaction and a viatical settlement transaction is that

A. The insured is about to die
B. The policy is about to end
C. A third party pays less than the face value of a life insurance policy
D. The policy is old

ID: MINZOPASSESEXC4Q50C4D1040522Q2DC

85. Uche, an insured, was covered in an employee group plan but terminated the group coverage. Which of the following is NOT correct?

A. Uche may choose to convert to a permanent or term coverage
B. Uche may convert coverage to an individual policy within 31 days
C. Uche's premium will be based on her attained age
D. To convert her policy, Uche would not need to show prove of insurability

ID: MINZOPASSEMADC6Q66C4D204042022Q2DC

86. Which of the following statements about noncontributory group life insurance is not true?

A. None of the premium is paid by the employee.
B. An employer pays 75% of the premium
C. 100% participation of all eligible group members is required
D. The participants do not have to submit evidence of insurability

ID: MINZOPASSEMADC7Q88C4E104042022Q3DC

87. A Roth IRA is unique for which of the following reasons?

A. Nondeductible Contributions and Nontaxable Distributions
B. Tax Deductible Contributions and Nontaxable Distributions
C. Tax Deductible Contributions and Taxable Distributions
D. Nondeductible Contributions and Taxable Distributions

ID: MINZOPASSJDADC5Q12C4E204032022Q2DC

88. What distinguishes a corporate-owned non-qualified annuity from a nonqualified annuity owned by an individual?

A. In the event of death, the beneficiary is not guaranteed the principal amount.
B. The Security and Exchange Commission (SEC) sets the earned interest rate
C. Interest and profits are taxable as income in the year they are received
D. Gains are taxable as capital gains and not as ordinary income

ID: MINZOPASSJDADC2Q46C4F104022022Q2DC
89. Which method for evaluating insurance needs takes into account the following information:

- Income replacement for at least ten years
- Total projected educational expenses for children
- Existing debt (including mortgage & personal loans)

A. Future coverage analysis
B. Needs analysis
C. Human life value
D. The DIME method

ID: MINZOPASSEMADC6Q76C4H204042022Q3DC
90. The following are characteristics of a key person, except

A. Not directly involved in production, sales, or service
B. Part of the management team
C. Admired by customers, lenders, or vendors
D. Receives significantly higher compensation than other employees

ID: MINZOPASSEMADC6Q65C4F2B04042022Q4DC
91. When business partners obtain life insurance policies on one another, this is referred to as a(n)__________ plan.

A. Industrial
B. Cross Purchase
C. Business Transfer
D. Ownership Transfer

ID: MINZOPASSEMADC7Q95C4H104052022Q2DC
92. Which of the following is false about the transactions that qualify as 1035 exchange?

A. Converting a variable annuity into an equity-indexed annuity
B. Converting a variable universal life insurance policy with an equity-indexed annuity
C. Converting a fixed annuity into a variable annuity
D. Converting a whole life policy into a universal life policy

ID: MINZOPASSEMADC6Q71C4F204042022Q6DC

93. A $1,800,000 Law Firm partnership with four equal partners is insured under a cross-purchase plan. The amount of the policy on each law partner's life under a Cross-Purchase Plan would be

A. $500,000
B. $150,000
C. $900,000
D. $1,800,000

ID: MINZOPASSEMEXSEXQ9C4H304052022Q2DC

94. Which purpose does the seven-pay test serve?

A. To keep premium payments level for seven years
B. Used to determine if an insurance policy is a MEC
C. Requires that the policy benefits be paid out in 7 years
D. It mandates a minimum interest rate

ID: MINZOPASSJDEXGEXQ85C5A104052022Q3DC

95. Bob has held on to a temporary insurance license for 90 days. How long does he have before his license expires?

A. 0 days
B. 180 days
C. 90 days
D. None of the above

ID: MINZOPASSJDXCSEXQ33C5A204062022Q5DC

96. During the financial examination of an insurance company, who bears the financial burden incurred by the Commissioner?

A. Office of the District Solicitor
B. Commissioner of Insurance
C. Insurance Guaranty Association
D. Insurer being examined

ID: MIINZOPASSJDEXGEXQ91C5A304062022Q1DC

97. If the commissioner believes that a producer has violated an insurance regulation and decides to hold a hearing, how many days before the hearing must the producer get written notice of the hearing's date?

A. 90
B. 14
C. 25
D. 10

ID: MINZOPASSJDEXGEXQ72C5B104052022Q3DC

98. Which of the following is NOT an example of a company's incorporation location?

A. Domestic
B. Alien
C. Foreign
D. Admitted

ID: MINZOPASSBMXCC1Q3C5B204012022Q6DC

99.___________is a primarily nonprofit social organization that provides life and health insurance ONLY to its members but does not have a capital stock.

A. A Fraternal Benefit Society
B. A Mutual Insurer
C. A Nonprofit Benefit Society
D. The Life and Health Insurance Guaranty Association

ID: MINZOPASSESXCSEQ13C5B3040622Q7DC

100. An insurer domiciled in Florida was permitted to conduct insurance business in this state under the state laws of The District of Columbia. What is this insurer called in The District of Columbia?

A. Non-admitted company
B. Non-Authorized Insurer
C. Domestic company
D. Foreign company

ID: MINZOPASSEMEXC5Q64C5C104052022Q6DC
101. In The District of Columbia, a producer license expires

A. June 1st of every odd-numbered year
B. On December 31st of each year with an even number
C. Every three years on the producer's birth month
D. Every two years on the producer's birth month

ID: MINZOPASSJDADC14Q15C5C2040522Q3DC
102. Within _________ days of signing the agency contract or submitting the first insurance application, the appointing insurer must file a notice of appointment with the Commissioner.

A. 21
B. 30
C. 15
D. 31

ID: MINZOPASSEMEXC5Q61C5C304052022Q4DC
103. The person or organization responsible for paying the fee for an insurance producer's appointment is known as whom?

A. The Insurance Guaranty Association
B. The appointing insurer
C. The insurance producer
D. The Department of Insurance

ID: MINZOPASSESXCSEQ5C5C4040622Q4DC
104. Legally, an agent may share their commissions with

A. The insured
B. Any person they decide to share it with as long as the insurance commissioner is notified within 30 days
C. Another insurance agent licensed for the same line of authority
D. An employee who isn't licensed yet works for the same insurer

ID: MINZOPASSJDADC1Q35C5C504012022Q1DC
105. If an applicant's credit report contains inaccurate information, the FCRA requires the reporting agency to

A. Only send the applicant a copy of the report
B. Send the updated and correct information to the insurance company
C. Do nothing
D. Send the updated and correct information to everyone who obtained a report in the last 24 months

ID: MINZOPASSESXCSEQ46C5C6040722Q5DC
106. Every reporting period, an insurance producer in The District of Columbia is required to complete _______ hour(s) of continuing education on law and ethics.

A. 0
B. 3
C. 1
D. 6

ID: MINZOPASSJDXCSEXQ20C5D104062022Q2DC
107. Of the following, which one is an example of false advertising?

A. A Producer buying client gifts worth more than $25
B. An insurance company placing an advertisement in a trade publication for insurance
C. Distributing policy brochures
D. An insurer exaggerating its dividends in an online advertisement

ID: MINZOPASSJDXCSEXQ15C5D204062022Q5DC
108. Which of these statements most accurately sums up rebating?

A. A stock insurer paying dividends to its policy owners
B. Issuing company brochures without NAIC approval
C. Giving the applicant a portion of the premium as an inducement to purchase insurance
D. Advertising significantly higher insurance rates than competitors

ID: MINZOPASSJDADC1Q32C5D304012022Q2DC
109. An applicant who falsified information on their application commits the following offense:

A. Misrepresentation
B. Concealment
C. Fraud
D. Rebating

ID: MINZOPASSESXCSEQ37C5D4040722Q7DC
110. Defamation happens when an agent intentionally makes a misleading statement that

A. Replaces an existing policy with a new policy
B. Induces an insured to purchase a new policy
C. Smears or maligns another insurance company
D. Increases sales

ID: MINZOPASSEMKAC2Q74C5D504112022Q8DC
111. All of the following are not used to determine insurance premium rates, except

A. The applicant's religion
B. The applicant's blindness
C. The applicant's race
D. The applicant's age

ID: MINZOPASSJDXCSEXQ18C5D604062022Q3DC
112. An insurance agent will be found guilty of ___________if he/she misrepresents a policy to induce an insured to lapse, cancel or surrender their policy.

A. Misrepresentation
B. Rebating
C. Twisting
D. Representation

ID: MINZOPASSEMKAC2Q4C5D704112022Q1DC
113. If a consumer report is obtained using false pretenses, what is the maximum penalty?

A. Imprisonment for one year, $7,000 fine, or both
B. Imprisonment for five years, $7,500 fine, or both
C. Imprisonment for two years, $10,000 fine, or both
D. Imprisonment for one year, $5,000 fine, or both

ID: MINZOPASSESXCSEQ1C5D8040622Q5DC
114. Which of the following describes an instance of an unfair claim settlement practice?

A. Requiring the insured or policyholder to give a statement under oath
B. Immediately honoring a claim after obtaining evidence of loss
C. Failing to effectuate a fair, equitable, and prompt settlement of a claim
D. Making the claim forms available for all client

ID: MINZOPASSEMEXSEXQ65C6F04052022Q6DC
115. Who is considered a fiduciary in insurance terms?

A. A banker
B. Any person who handles other people's money
C. An agent who handles insurance company money in a trust capacity
D. An insurance company accountant

ID: MINZOPASSBMC5F08052022Q3DC
116. Insurers can contest a policy for three years in The District if

I. After it had been issued, renewed, or amended, the insured intentionally did not disclose that they had AIDS at the time of the application
II. The insurer was not permitted to test for AIDs at the time of application, renewal, or amendment
III. The insurer was allowed to test for AIDs during application, renewal, or amendment
IV. Insurers are ONLY authorized to contest a policy for the first two years, not 3

A. IV
B. I & II
C. I & III
D. II

ID: MINZOPASSJDADC14Q29C5G04052022Q2DC
117. Which of these statements about the Life and Health Insurance Guaranty Association is false?

A. The association requires all insurers allowed to transact life and health insurance in The district to be members
B. It protects policyholders against financial loss if an insurer goes bankrupt
C. In no case will the association be responsible for more than $300,000 in total for any single individual
D. An insurer can join the association by choice

ID: MINZOPASSJDADC14Q24C6A104052022Q1DC
118. A flexible premium contract's grace period must be at least _____________.

A. 31 days
B. 61 days
C. 30 days
D. 90 days

ID: MINZOPASSEMEXSEXQ83C6A204072022Q3DC
119. Which statement is true about the reinstatement provision?

A. It mandates reinstatement within seven years after an insurance policy lapses
B. It mandates reinstatement within two years after an insurance policy lapses
C. It requires reinstatement of a policy within six months if the policy lapsed because of the insured's inability to pay premiums due to disability suffered during active-duty military service
D. It requires the policyowner to submit a new application, pay with interest all overdue premiums, and submit evidence of insurability for the policy to be reinstated.

ID: MINZOPASSJDEXGEXQ71C6B104052022Q5DC
120. How long does an insurance policy have to be in effect before its owner is eligible to borrow against its cash value?

A. 3 years
B. 5 years
C. 4 years
D. 6 years

ID: MINZOPASSJDEXGEXQ73C6B204052022Q5DC
121. Who does the spendthrift clause protect when added to a policy?

A. The agent
B. The beneficiary
C. The insured
D. The home office underwriter

ID: MINZOPASSEMEXC6Q89C6C104052022Q4DC

122. Leaving or terminating a group insurance plan and switching to an individual life policy without proof of insurability can be related to which of the following?

A. Conversion
B. Reinstatement
C. Renewable
D. Risk sharing

ID: MINZOPASSJDADC5Q17C6D104042022Q3DC

123. Beko owns a variable annuity with a 5% monthly assumed interest rate (AIR) . If the insurer's separate account(s) gained 4.5% interest last month, Beko could expect this month's income payment to

A. Stay the same because variable annuity income payments are fixed and guaranteed
B. Stay the same because the difference between the AIR and actual earned interest rate is less than 1%
C. Decrease
D. Increase

ID: MINZOPASSBMXCC3Q24C6E04022022Q1DC

124. A whole life policy with defined benefits (such as death benefit and cash value) that changes according to market performance is known as

A. Universal life
B. Variable Life
C. Variable Universal Life
D. Whole Life

ID: MINZOPASSEMEXC6Q78C6F04052022Q4DC

125. Chinedu is a professional scuba diver who wants a loan to purchase his dream vehicle. What protects a lender if he is involved in an accident and unable to continue making payments?

A. Credit life insurance
B. Credit accident and health insurance
C. Lender's guarantee insurance
D. None of the above

ID: MINZOPASSJDADC14Q8C6G04052022Q1DC

126: After _________ years, nonforfeiture benefits and cash surrender values will be available to the insured in the event of default in premium payments in The District.

A. 1
B. 5
C. 3
D. 2

District of Columbia Simulated Exam 2 Answers

ID: MINZOPASSBMXCC3Q23C1A104022022Q2DC
1. Correct Answer: C
With a whole life policy, you can borrow from your cash value.

Different Types of Whole life policies:

- Straight Life
  - pay premium until age 100 or insured's death, whichever occurs first
- Limited Pay Whole life
  - pay premium for a limited time, but coverage lasts a lifetime
    Ex: Like paying off your house early
- Single Premium Whole Life
  - Paying one lump sum premium to cover you for life
- Modified Premium Whole Life
  - low premium to start with, but premium increases in the future & stays fixed. Premium only increases once
- Graded Whole Life
  - Premium increases yearly for a certain number of years, then stays level
- Variable Whole Life (Variable Life)
  - Cash value not guaranteed and the policyowner bears the investment risk

ID: MINZOPASSEMADC3Q78C1A104042022Q3DC
2. Correct Answer: A
With a limited pay life insurance, a type of whole life policy, the policy owner pays the required premium for the entire policy in a short time or before a stated age, whichever occurs first. Although all the premium payments were made over a short time, the policy will remain in force until it endows at age 100 or until the insured dies, whichever occurs first.

ID: MINZOPASSBMXCC3Q26C1B04022022Q2DC
3. Correct Answer: B
A universal life policy is also known as an unbundled life policy because the expense charges, the interest earned, and the cost of insurance can be seen by the policyowner.

ID: MINZOPASSESEXC2Q17C1B040422Q4DC
4. Correct answer: D
To be granted permission to sell variable life products in a state, an agent must be registered with FINRA and the SEC, in possession of a securities license, and must be life insurance licensed.

ID: MINZOPASSEMEXSEXQ56C1B104072022Q21DC

5. Correct Answer: A

Both universal and variable universal life policies have a FLEXIBLE premium and flexible death benefit. The policyowner can increase or decrease the premium and the death benefit anytime. Remember, to increase the death benefit, the insured must show evidence of insurability if they did not purchase the guaranteed insurability rider.

ID: MINZOPASSBMC1B4061422Q2DC

6. Correct answer: D

Another name for the *current assumption whole life* is interest-sensitive whole life. With an interest sensitive whole life policy, the insurer can either change the premiums or change the interest rate that it credits to the cash value based on the current interest rates on the market.

More on interest-sensitive whole life:

- Has guaranteed minimum death benefit
- Death benefit may increase if the cash value grows based on higher interest rates
- Higher current interest rate results in
  - reduced premium or
  - Cash value increases very quickly
- Note: the policy could endow before age 100 if the cash value equals the face amount before age 100. For this reason, the insurer will usually automatically increase the death benefit to prevent early endowment. When this happens, it is generally called protection or a corridor.

ID: MINZOPASSESXCC3Q39C1B040522Q17DC

7. Correct Answer: A

The premium cannot be lowered or raised because it is fixed.
Accumulated cash values are tied to the stock market index in the Equity Indexed Life Insurance policy.

ID: MINZOPASSESKAC4Q2C1C041122Q20DC

8. Correct Answer: A

Level term life insurance policy refers to the type of insurance in which the face amount and coverage issued stay unchanged during the policy's life. Term(temporary) insurance is always cheaper than permanent life insurance because it does not have a cash value attached. When a client wants life insurance for a limited number of years at a very low cost, term insurance will be the best option. In this case, term insurance will be the cheapest option for Clara because it will offer her the protection she needs at the lowest cost.

ID: MINZOPASSESKAC4Q34C2A4041322Q29DC

9. Correct Answer: C

A decreasing term insurance policy protects decreasing insurance needs. In this case, the daughter's total college tuition needs to decrease every year. Therefore, a decreasing term policy would be required to pay her daughter's remaining policy in the event of her premature death. The decreasing term would not be used to provide funds for the son's college education.

Remember that term insurance cannot be used for retirement savings because it does have a savings account attached.

ID: MINZOBMC1C3ID060922Q2DC

10. Correct Answer: C

The Return of Premium (ROP) is an increasing term policy. It is not banned in any state, and it is ALWAYS more expensive than regular level term insurance. In addition to the death benefit, the full premium is paid if the insured dies within a specific time period or outlives the term policy. The ROP can also be added as a rider to a level term policy.

ID: MINZOPASSESEXC2Q30C1C040422Q7DC

11. Correct answer: C

Annually Renewable Term (ART) provides the lowest insurance cost. ART is a type of level term insurance.

More on Term Insurance:

- Temporary insurance
- Provides PURE DEATH PROTECTION
- No cash value or additional living benefits
- Three categories: level, increasing and decreasing
- Level term = most common type
- Annually Renewable Term (ART) is a level term insurance
    - Premium increases annually
    - May be guaranteed to be renewed every year without proof of insurability
- Decreasing Term
    - Usually used for mortgage or other types of death for protection against premature death
- Return of Premium (ROP)
    - is a type of Increasing Term Policy
    - Full premium is paid in addition to death benefit if Insured dies within a specified time or outlives the term policy

ID: MINZOPASSEMEXSEXQ25C1C104052022Q11DC

12. Correct answer: A

The death benefit can either increase, decrease, or remain level during an insurance policy term. Convertible is a feature that allows a term insurance policy to be converted to a permanent one without proving insurability.

ID: MINZOPASSESKAC4Q35C2A4041322Q30DC

13. Correct Answer: B

A renewable term insurance provides a fixed death benefit and a premium that increases every five years.

ID: MINZOPASSPCXCC9Q49C1D104092022Q68DC

14. Correct answer: C

A single lump-sum deposit is required for single premium deferred annuities. After this, the annuity immediately becomes annuitized, and no further premium payments can be made. However, the insured could make additional premium payments if this was a deferred annuity.

ID: MINZOPASSTAXCC9Q30C1D204092022Q71DC

15. Correct answer: B

There is no accumulation period with an immediate annuity because benefit payments begin WITHIN 30 days of the lump sum payment. On the exam, they may use 30 days or 12 months. If given these two options, select WITHIN 12 months because it is the most correct answer. However, if only WITHIN 30 days is in the answer options, choose WITHIN 30 days.

ID: MINZOPASSTAXCC9Q54C1D304112022Q74DC

16. Correct answer: B

Fixed Life Annuities provide a guaranteed income for the rest of a person's life, preventing the annuitant from outliving their money. Protection against untimely/premature death is the main objective of life insurance, not annuities. If it were an indexed annuity, it would protect against inflation due to the higher guaranteed minimum interest rate.

ID: MINZOPASSADXCC9Q20C1D404092022Q20DC

17. Correct answer: A

An equity-indexed annuity is linked to a stock index, such as the S&P 500, but offers a guaranteed minimum interest rate. The annuitant can outperform the inflation rate by usually providing at least 5 % guaranteed interest rates. Equity-indexed annuities usually provide a higher rate of return than fixed index annuities.

ID: MINNZOPASSJDADC5Q15C1D104042022Q12DC

18. CORRECT ANSWER: D

When the contract owner and annuitant are the same person, and the specified beneficiary is the annuitant's spouse, the IRS code enables the spouse to inherit the annuity following the annuitant's death. All ownership rights, including tax deferment, are assumed if a person dies within the accumulation period.

ID: MINZOPASSPCXCC9Q37C1D304092022Q54DC

19. Correct answer: D

During the liquidation phase of an annuity, an annuitant usually gets benefit payments at regular intervals. This is also called the Payout Phase. There are 2 phases for annuities: the accumulation/pay-in phase and the annuitization/pay-out/liquidation.

ID: MINZOPASSEMEXSEXQ49C1E104072022Q88DC

20. Correct Answer: D

Joint Life Policy is a permanent life insurance policy that provides coverage for two or more insureds, usually a husband and wife. The average age of both insureds is used to determine the premium amount. This policy pays death benefits when one of the insured dies.

Another name for Joint Life is the First to Die Policy.

Unlike Joint Life, Joint Survivorship policies pay death benefits ONLY when the last insured dies. Joint Survivorship Policies are also called

- Second-To-Die
- Joint And Survivor Policy
- Survivorship Life Policy
- Last To Die Policy

ID: MINZOPASSBMXCC3Q22C4C04022022Q1DC

21. Correct Answer: D

Designed to insure two people, a survivorship life insurance policy will only pay the face amount upon the death of the second insured.

ID: MINZOPASSESEXC3Q41C2A1040522Q3DC

22. Correct answer: C

Policy Riders

- Waiver of premium rider
    - waives the premium if the policyowner is totally disabled for a certain period. The policy remains in force until the insured returns to work. There is usually a 6-month waiting period.
- The payor benefit rider

    - waives the premium payment for a certain period if the owner (the payor) becomes disabled for at least six months. The payor benefit rider is usually added to Juvenile policies. This rider can also be used if the owner and the insured are two different persons.
- Waiver of cost of insurance
    - is found in Universal Life Insurance Policies

ID: MINZOPASSEMADC3Q91C2A204042022Q1DC

23. Correct answer: A

Anytime an individual purchases an insurance policy, the underwriting will always be based on the Attained(current) Age of the insured.

ID: MINZOPASSESXCC3Q59C2A3040622Q2DC

24. The correct answer: D

"Payor clause" is the correct answer.

With a payor clause or rider, the insurer will waive the premium payments for a Juvenile Life policy if the owner becomes disabled or dies. They will usually waive the premium payment up until the juvenile turns 21.

ID: MINZOPASSJDEXGEXQ4C2A404052022Q2DC

25. Correct answer: A

An accidental death rider pays double or triple the face amount if the insured dies of an accident or 90 days after an accident. Death resulting from illness is not covered.

Accidental Death Benefit Rider (Double Indemnity)

- Provides an additional amount of insurance equal to the death benefit if the death was caused by an accident. This could be double or triple the original death benefit
- Cheapest way to purchase additional coverage for a fixed period

Accidental Death & Dismemberment Rider

- Pays benefits for accident death or dismemberment
- Pays principal sum for loss of both legs, loss of vision in both eyes, both hands or both arms

Guaranteed Insurability Rider

- With this rider, a policyowner can purchase additional insurance at specified dates without showing evidence of insurability

ID: MINZOPASSJDEXGEXQ38C2A504052022Q2DC

26. Correct Answer: D

Term insurance, when used to provide extra benefits to a base policy, is called a term rider. Another name for a term rider is Base Insured Rider.

ID: MINZOPASSJDEXGEXQ10C2A504052022Q2DC

27. Correct answer: D

A family rider provides a combination of coverage for the spouse and children.

ID: MINZOPASSJDEXGEXQ2C2A704052022Q2DC

28. Correct answer: B

Paying out LTC benefits to the insured will reduce the death benefit of the original policy.

ID: MINZOPASSEMKAC5Q1C2A804122022Q2DC

29. Correct Answer: B

Return-of-Premium (ROP) policy is the correct answer.

This is a rider that can be attached to term policies. ROP rider returns a portion or all of the paid premium at the end of a term policy if the insured outlives the term coverage. Remember that this term policy is usually more expensive than a regular level term policy for the same age and face amount.

ID: MINZOPASSBMC2A9061922Q1DC

30. Correct Answer: D

All of the other riders are disability riders except accelerated death benefit rider.

ID: MINZOPASSEMKAC5Q6C2A204122022Q10DC

31. Correct Answer: A

The S&P 500 Index is linked to the cost-of-living rider. The consumer price index (CPI) is the most common index tied to the automatic increases in death benefits with this rider. The cost-of-living rider is sometimes called the cost-of-living adjustment (COLA) rider. For example, if the CPI increases by 3% this year, the death benefit will automatically increase by 3% if this rider is attached to that policy.

ID: MINZOPASSESXCC3Q46C2B1040522Q5DC

32. Correct Answer: D

The entire contract provision states that the application attached to the policy, the insurance policy, and any attached riders and amendments constitute the ENTIRE CONTRACT.

ID: MINZOPASSJDEXGEXQ51C2B204052022Q2DC
33. Correct Answer: B
The Insuring Clause is the part of an insurance policy that describes the risks the insurer takes on. In other words, this provision outlines the risks that the insurance company will have to pay for and establishes the scope of the coverage. The *insuring* rider can be described as the heart of the policy.

ID: MINZOPASSESXCC5Q81C2B3040622Q2DC
34. Correct Answer: A
An insurance policy will go into effect after all these actions are taken except the expiration of the free-look period. The free look period becomes important AFTER the policy is approved and delivered. The free look period (aka refund period) is the time after a policy is delivered that a policyowner has to return their policy and receive a full refund of all premiums paid.

ID: MINZOPASSESXCC3Q57C2B4040622Q1DC
35. Correct answer: B
According to the consideration clause, in order for the insurance company to consider the applicant for the policy, they must submit an application and pay the first premium.

More on the Consideration Clause:

- The amount and premium payment mode are included in the consideration clause
- The exchange of something valuable is called consideration
- It is one of the four elements of a LEGAL contract
- The insurer's consideration is approving and issuing the policy and agreeing to pay future claims

ID: MINZOPASSJDEXGEXQ54C2B504052022Q2DC
36. Correct answer: D
All rights to the policy belong to the policy owner. Some rights are the right to change or name a beneficiary, borrow against the cash value, receive dividends, surrender the policy, pay premiums, and assign the policy.

ID: MINZOPASSJDADC4Q6C2B604022022Q1DC
37. CORRECT ANSWER: C
A contingent beneficiary has no claim to the policy benefit. If there is a surviving primary beneficiary, the death benefit is not shared between contingent and primary beneficiaries. In a life insurance policy, only an irrevocable primary beneficiary has the authority to interfere with some of the owner's rights.

BENEFICIARY PROVISIONS:

Types of Beneficiaries

- Revocable
    - A revocable beneficiary may be changed at any moment by the policyowner.
- Irrevocable
    - An irrevocable beneficiary cannot be changed unless they die or give written approval
    - When an irrevocable beneficiary is selected, the owner of the insurance cannot make changes to the coverage or benefits without the beneficiary's approval
    - There is a vested interest in the insurance contract for the irrevocable beneficiary.

Succession of Beneficiary

- Primary Beneficiary
    - When the insured dies, the primary beneficiary is the first to receive the death benefit
- Contingent or Secondary Beneficiary
    - The secondary beneficiary gets the death benefit if no primary beneficiary survives the insured's death.

If the primary and contingent beneficiaries pass away before the insured, the policy proceeds are paid to the tertiary beneficiary.

When there is no surviving designated beneficiary at the time of the insured's death, the insurer will pay the benefits to the policyowner if they are alive or to the insured's estate if the policyowner is deceased.

ID: MINZOPASSJDADC4Q23C2B604022022Q4DC

38. CORRECT ANSWER: C

Once the policy owner has designated an irrevocable beneficiary, the beneficiary designation cannot be altered without the irrevocable beneficiary's prior written consent. There is a vested interest that the irrevocable beneficiary has in the policy.

ID: MINZOPASSJDADC4Q14C2B604022022Q3DC

39. CORRECT ANSWER: D

Contingent beneficiaries receive the policy funds in the event that the primary beneficiary is unavailable. If both are killed in the same accident or as a result of the same accident, usually within 90 days, then the *common disaster clause* states that the primary beneficiary perished before the insured.

Common Disaster Clause

If an insured and primary beneficiary are in the same accident, the primary beneficiary must survive the insured for a certain number of days, usually 90 days; otherwise, the insurance company will assume the insured died last and the primary beneficiary died first.

The purpose of this provision

- to guarantee that in the event that both the primary beneficiary and the insured die in the same accident, the contingent beneficiary will get the death benefit.

ID: MINZOPASSEMEXSEXQ57C2B604072022Q20DC

40. Correct Answer: D

The contingent beneficiary can only receive the death benefit if the primary beneficiary predeceases the insured.

ID: MINZOPASSESXCC466C2B6040622Q13DC

41. Correct answer: B

"Irrevocable" is the correct answer.

A policyowner cannot change an irrevocable Beneficiary unless the beneficiary dies or grants written approval.

ID: MINZOPASSESXCC4Q65C2B6040622Q13DC

42. Correct answer: B

The Mode of Premium is a provision allowing the insured (or policyowner if different from the insured) to pay premiums more than once yearly.

The modes of premium payment are:

- Single premium (one time)
  - Accumulates instant cash value
- Annual
  - Least expensive mode of payment
- Biannual
  - Every six months
- Quarterly
- Monthly
  - Most common
  - Most expensive

ID: MINZOPASSEMEXSEXQ54C2B704072022Q17DC

43. Correct Answer: B

The automatic premium loan provision is activated at the end of the grace period. An automatic premium loan occurs when the insurer uses an insured's policy cash value to pay an overdue premium. This provision has now become standard in most permanent life insurance policies.

ID: MINZOPASSEMKAC6Q21C2B1004122022Q16DC

44. Correct Answer: C

The automatic premium loan clause permits the insurer to use a portion of the cash value to pay the outstanding premium for a permanent life insurance policy if the grace period ends without the premium being paid. This is one of the standard provisions that comes with all permanent life insurance policies.

ID: MINZOPASSESEXC2Q27C2B7040422Q10DC

45. Correct answer: D

For annual renewable terms, the death benefit is level throughout, but the premium increases yearly as the insured's attained age increases.

The annually renewable term (ART) is the most basic type of term insurance. Most group life insurance is written as an annual renewal term.

<u>More on Types of Term Insurance</u>: Only the face amount is subject to change during the term, not the premium. The premium only changes when renewing or converting the term policy based on the ATTAINED age. Attained age is the applicant's age at the time of application.

Decreasing Term

- Death benefit decreases
- The premium doesn't change over the course of the policy.

Level term

- The premium and death benefit stay level.

Increasing term

- The death benefit increases
- Premium remains the same

ID: MINZOPASSJDEXGEXQ20C2B804052022Q3DC

46. Correct answer: B

Reinstatement is bringing back into force a policy that has lapsed. The policy owner must pay back all premiums from the lapsed date with interest plus any outstanding loans. In addition, the policy owner must fill out the reinstatement application (if the insurer demands it) and a statement of good health.
The standard reinstatement period for most states is **three years** from the date that a policy lapsed.

ID: MINZOPASSESXCC3Q52C2B9040522Q4DC

47. Correct Answer: B

A loan's variable interest rate is one that changes over time.

ID: MINZOPASSJDADC4Q13C2B1004022022Q2DC

48. CORRECT ANSWER: C

Settlement Options, not Nonforfeiture Options, are employed when the insured lives until the policy's endowment date or when the insured dies.

Nonforfeiture options

These options are offered in plans that build cash values and safeguard the policyowner from losing all benefits if the policy lapses due to nonpayment of premiums or is surrendered.

The nonforfeiture options are:

- Cash Surrender
  - When the insurance policy is surrendered in to the insurer, the policy owner will get the cash surrender value specified in the policy, minus any outstanding loans and interest that has accrued.
- Reduced Paid-Up
  - A single premium permanent policy with a reduced face amount is purchased using the present cash value. Because no extra premiums are due, this policy is considered paid-up.
- Extended Term
  - The current cash value is used to purchase a single premium term policy with about the same face amount for as long as it will last, indicated in years and days. If no other option has been selected, this option provides the biggest death benefit and is sometimes known as the **Default** or Automatic Option.

ID: MINZOPASSJDADC4Q24C2B1104022022Q2DC

49. CORRECT ANSWER: D.

Dividends are paid out to mutual(participating) insurance policyholders. They aren't guaranteed, and the dividend is not taxed because it is a return of excess premium. The policy owner can withdraw the dividend option anytime if there is enough accumulated cash dividend.

ID: MINZOPASSJDADC4Q4C2B1204022022Q2DC

50. CORRECT ANSWER: B

Reinstatement brings the policy back to its original state as if it had never expired. Even if the insurance is reactivated at a later age, the insurer will only require the initial issue premium.

The reinstatement clause states:

- If a policy has lapsed accidentally for three years due to nonpayment, the owner can reactivate it.

- The insured must produce proof of insurability to be reinstated.
- All retroactive premiums, including interest, must be paid by the owner from the lapse date.
- A new incontestability period begins upon reinstatement.

ID: MINZOPASSESXCPC11Q29C2B13040822Q2DC

51. Correct Answer: A

An insured can assign(transfer) up to **100%** ownership for an individual life insurance policy.

ID: MINZOPASSESXCC3Q55C2B14040522Q2DC

52. Correct answer: A

The suicide clause is added to life insurance contracts to deter people who are actively considering suicide from buying an insurance policy. If the insured commits suicide during the contestability period, no death benefit will be paid.

ID: MINZOPASSJDXCSEXQ29C2B1504062022Q2DC

53. Correct Answer: C

Misstatement of age or gender is exempt from the incontestability provision in insurance. Therefore, Weah's beneficiaries will receive the full benefits he would have been entitled to at the correct age.

Incontestability Clause

The insurer has the authority to refuse a claim and terminate the contract if evidence of a material misrepresentation or fraud is discovered within the first two years of a life insurance policy.

If the insurer had known the truth, they would not have issued the policy—this is known as a material misstatement.

The insurance policy will become incontestable when it has been in effect for two years, typically, from the date of policy issuing, except for nonpayment of premiums or fraud.

ID: MINNZOPASSJDADC4Q12C2B1604022022Q2DC

54. CORRECT ANSWER: A

Only Life Income ensures that the beneficiary will be paid for the rest of their life.

ID: MINZOPASSEMADC7Q80C2B1704042022Q2DC

55. CORRECT ANSWER: B

To be considered terminally ill according to federal law, the illness must be expected to result in the person's death within 24 months. However, for an insurance company to implement the accelerated death benefit rider and to limit such claims, insurance companies often define terminal illness as one that would result in death within 12 months. As you can see, insurance companies have a stricter definition of terminal illness than the federal government. However, for your exam, the correct answer is always **24 months**.

ID: MINZOPASSBMC2C207262022Q9DC

56. Correct answer: A

With the Status Clause, any death that occurs during the course of active-duty military service is not covered. With this clause, it does not matter whether or not the insured's death was directly caused by military service or war as long as the insured's status at the time of death was *active-duty military service.* The Results Clause excludes ONLY death due to war or military service. If the insured does not pass away as a direct result of a war or military duty, the insurer is nonetheless required by the Results Clause to pay the death benefit. For example, suppose you are killed in a car accident while spending time with your family. In that case, the insurer will still pay the death benefit even if you are currently on active military service.

ID: MINZOPASSJDEXGEXQ8C2C04052022Q4DC

57. Correct answer: C

Disability is not a typical exclusion in life insurance contracts.

ID: MINZOPASSBMC2C307262022Q7DC

58. Correct Answer: A

If an insured dies due to a hazardous occupation or hobby, the insurer will not pay claims because this is a common exclusion in life insurance policies. The two other standard exclusions are war and aviation. Exclusions are a common feature of life insurance policies where the insurer explicitly states certain risks that will not be covered.

ID: MINZOPASSJDADC2Q39C3A1040122Q2DC

59. Correct answer: A

The beneficiary does NOT have to sign an insurance application. The legal guardian or parent must also sign the application if the insured is a juvenile.

ID: MINZOPASSJDEXGEXQ48C3A204052022Q2DC

60. Correct answer: C

Any corrections that need to be made to the application should be done with the applicant's consent before being submitted to the insurer. The applicant MUST initial any change to the application. The incorrect information should be *crossed out,* not white-out.

ID: MINZOPASSJDEXGEXQ57C3A304052022Q2DC

61. Correct answer: C

Applying for a life insurance policy does not require the existence of an active health insurance policy.

ID: MINZOPASSJDADC1Q17C3A404012022Q2DC

62. Correct Answer: C

A representation is a statement on the application that the applicant believes is true to the best of their knowledge.

ID: MINZOPASSESXCC5Q48C3A504022Q2DC

63. Correct Answer: C

Upon completing the application.

ID: MINZOPASSEMADC7Q93C3A604042022Q1DC

64. CORRECT ANSWER: A

The exchange of an annuity policy for any type of life insurance policy is prohibited by Internal Revenue Code (IRC) section 1035.

ID: MINZOPASSJDADC2Q38C3A704012022Q2DC

65. Correct answer: D

A buyer's guide gives general information to help potential life insurance buyers make informed decisions. Included in the buyer's guide is the following information:

- How to choose a policy
- Price comparison of various policies
- Comparison of various policies and their benefits

Policy Summary

- A computer-generated image that shows the current and guaranteed premiums, as well as the current and guaranteed interest rates.

ID: MINZOPASSESXCC5Q86C3A8040622Q2DC

66. Correct Answer: B

The Patriot Act was enacted to detect and deter money laundering and terrorism.

ID: MINZOPASSBMC3A907282022Q2DC

67. Correct Answer: B

The Gramm-Leach-Bliley Act (GLBA) stipulates that application information remains confidential and should ONLY be used for other purposes or shared with third parties not specified in their financial contract with the consumer's consent. The GLBA is a federal law that requires that consumers receive a privacy notice when they enter into a financial relationship with a financial institution (including insurance companies) and every year after that. This law grants consumers the right to opt-out of having their information shared with third parties or used for purposes not specified in their contract.

ID: MINZOPASSBMXCC2Q6C3B104012022Q2DC

68. Correct Answer: C

The correct answer is Frank.

The death benefit from Elvis' life insurance policy will go to his primary beneficiary, Frank, named in the application. Insurable interest describes a relationship that must exist at the time of application.

Note: It is not necessary for an insurable interest to exist at the time of the loss. Only at the time of application must it exist.

ID: MINZOPASSEMEXSEXQ560C3C204072022Q2DC

69. Correct Answer: A

The buyer's guide must be delivered to the policy owner no later than at policy delivery.

ID: MINZOPASSBMXCC1Q1C3B304012022Q2DC

70. Correct Answer: C

Upon completion of an application, an applicant should be informed of their rights.

More about the Fair Credit Reporting Act:

- Protects consumers by mandating fair and accurate credit reporting and consumer privacy
- Insurance companies are required to inform clients if a credit check will be performed on them
- Maximum $5,000 penalty for producers who obtain consumer credit information under false pretense
- The insurer should inform the applicant in writing if a credit check will be performed

ID: MINZOPASSJDADC1Q9C3B4033122Q2DC

71. Correct answer: B

The three types of hazards are moral, morale, and physical.

Morale

- Is apathy or carelessness, while physical is a bodily condition.

Physical Hazards

- Are risks that can be seen, heard, felt, tasted, or smelled quite frequently.

Morale hazard

- An attitude of indifference toward the risk of loss, which enhances the likelihood of a loss.

ID: MINZOPASSBMXCC2Q8C3B504012022Q2DC

72. Correct Answer: A

The practice of investor-originated life insurance (IOLI) has resulted in fraudulent abuses causing many states to outlaw the policy due to lack of insurable interest.
OILI is essentially the insured selling their mortality. With IOLI, an investor usually convinces a person to get a life insurance policy to sell it to that investor. The investor will make the premium payments. In addition, the investor who paid the policy's premium also will pay the insured and collect the death benefit when the insured dies.

ID: MINZOPASSEMEXSEXQ12C3C104052022Q2DC

73. Correct Answer: C

If the initial premium was received with the application and the policy was issued as applied for, then the EFFECTIVE date will be the date of the application.

If no premium was received with the application, then the effective date would be the date that the policy was issued and the premium received.

ID: MMINZOPASSJDADC1Q30C3C204012022Q2DC

74. Correct answer: A

Having the applicant agree to a change in the application by the insurer is considered a counteroffer. The applicant accepts the counteroffer when he/she accepts the change by signing the amendment and paying the required premium.

ID: MINZOPASSESEXC1Q7C3D2040422Q12DC

75. Correct answer: A

The four major elements of an insurance contract that makes it legally binding are: *agreement* (offer and acceptance), *consideration*, *competent parties*, and *legal purpose*.
Counteroffer is not required.

ID: MINZOPASSBMXCC2Q10C3D104012022Q5DC

76. Correct Answer: B

The elements of a legal contract are legal purpose, legal purpose, agreement (Offer and acceptance) and consideration.
Estoppel: the legal name for preventing a person/company from reclaiming a right already waived.

ID: MINZOPASSESADC1Q12C3D103312022Q2DC

77. Correct answer: B

Indemnity is not an element of a legal contract.

Elements of a legal Contract

A contract is an arrangement whereby two or more parties agree to carry out a certain task in exchange for a valuable reward known as consideration.

.

A legal contract consists of four components:

1. Competent Parties
    a. All parties to a contract, including the insurer and policyowner, must meet the legal competence to enter into a contract.
2. Legal Purpose
    a. All parties to a contract must enter into it for a legal reason. A legal contract cannot violate current laws.
3. Agreement
    a. One party must make and submit to the other party an offer, which the other party must accept.
4. Consideration
    a. Each contracting party exchanges something of value called consideration. The consideration for the applicant is the money (just the first premium and the application) in exchange for the insurer's consideration (issuing the policy and agreeing to pay future claims).

ID: MINZOPASSEMEXSEXQ8C3D104052022Q9DC

78. Correct answer: C

An insurance contract consists of a legal purpose, competent parties, consideration and agreement (offer and acceptance). These are the four elements of any LEGAL contract, not just insurance. Note, the UNIQUE features of insurance contracts are:

- Adhesion
- Aleatory
- Unilateral
- Conditional
- Personal (not for life insurance, but insurance in general)

ID: MINZOPASSESEXC1Q5C3D2040422Q11DC

79. Correct answer: D

In a conditional contract, the insurer and the policy owner agree on certain conditions to execute the contract successfully.

Four Unique Characteristics of Insurance Contracts [test alert]:

1. Adhesion
    a. Take-it-or-leave-it
2. Aleatory
    a. Unequal exchange of value

3. Unilateral
    a. ONLY one party, the insurer, is legally bound to enforce the contract
4. Conditional
    a. Both parties must meet certain conditions before the contract is executed

ID: MINZOPASSEMADC1Q16C3D2033122Q2DC
80. Correct Answer: B
A unilateral contract is one in which the insurance company is the sole party legally bound to fulfill its end of the bargain.

ID: MINZOPASSJDADC1Q19C3D204012022Q4DC
81. Correct Answer: D
One party, the insurer, prepares the contract. The contract is not negotiable. When you think Adhesion, think about a TAKE-IT-OR-LEAVE-IT contract

ID: MINZOPASSEMEXSEXQ10C3D204052022Q14DC
82. Correct answer: B
Aleatory means an exchange of unequal value.

ID: MINZOPASSEMADC6Q68C4A04042022Q3DC
83. CORRECT ANSWER: D
When an applicant purchases insurance on someone other than themselves, this is known as third-party ownership.

Third-Party Ownership
- An insurance that is owned by one person that insures the life of another person. The policyowner, insured, and insurer are the three parties involved in third-party ownership.

Examples of Third-Party Ownership
- A business partner purchases insurance on his business partner
- A husband purchases a policy for his wife
- A wife buys her husband an insurance policy.
- A parent purchases a policy for one of their children
- A company purchases a policy for a key employee

Test Alert:
The insurance contract is ALWAYS between only the policyowner and the insurer, even in the case of third-party ownership. The signatories to the insurance contract are the policyowner,

producer, insured (if different from the applicant/policy owner) and the insurer. However, there are only two parties to the insurance contract: The applicant/policy owner and the insurer.

ID: MINZOPASSEMADC3Q76C4C04042022Q2DC
84. Correct answer: C
A life settlement is similar to a viatical settlement because it refers to selling an existing life insurance policy to a third party for a sum smaller than the face amount but more than the cash surrender value. One distinction between the two is that a life settlement does not require the insured to be terminally ill. A policyowner might sell their policy because they cannot afford their premium due to a job loss or they just want to acquire a different policy. Unlike that, a viatical settlement can only be made for terminally ill clients.

ID: MINZOPASSESEXC4Q50C4D1040522Q2DC
85. Correct answer: A
It is usually the insurer that determines the type of coverage when group coverage is converted to individual policies. When a policy is converted, insurers usually convert it to a permanent policy.

Note: To be eligible for group insurance, the group must have been founded for a non-insurance purpose.

ID: MINZOPASSEMADC6Q66C4D204042022Q2DC
86. CORRECT ANSWER: B
Types of Group Insurance

Non-Contributory Plan
- Employees don't participate in premium payment. With a Noncontributory plan, 100% of eligible employees are required to enroll. A noncontributory group life policy must cover all eligible employees to reduce the effects of adverse selection. The premium is usually paid in full by the employer.

Contributory Plan
- This plan is the direct opposite of a noncontributory plan. In this plan, employees participate in premium payments, and it usually requires at least 75% of eligible employees to enroll in this group plan.

ID: MINZOPASSEMADC7Q88C4E104042022Q3DC
87. CORRECT ANSWER: A
After-tax (nondeductible) funds are used to contribute to Roth retirement plans. Distributions, including all gains, are tax-free under existing tax rules.

ID: MINZOPASSJDADC5Q12C4E204032022Q2DC

88. CORRECT ANSWER: C

To avoid current income taxation, a corporation's owned annuities must be linked to a qualified retirement plan. The Internal Revenue Code has no interest rate ceilings for annuities. Before annuitization, all annuities include a death benefit guarantee, and the annuity's corporate owner will name itself the beneficiary.

Non-Qualified Annuity

- A nonqualified annuity is funded by after-tax monies, meaning the money has already been taxed before it is deposited into the annuity. Only the earnings are taxable as ordinary income when they are distributed.

Qualified Annuity

- Because a qualifying annuity is funded with pre-tax funds, the contribution may be eligible for a tax deduction, lowering taxable income. Ordinary income taxes apply to the entire distribution from a qualifying annuity.

ID: MINZOPASSJDADC2Q46C4F104022022Q2DC

89. Correct answer: B

When producers use a needs approach, they consider various factors relating to lost future income. There are two approaches an agent uses to evaluate the need for coverage and the amount of coverage: Needs Analysis and the Human Life Value Approach.

Need Analysis

- This method assesses whether or not coverage is required in the event of an individual's early death. It always assumes the individual's death is imminent and considers the following considerations when determining the appropriate amount of coverage:
    - Calculate all financial needs resulting from sudden death, including debts, medical bills, and funeral costs
    - Ensure that the spouse has a steady source of income for the at least ten years
    - Getting rid of a mortgage or other debt
    - Invest in the education of children
    - An emergency fund or lump-sum needs may be included in the calculation to cover unexpected expenses that the insured's family may face soon after their death.
    - Any assets available to fulfill financial demands after death are subtracted.

Human Life Value Approach

- This approach just takes into account an individual's economic value in determining the need for life insurance
- Insurance need is calculated with this formula:
    - (applicant's annual income) X (the number of years remaining until retirement)

ID: MINZOPASSEMADC6Q76C4H204042022Q3DC

90. CORRECT ANSWER: A

Employees who have a substantial impact on the company's income and profitability, especially in small enterprises, are referred to as key employees. They are usually part of the management team, paid significantly more, respected by creditors, suppliers, vendors, and customers, and have direct sales, production, or service duties.

ID: MINZOPASSEMADC6Q65C4F2B04042022Q4DC

91. CORRECT ANSWER: B

The partners buy life insurance policies on each other under a cross-purchase arrangement. An entity plan entails the business entity purchasing life insurance for the company's proprietors.

Types of buy-sell agreements

Entity Plan — Under this plan, a business entity agrees to buy the dead owner's share of the company.

A *stock redemption* agreement is a contract between a company and its shareholders. Each shareholder undertakes to sell their shares to the corporation at the price, terms, and conditions indicated in the agreement when they die.

Cross Purchase Plan — When business partners buy life insurance for each other. When one of the partners dies, the profits from the policy are used to buy that person's share of the business from their heirs.

Note that cross-purchase and entity plans are the two types of buy-sell agreements.

ID: MINZOPASSEMADC7Q95C4H104052022Q2DC

92. CORRECT ANSWER: B

Annuities cannot be converted into a life insurance policy under Section 1035 of the Internal Revenue Code (IRC). However, a policy owner can convert a life insurance policy to an annuity under Section 1035 of the IRC.

ID: MINZOPASSEMADC6Q71C4F204042022Q6DC

93. CORRECT ANSWER: B

Each partner's ownership portion is $450,000, so under a Cross-Purchase Plan, each partner would hold a $150,000 policy on the lives of the other three partners (3 x $150,000 = $450,000). There would be 12 policies (4 x 3) for $1,800,000 (12 x $150,000 each).

ID: MINZOPASSEMEXSEXQ9C4H304052022Q2DC

94. Correct answer: B

It determines whether the policy is a MEC or not.

Modified Endowment Contracts (MEC):

- An overfunded life insurance policy according to IRS Guidelines
- Policies that fail the 7-pay test are considered MECs and will lose their tax-advantaged treatment
- The 7-pay test sets a limit on the total amount that a policy owner can pay into the policy in the first seven years after the policy is issued
- For example, if the monthly premium is $100, then the maximum payment allowed in 7 years is ($1,200/year X 7 years) = $8,400. If the insured pays more than $8,400 within seven years, then the policy automatically becomes a MEC
- 10% withdrawal penalty if made prior to age 59 ½
- Taxation only happens when money is distributed.
- When money is taken out of a MEC, last-in, first-out (LIFO) applies
    - This means that gains are taxed first before the cost basis
    - Unlike MECs, withdrawals from life insurance are taxed on a FIFO (first-in-first-out) basis, which means that the policy owner's cost basis (total amount paid into the policy) is received tax-free first.

ID: MINZOPASSJDEXGEXQ85C5A104052022Q3DC

95. Correct Answer: C

In Washington DC, a temporary license is valid for 180 days and shall be immediately terminated upon the producer failing the required examination. A temporary license cannot be renewed, nor can it be extended.

ID: MINZOPASSJDXCSEXQ33C5A204062022Q5DC

96. Correct Answer: D

During a financial examination of an insurance company, the insurer being examined or investigated is responsible for the cost of the examination.

If the commissioner determines that insurance laws were violated, they may issue a cease-and-desist order. The cease-and-desist order will be entered as final if the person does not request a hearing within **15 days** of receiving it.

ID: MIINZOPASSJDEXGEXQ91C5A304062022Q1DC

97. Correct answer: D

The producer needs written notice **ten days** before a hearing.

ID: MINZOPASSJDEXGEXQ84C5B104052022Q3DC

98. Correct answer: D

A company's domicile(location) can be domestic, foreign, or alien.

ID: MINZOPASSBMXCC1Q3C5B204012022Q6DC

99. Correct Answer: A

A primarily non-profit social organization that provides Life and Health Insurance to its members is known as a Fraternal Benefit Society. This organization exists for the sole benefit of its members.

ID: MINZOPASSESXCSEQ13C5B3040622Q7DC

100. Correct answer: D

A foreign insurer is an insurance company headquartered in another state but authorized to conduct business in Washington, DC.

ID: MINZOPASSEMEXC5Q64C5C104052022Q6DC

101. Correct answer: D

Every two years (biennial), on the last day of the producer's birth month, a producer's licence expires.

Note: Biennial means every two years. So, you may see "biennial" on the exam instead of every two years. Remember, it represents the same thing.

Other license requirements:

- The duration of a producer license is two years
- Producer has one year to reinstate a lapsed license without retaking the exam
    - Note: the producer must complete required continuing education and pay any required fees
- Minimum age for producers is 18
- Producers have 30 days to report a change of address or name
- 24 hours of CE (continuing education) must be completed every two years
    - 3 hours of the 24 hours must be ethics
- A temporary producer license may be issued for up to 6 months (180 days)
- The producer has thirty days to disclose any action taken against them (such as a criminal conviction, suspension or revocation of their license in another state, etc.)

ID: MINZOPASSJDADC14Q15C5C2040522Q3DC

102. Correct Answer: B

Within **30** days of signing the agency contract or submitting the first insurance application, the appointing insurer must file a notice of appointment with the Commissioner.

DC Laws on Appointments

- If an insurance producer is not working as an agent for an insurer, they may be exempt from becoming appointed
- The Commissioner must verify that the insurance producer is eligible for appointment within **ten days** of receiving the notice of appointment
- If the Commissioner determines that the insurance producer is ineligible for appointment, the insurer must be notified within **five days** of the determination
- A commissioner-set appointment fee must be paid by an insurer
- A renewal appointment fee set by the Commissioner must be paid by an insurer

ID: MINZOPASSEMEXC5Q61C5C304052022Q4DC

103. Correct answer: B.

When a producer is appointed, the insurer has to pay the appointment fee. An appointment is the power granted to an agent by an insurance company to do business on their behalf.

More on Appointments:

- The Insurance Commissioner has **10 DAYS** to verify agent's appointment eligibility
- Insurer must file a notice WITHIN **30** days from the date that
    - The agent submits their first application or
    - The agency contract goes into effect
- The Commissioner must notify the insurer within **5 DAYS** of determining that the producer is ineligible for appointment
- Insurers must notify The Commissioner WITHIN **30** days after terminating a producer's appointment.

ID: MINZOPASSESXCSEQ5C5C4040622Q4DC

104. Correct Answer: C

Only another producer licensed in the same line of insurance in the insured's state of residence may legitimately share commissions with the licensed producer.

ID: MINZOPASSJDADC1Q35C5C504012022Q1DC

105. Correct answer: D

The reporting agency must send the correct information to all individuals/entities that received the incorrect information during the last two years.

ID: MINZOPASSESXCSEQ46C5C6040722Q5DC

106. Correct Answer: B

Every two years, producers need to complete 24 hours of continuing education for them to renew their licence. The producer must dedicate three of those 24 hours to law and ethics.

ID: MINZOPASSJDXCSEXQ20C5D104062022Q2DC

107. Correct Answer: D

False Advertising

- A false advertising intentionally misleads customers. It is illegal. An insurer exaggerating its dividends in an online advertisement is an example of false advertising.
- Examples include:
    - Misrepresenting the terms of the policy
    - Persuading an insured to abolish an existing policy with false details of the new policy
    - Representing an insurance policy as a share of stock
    - Insurance company advertising to prospective clients that the Insurance Guaranty Association backs its coverage.

An insurance must use its ***true*** legal corporate name when advertising.

ID: MINZOPASSJDXCSEXQ15C5D204062022Q5DC

108. Correct Answer: C

Rebating is the unlawful practice of enticing someone to buy insurance by providing "something of value" that isn't specifically mentioned in the policy. In The District, something of value is considered worth more than $10(ten dollars). “Something of value” does not include brochures, educational, or promotional materials that cost less than $10. An example of rebating would be a producer sharing their commission with an applicant as an incentive to purchase insurance.

ID: MINZOPASSJDADC1Q32C5D304012022Q2DC

109. Correct answer: A

A false statement on the application is called *misrepresentation*.

Fraud is the deliberate misrepresentation of facts to gain something of value.

Deliberately withholding material facts important to issuing an insurance policy or a claim is considered *concealment*.

ID: MINZOPASSESXCSEQ37C5D4040722Q7DC

110. Correct Answer: C

Producers who make misleading comments intending to slander another insurance business or person involved in the business of insurance may be guilty of defamation.

ID: MINZOPASSEMKAC2Q74C5D504112022Q8DC

111. Correct answer: D

Age is one of the underwriting factors used to determine insurance premium rates. A person's blindness is not a determining factor for insurance premium rates.

ID: MINZOPASSJDXCSEXQ18C5D604062022Q3DC

112. Correct Answer: C

Twisting is the unfair trade practice of misrepresenting facts to get someone to lapse, forfeit, surrender, retain, exchange, or convert an existing insurance policy.

ID: MINZOPASSEMKAC2Q4C5D704112022Q1DC

113. Correct answer: D

A fine of $5,000,1 year of imprisonment, or both are the maximum penalties for obtaining consumer reports under false pretenses.

Information gathered by consumer reporting organizations, including credit bureaus, companies that provide medical information, and tenant screening services, is protected by the Fair Credit Reporting Act (FCRA). A consumer report's information cannot be given to anyone for an unspecified purpose as defined by the Act.

ID: MINZOPASSESXCSEQ1C5D8040622Q5DC

114. Correct Answer: C

Failing to effectuate a fair, equitable, and prompt settlement of a claim is an example of unfair claims practices, one of the unfair trade practices. Other unfair trade practices include:

- Rebating
- Twisting
- Misrepresentation
- Discrimination
- Defamation
- False advertising

ID: MINZOPASSEMEXSEXQ65C6F04052022Q6DC

115. Correct Answer: C

In insurance, a fiduciary is an agent who receives and handles applicants' premiums in a trust capacity.

ID:MINZOPASSBMC5F08052022Q3DC

116. Correct answer: B

Insurers are permitted to contest a policy for ***three*** years after it has been issued, renewed, or amended if the insured intentionally did not disclose that they had AIDS at the time of application AND the insurer was not permitted to test for AIDs at the time of application, renewal, or amendment.

Note: The regular contestability period in The District is two years. However, an insurer is ONLY allowed to contest a policy within the first three years if, after it has been issued, renewed, or amended, the insured intentionally did not disclose that they had AIDS at the time of application. The insurer was not permitted to test for AIDs at the time of application, renewal, or amendment.

ID: MINZOPASSJDADC14Q29C5G04052022Q2DC

117. Correct Answer: D

The Association requires all insurers doing business in The District to be members.

ID: MINZOPASSJDADC14Q24C6A104052022Q1DC

118. Correct Answer: B

A flexible premium contract must have a grace period of at least 61 days. A planned premium contract has a 30-day grace period.

ID: MINZOPASSEMEXSEXQ83C6A204072022Q3DC

119. Correct answer: D

The reinstatement provision requires the policyowner to submit a new application, pay with interest all overdue premiums, and submit evidence of insurability for the policy to be reinstated.

ID: MINZOPASSJDEXGEXQ71C6B104052022Q5DC

120. Correct answer: A

A policy has to be in force for **three** years before a policy owner can take a policy loan from the cash value.

ID: MINZOPASSJDEXGEXQ73C6B204052022Q5DC

121. Correct answer: B

A "spendthrift provision" is a clause in an insurance policy that protects a beneficiary against the insured's creditors.

ID: MINZOPASSEMEXC6Q89C6C104052022Q4DC

122. Correct answer: A

Conversion occurs when a group member terminates or forfeits membership in a group insurance plan and converts their policy to an individual whole life without proof of insurability.

ID: MINZOPASSJDADC5Q17C6D104042022Q3DC

123. CORRECT ANSWER: C

Because the actual return is less than the assumed interest rate (AIR), the monthly annuity payout will be smaller.

The monthly annuity payout will remain the same as it did the previous month if the actual return matches the AIR. The monthly annuity payment will increase from the prior month if the actual return is higher than the AIR.

Remember that variable annuity payments are not guaranteed, unlike fixed annuity payments. The assumed interest rate is used to predict future annuity payments. However, depending on how the separate account really performs, the payouts could change.

ID: MINZOPASSBMXCC3Q24C6E04022022Q1DC

124. Correct Answer: B

Variable life is a whole life policy with certain benefits, for example, cash value and death benefits, that will vary based on the market performance of its underlying account (a separate account). Variable Whole Life is the same as Variable Life. Expect to see Variable Life Instead of Variable Whole Life on the exam.

ID: MINZOPASSEMEXC6Q78C6F04052022Q4DC

125. Correct answer: B

As defined in the policy, insurance on a debtor that covers debt payments on specific credit transactions during the disability of the debtor is a "Credit accident and health" insurance.
Credit life insurance is a policy usually written as decreasing term insurance.

ID: MINZOPASSJDADC14Q8C6G04052022Q1DC

126. Correct Answer: C

In the event of premium payment default after three years, the insured will be eligible for nonforfeiture benefits and cash surrender values.

Mandatory Provisions

- The company will award a paid-up nonforfeiture benefit if the insured defaults on a premium payment only after policy premiums for regular insurance have been paid for an entire year and if petitioned no later than **60 days** after the premium due date
- The company will pay a cash surrender value rather than a paid-up nonforfeiture value if the insured defaults on a premium payment for conventional insurance after the policy premiums have been paid for three years and if requested no later than **60 days** after the premium due date

- Unless the policyholder chooses another accessible choice no later than 60 days from the defaulted premium due date, a specified paid-up nonforfeiture benefit will automatically become effective
- If the client surrenders the policy during **30 days** of any policy anniversary or the insurance company continues the policy under a paid-up nonforfeiture benefit that became applicable after the policy has been in force for 3 years, the firm will pay the cash surrender value
- The mortality table, interest rate, and method used to determine cash surrender values and paid-up nonforfeiture options must be described or shown in guaranteed policies that allow for unscheduled changes in benefits or premiums

Helpful Resources

1. Email us at MinzoPass@MinzoPass.com.

2. Subscribe to our email list

3. Join our private Facebook group https://www.facebook.com/groups/1513896509443066/

4. Visit our website www.MinzoPass.com

5. Our Instagram https://www.instagram.com/minzopass/

6. Become an affiliate and earn up to $3,000 every month
   https://www.minzopass.com/affiliate_users/sign_up

7. Listen to our Pass Your Life and Health Insurance Exam Podcast
   https://minzopass.podbean.com/

8. Our Youtube Channel https://www.youtube.com/@minzopass3325

9. Our TikTok Page https://www.tiktok.com/@minzopass_lifeinsurance

10. Washington DC Life Insurance Exam Content Outline
    https://tinyurl.com/DCExamOutline

District of Columbia Simulated Exam 3 Questions

ID: MINZOPASSBMXCC3Q28C1A104022022Q3DC
1. A(n) _____________ is a type of insurance in which the insured is offered permanent life coverage with premiums that are payable for life.

A. Renewable Permanent Term Life
B. Renewable Term Life
C. Combo Life
D. Whole Life

ID: MINZOPASSEMEXSEXQ4C1A204052022Q4DC
2. As 45-year-old Roberto's agent, which policy would you recommend to him if he wants to pay premiums until age 65 and get life insurance protection with an attached savings component?

A. Whole life
B. Increasing term
C. 20-Pay Life
D. Decreasing term

ID: MINZOPASSESEXC2Q21C1B040422Q5DC
3. The premium that Variable Life and Universal Life policies have in common is known as what?

A. Decreasing
B. Level fixed
C. Increasing term
D. Flexible

ID: MINZOPASSEMADC3Q79C1B204042022Q13DC
4. Which of the following is true about a variable whole life policy's death benefit?

A. The death benefit is reduced by policy loans. The loans can be taken from the separate account or the general account
B. The contract will never pay less than the general account's guaranteed death benefit, even if the value of the separate account declines
C. The death benefit fluctuates based on the performance of the separate account
D. All of the above

ID: MINZOPASSEMADC3Q88C1B104042022Q19DC
5. What features do Equity Universal, Variable, and Variable Universal Life Insurance policies have in common?

A. The cash value and overall policy performance depend on the performance of the linked stock market index(es)
B. They are temporary insurance policies
C. A life insurance license and securities license are required to sell them
D. They do not protect against inflation

ID: MINZOPASSBMC1B4061422Q3DC
6. All of the following are true about Interest-sensitive whole life, EXCEPT

A. Has a guaranteed minimum death benefit
B. Depending on the current interest rate, a higher interest rate can be credited to the cash value.
C. The policy may endow before age 100 if the policy cash value matures too quickly
D. Has a guaranteed maximum death benefit

ID: MINZOPASSEMEXSEXQ33C1B204062022Q20DC
7. Which type of life insurance policy will provide permanent protection?

A. Credit life
B. Group life
C. Variable Life
D. Term life

ID: MINZOPASSESKAC4Q3C1C041122Q21DC
8. Eddie pays for a $100,000 10-year level term insurance. Which of the following statements about his term policy is INACCURATE?

A. If Eddie dies before the 10-year duration of the contract, his beneficiaries will be entitled to nothing
B. The policy does not provide a savings account
C. If Eddie dies at any time during the ten years, the policy's face value will be paid to his beneficiaries
D. Absolutely no benefits are payable if Eddie dies after the 10-year term and the policy expires.

ID: MINZOPASSESKAC4Q49C2A4041322Q37DC

9. Which category below best describes a need that decreasing term life protection is often used to satisfy?

A) Retirement savings
B) LTC coverage
C) Funds to cover burial and final expenses at a reasonable premium
D) Paying off outstanding loans when the borrower prematurely dies

ID: MINZOBMC1C3ID060922Q1DC

10. All the following are true about the Return of Premium Term, Except

A. It is a type of increasing term policy
B. If the insured passes away within a specified period of time or outlives the term insurance, the full premium will be paid plus the death benefit
C. It is more expensive than a regular level term policy
D. It is cheaper than a regular level term policy

ID: MINNZOPASSJDEXGEXQ15C1C104052022Q8DC

11. Annually renewable term insurance is associated with the following options, EXCEPT

A. The policy renews regardless of the insured's heath
B. No need for medical exams
C. The premium increases as the insured attains age increases
D. There must be proof of insurability upon renewal

ID: MINZOPASSESXCC3Q40C1C040522Q15DC

12. Included in a 30-year Term Life policy is a renewability provision.
This means the policy will renew

A. Without evidence of insurability
B. Only if the producer who sold the policy consents in writing
C. Only with proof of insurability
D. Only if the insurer consents in writing

ID: MINZOPASSESKAC4Q6C1C041122Q23DC
13. Which of the following statements regarding term insurance is true?

A) Cannot be renewed
B) Cannot be converted to a permanent policy
C) Term insurance contracts provide coverage for only a temporary time
D) Jessy and Sarah are 25 years old and have term policies with the same face amounts. Jessy's contract is convertible, and Sarah's contract cannot be renewed. Therefore, Sarah will pay a higher premium than Jessy.

ID: MINNZOPASSJDADC5Q22C1D104042022Q18DC
14. What type of annuity is purchased in June, and monthly benefit payments begin in July with a fixed and guaranteed interest rate and monthly income payments of $2,000?

A. Periodic Premium Fixed Immediate Annuity
B. Single Premium Fixed Immediate Annuity
C. Single Premium Deferred Annuity
D. Single Premium Deferred Variable Annuity

ID: MINZOPASSESXCC7Q2C1D040622Q34DC
15. Richard, a 50-year-old banker, purchased an annuity he will fund with $2,000 every month for 15 years. What type of annuity did Richard buy if the annuity is to pay him retirement after 15 years?

A. Deferred
B. Immediate
C. Multiple premium immediate annuity
D. Single Premium deferred annuity

ID: MINZOPASSESXCC7Q5C1D040622Q37DC
16. A 55-year-old business woman just bought an annuity that will pay a guaranteed $3,000 monthly benefit starting at age 65. What type of annuity did this woman buy?

A. Fixed Deferred
B. Deferred Variable
C. Fixed Immediate
D. Immediate Variable

ID: MINZOPASSESEXC2Q18C1D040422Q20DC
17. Which of the options is NOT associated with Equity Indexed Annuities?

A. Guaranteed minimum interest rates
B. Less risky than variable annuities
C. A portion of the returns are retained by the insurer
D. Lower interest rates are earned than fixed annuities

ID: MINZOPASSPCXCC9Q42C1D304092022Q61DC
18. In a tax-sheltered annuity (TSA), how are monthly life annuity benefit payments handled?

A. During the accumulation phase, they are taxed like regular income
B. Not subject to taxes
C. During the accumulation period, they are taxed as capital gains
D. In the year they are received; they are taxed as ordinary income

ID: MINZOPASSADXCC9Q16C1D2022Q16DC
19. An annuitant gets $600 every month until the contract value is depleted at some future date; this type of annuity option is called

A. Life period certain
B. Fixed amount
C. Period certain
D. Joint & Survivor Life

ID: MINZOPASSPCXCC9Q34C1E204092022Q10DC
20. Which one of the following annuities distributes an income to two or more annuitants until the last annuitant dies?

A. Joint and survivor
B. Joint Life
C. Fixed Amount
D. Survivorship

ID: MINZOPASSEMADC3Q69C1E2040222Q4DC
21. Which of the following uses for the Last-to-Die policy is most appropriate?

A. A wife who wants to receive a lump sum death benefit after her husband dies
B. Key Person Insurance
C. Buy-Sell Agreement
D. A husband and wife who are worried about having to pay inheritance taxes after they
Die

ID: MINZOPASSEMKA5Q9C2A104122022Q14DC
22. During Melvin's two (2) years of total disability, the insurer paid $2,400 of his premiums on his $50,000 life insurance coverage, which has a *waiver of the premium* rider. If Melvin should die then how much will the insurer pay Melvin's beneficiary?

A) $25,000
B) $50,000
C) $47,600
D) $52,400

ID: MINZOPASSEMEXSEXQ16C2A204052022Q4DC
23. As the policyholder, Olafemi's life insurance policy allows him to periodically purchase additional death benefit coverage at standard rates without submitting evidence of insurability. Olafemi would like to know what option in his life insurance policy allows this. As Olafemi's agent, what should you tell him?

A. Guaranteed insurability rider
B. Nonforfeiture option
C. Paid-up additions option
D. Guaranteed renewability rider

ID: MINZOPASSEMKAC5Q8C2A304122022Q4DC
24. When does the *payor* rider waive premiums on a juvenile policy?

A. The premium payor is actively serving in the United States Military
B. The insured child dies before their 18th birthday or first semester of college, whichever occurs first
C. When the parent is unemployed for more than one year
D. In the event that the premium payer passes away or becomes incapacitated before the insured child reaches a policy-specified age

ID: MINZOPASSEMADC3Q87C2A404042022Q6DC

25. What is the name of the rider that pays double or triple the death benefit amount if death occurs as a result of an accident?

A. Accidental Death
B. Guaranteed Insurability
C. Accelerated Death Benefit
D. Accident Life

ID: MINZOPASSEMEXSEXQ6C2A504052022Q3DC

26. A rider, when added to a permanent life insurance policy that provides additional coverage for the insured or coverage for the insured's family members for a period of time, is known as what?

A. Guaranteed insurability rider
B. Guaranteed renewability rider
C. Child rider
D. Term rider

ID: MINZOPASSESKAC3Q77C2A6041122Q4DC

27. A juvenile policy can be purchased for all of the following reasons, except

A. Funds for the kid's final expenses
B. Low insurance premiums for life
C. Permanent life insurance coverage for life
D. All of the above

ID: MINZOPASSEMADC3Q71C2A7040222Q1DC

28. What advantages does a long-term care rider have over a living needs rider?

A. Only pays benefits if a licensed medical provider certifies that an insured is expected to die within 24 months
B. Pays a monthly income based on a proportion of the death benefit to an insured who is unable to do any of the six activities of daily living
C. Permits a chronically ill individual to receive up to 100% of the death benefit in a daily or monthly amount for non-hospital expenses if they are unable to conduct any four of the six activities of daily life (eating, bathing, walking, toileting, etc.)
D. Permits a chronically ill individual to receive up to 100% of the death benefit in a daily or monthly amount for non-hospital expenses if they are unable to carry out any two of the six activities of daily life (eating, bathing, walking, toileting, etc.).

ID: MINZOPASSEMKA5Q7C2A804122022Q3DC
29. Frank owns a life insurance policy with a $60,000 face amount and a 20-year return-of-premium rider. He pays a $800 annual premium. If he were to die five years after purchasing the policy, what should be the total amount payable to the policy's beneficiary?

A) $60,800
B) $76,000
C) $60,000
D) $64,000

ID: MINZOPASSBMC2A9061922Q1DC
30. All of the following are disability riders, except

A. Waiver of Premium
B. Disability Income Benefit
C. Payor Benefit
D. Accelerated Death Benefit

ID: MINZOPASSEMKAC5Q18C2A104122022Q15DC
31. Which one of the following statements about the cost-of-living (COLA) rider is false?

A. Increases in the death benefit results in an increase in premium
B. Evidence of insurability is not required for the increase in death benefit
C. The death benefit will be reduced by the corresponding percentage drop in the consumer price index (CPI)
D. All of the above

ID: MINZOPASSJDADC2Q42C5C104012022Q42DC
32. Which one of the following statements about life insurance applications is not correct?

A. The producer attaches an agent's report to the completed life insurance application and forwards it to the insurer

B. Life insurance applications are usually broken into two sections: Medical History and General information

C. The agent's report forms a part of THE ENTIRE CONTRACT

D. The application contains identifying information about the insured

ID: MINZOPASSESXCC3Q43C2B2040522Q3DC
33. What constitutes an insuring agreement in life insurance?

A. The insurer's promise to maintain their license
B. The insurer's promise to reinstate a lapsed policy
C. An Insurer's required Reserve Amount
D. An Insurer's basic promise

ID: MINZOPASSEMXCPC11Q54C2B304072022Q4DC
34. Which of the following is the Free-Look period, also called the Right to Examine period?

A. 5 days
B. 10 days
C. 30 days
D. 90 days

ID: MINZOPASSESXCC3Q57C2B4040622Q1 DC
35. What relevant detail is included in the Consideration Clause of a life insurance contract?

A. The offer and acceptance
B. States that the policyowner must complete the application and pay the initial premium
C. The absolute assignment
D. The frequency of application

ID: MINZOPASSESXCC3Q56C2B5040622Q3DC
36. Which statement about the ownership clause in a life insurance policy is TRUE?

A. Specifies the beneficiary and what rights the beneficiary is entitled to
B. Ownership can NEVER be assigned after the incontestable period
C. States who the policyholder is and what rights the policyholder is entitled to
D. Permits the policyholder to change the premium amount and death benefit at any time

ID: MINZOPASSJDEXGEXQ24C2B604052022Q7DC
37. Who should annuity benefits be paid to if a beneficiary was named before the death of an annuitant during the accumulation period?

A. Annuitant's estate
B. Named beneficiary
C. Contingent beneficiary ONLY
D. The annuitant's next of kin

ID: MINZOPASSESXCC4Q61C2B6040622Q10DC
38. Caprice wants to retain her rights to change a beneficiary without proof of the beneficiary's death or approval. What type of beneficiary designation should she select?

A. Revocable beneficiary
B. Irrevocable beneficiary
C. Volatile beneficiary
D. Contingent beneficiary

ID: MINZOPASSESEXC3Q37C2B6040522Q5DC
39. Under which circumstance can an irrevocable beneficiary be changed?

A. With written permission from the beneficiary
B. The owner can change the beneficiary anytime they please
C. Beneficiary can NEVER be changed under any circumstance
D. The beneficiary cannot be changed for at least five years

ID: MINZOPASSESEXC3Q43C2B6040522Q6DC
40. Upon the death of Kiesha, the insured, which of the following beneficiaries named in the policy would NOT directly receive death benefits?

A. Keisha's former husband
B. Keisha's estate
C. Keisha's business partner
D. Keisha's 14-year-old daughter

ID: MINZOPASSJDADC4Q23C2B604022022Q4DC
41. Which statement is most accurate about changing an irrevocable beneficiary?

A. It is impossible to change the beneficiary
B. The beneficiary can, at any time, be changed by the policyholder
C. The beneficiary can only be changed if they give a written consent or dies
D. The beneficiary can only be changed if they give oral consent or dies

ID: MINZOPASSESXCC4Q67C2B6040622Q14DC
42. Which frequency of premium payments has the lowest premium outlay?

A. Annual
B. Semi-annual
C. Quarterly
D. Monthly

ID: MINZOPASSJDKAC23Q8C2B0412202Q33DC
43. __________ is the mandatory provision specifying that the insured has either 31 days or one month to pay any unpaid or overdue premium and that the coverage will remain active within that time frame.

A. Reinstatement
B. Grace period
C. Conversion
D. Nonforfeiture

ID: MINZOPASSJDEXGEXQ37C2B704052022Q11DC
44. How soon should a loan requested for the payment of premiums be issued?

A. After six months of request
B. Within ten days
C. Immediately
D. Within 90 days

ID: MINZOPASSESKAC3Q36C2B7041122Q24DC
45. What is indicated in the routine notification sent to policyholders for timely premium payment for their life insurance coverages?

A. The gross premium
B. The gross single premium
C. The net level premium
D. The net single premium

ID: MINZOPASSESXCC3Q58C2B8040622Q4DC

46. An opportunity for a policy owner to restore a life insurance coverage that had lapsed unintentionally for some time or due to nonpayment is made available under which provision?

A. Reinstatement provision
B. Restoration provision
C. Automatic Premium Loan provision
D. Waiver of Premium provision

ID: MINZOPASSTAXCC9Q29C2B904092022Q5DC

47. Which of the following elements of an annuity contract is intended to discourage withdrawals as well as exchanges?

A. Withdrawal penalty
B. Surrender charges
C. Withdrawal tax
D. The Bailout Provision

ID: MINZOPASSJDADC4Q18C2B1004022022Q3DC

48. Which nonforfeiture option is automatically selected when a policy lapses due to nonpayment of premium?

A. 20-Pay whole life
B. Extended term
C. Cash surrender value
D. Reduced paid-up

ID: MINZOPASSESEXC3Q42C211040522Q3DC

49. When dividends are used to buy a one-year term policy, what is this called?

A. One-year term option
B. Semi-annual term
C. Paid-up option
D. Endowment

ID: MINZOPASSJDXCC8Q7C2B1204112022Q3DC
50. Which of the following assertions about a life insurance policy's contestability is correct?

A. The insurer will never contest the policy
B. The insurer can always contest the policy
C. Only within the contract's first two years can the insurer contest the policy
D. None of the above

ID: MINZOPASSEMEXSEXQ26C2C1704052022Q7DC
51. What is an absolute assignment?

A. Temporary transfer of all ownership rights in a policy
B. Permanent transfer of all ownership rights in a policy
C. Transfer of partial ownership rights in a policy
D. Change of insured

ID: MINZOPASSESXCC3Q50C2B14040522Q1DC
52. What does the insurer do to resolve a case where the insured takes his own life during the policy's contestability period?

A. Pays twice the face amount under the double indemnity clause
B. Pays only 50% of the death benefit
C. Denies claims under the Suicide Clause of the policy
D. Pays only 25% of the death benefit

ID: MINZOPASSESXCC11Q1C2B15040722Q3DC
53. If Annie's age was misstated on her life insurance application, what would be required under the Misstatement of Age provision regarding her death benefit?

A. An amount that the premiums paid would have purchased at the correct age
B. Reduced by 25%
C. No death benefit will be paid
D. Both A & B

ID: MINZOPASSJDADC4Q17C2B1604022022Q3

54. Gary made Candy the beneficiary of his will, but he did not select a Settlement Option. Who decides which option to employ to obtain benefits at the time of Gary's death?

A. When no option was pre-selected before the insured's death, a lump sum is the default option and cannot be changed
B. Gary's estate
C. Candy
D. When the policyowner does not make the election before death, the insurer makes the decision

ID: MINZOPASSESEXC3Q34C2B17040422Q3DC

55. Accelerated death benefits are paid under which of the following circumstances?

A. An insured needs help to pay for medical treatment after being diagnosed with a terminal illness
B. First-time homebuyers or total disability
C. Going for an important family meeting
D. A senior citizen living on a fixed income who needs additional income stream

ID: MINZOPASSBMC2C207262022Q9DC

56. Military service is a common exclusion in life insurance policies, and it has two clauses: STATUS and RESULTS. What is the difference between the STATUS and RESULTS Clauses?

A. With the Status Clause, any death that occurs during the course of active-duty military service is not covered, and with the Results Clause, ONLY death that occurs as a result of war is not covered

B. With the Status Clause, ONLY death that occurs as a result of war is not covered, and with the Results Clause, any death that occurs during the course of active-duty military service is not covered

C. With the Status Clause, any death that occurs during active-duty military service is not covered, and with the Results Clause, any death that occurs during the course of active-duty military service is not covered

D. None of the above

ID: MINZOPASSESEXC3Q36C2C040522Q2 DC
57. The clause that denies death benefit if death was caused by war is____________.

A. Result or war clause
B. Aviation
C. Hazardous occupation
D. Exclusions

ID: MINZOPASSBMC2C307262022Q7DC
58. If an insured dies due to a hazardous occupation or hobby, the insurer will

A. Not pay claims
B. Pay claims
C. Pay claims only after the contestability period
D. Pay claims only if the policy had a double indemnity rider

ID: MINZOPASSESEXC1Q1C3A1040422Q3DC
59. What is the best course of action an agent should take if an applicant did not sign an application and he, the agent, is just realizing it?

A. Sign the application and attest it was the agent
B. Let the insurer receive the application with written communication about the absence of signature
C. Let the applicant sign the application before submitting it to the insurer
D. Sign the application for the applicant

ID: MINZOPASSESXCC5Q76C3A2040522Q5DC
60. Which statement is true about an agent accepting an insurance contract?

A. The agent will only accept the application in the presence of a lawyer
B. The agent should avoid asking the applicant personal questions
C. If the applicant makes any change to the application, the agent should make sure they initialed it
D. For the applicant, the agent may respond to common questions on the application

ID: MINZOPASSESXCC589C3A3040622Q3DC
61. What action is taken by the insurer when an incomplete application is submitted?

A. The insurer will approve the incomplete application with restrictions
B. The insurer will automatically decline the application
C. The insurer will return the incomplete application to the writing agent
D. The application process will be delayed by the insurer until they receive a MIB report.

ID: MINZOPASSBMXCC2Q7C3A404012022Q3DC
62. On an insurance application, the statements made by the applicant believed to be true to the best or their knowledge are

A. Guarantees
B. Considerations
C. Representations
D. Warranties

ID: MINZOPASSESXCC5Q80C3A504022Q3DC
63. What specific step is essential when a producer is submitting an application without the initial premium?

A. Halt the application process
B. Send in your application to the insurance company without paying the initial premium.
C. Submit the application to the insurer only after giving the applicant a binding receipt
D. Withhold the application until the premium is paid

ID: MINZOPASSEMADC7Q93C3A604042022Q1DC
64. All of the following are permitted transactions in Section 1035 Exchange transactions, Except

A. An annuity is traded for a Whole Life insurance Policy
B. One annuity contract is traded in for another one.
C. A Whole Life Insurance Policy is traded for a Universal Life Policy
D. A Variable Universal Life Policy is exchanged for an Equity-Indexed Annuity

ID: MINZOPASSJDEXGEXQ18C3A704052022Q3DC
65. When must the policy summary be given to the policy owner if it wasn't given when the application was submitted?

A. When requesting reinstatement
B. When the policy is delivered
C. Within 30 days after the insurance contract is issued
D. When the policy is forfeited

ID: MINZOPASSESXCC5Q87C3A8040622Q2DC
66. The enactment of the USA Patriot Act was done in the year ____________.

A. 2018
B. 2002
C. 2008
D. 2001

ID: MINZOPASSBMC3A907282022Q3DC
67. According to the Gramm-Leach-Bliley Act (GLBA), when do consumers have the right to receive a privacy notice from a financial institution (including insurers)?

A. When the contract becomes effective
B. Every year after the contract's effective date
C. When the financial institution's privacy practices have been altered
D. All of the above

ID: MINZOPASSBMXCC2Q11C3B104012022Q3DC
68. When must insurable interest exists for a life insurance contract to be valid?

A. Throughout the entire length of the contract
B. When the insured dies
C. At the inception of the contract
D. During the contestable period

ID: MINZOPASSEMKAC2Q8C3B204112022Q3DC
69. All of the following statements relating to credit reports and inspection reports when applying for insurance coverage are true, except

A. Applicants must be notified and give their consent to an inspection report
B. Inspection reports examine risk from a physical, moral, and financial perspective
C. Consumers should be notified of their Inspection reports only when they being are conducted.
D. Applicants with a history of moral hazard are usually poor prospects for life insurance

ID: MINZOPASSBMXCC1Q1C3B304012022Q3DC
70. Which of the following laws gives consumers the right to request disclosure and correction of any inaccurate information obtained by consumer reporting agencies?

A. State Guaranty Association
B. Fair Consumers Correction Act
C. Fair Credit Reporting Act
D. National Association of Insurance Commissioners

ID: MINZOPASSJDADC1Q21C3B404012022Q3DC
71. The following are things underwriters consider, except:

A. Age
B. Gender
C. Marital status
D. Hazardous occupation

ID: MINZOPASSBMXC2Q17C3B504022022Q3DC
72. Which of the following contractual elements does Stranger Originated Life Insurance (STOLI) violate?

A. Competent Parties
B. Offer/Acceptance
C. Legal Purpose
D. Minimum $100 value

ID: MINZOPASSJDEXGEXQ47C3C104052022Q3DC
73. An insurer mails an insurance policy to a new policy owner. When the insurance company relinquish control of the policy, the policy is regarded as

A. Delivered
B. Finalize
C. Issued
D. Mailed

ID: MINZOPASSESEXC1Q2C3C2040422Q3DC
74. When delivering a policy to a policyowner, all of the following are responsibilities of an agent, EXCEPT:

A. Collect due premiums
B. Share information on commissions earned from selling policies
C. Explain policy provisions, exclusions, and riders.
D. Explain the rating procedures if the policy was rated differently other than applied for

ID: MINZOPASSEMEXSEXQ8C3D104052022Q9DC
75. Which of the following does NOT constitute an essential element of an insurance contract?

A. Consideration
B. Legal purpose
C. Counteroffer
D. Agreement

ID: MINZOPASSESEXC1Q9C3D1040422Q8DC
76. Which of the following is NOT a competent party to a contract?

A. Jeremiah, who is not under the influence of alcohol or drugs
B. David, because he is under the influence of drugs or alcohol
C. Sarah, because she is mentally competent to understand the contract
D. Jessica, because she is not a minor

ID: MINZOPASSESEXC1Q7C3D2040422Q12DC
77. __________is NOT an important element of an insurance contract

A. Counteroffer
B. Agreement
C. Consideration
D. Legal Purpose

ID: MINZOPASSBMXCC2Q10C3D104012022Q5DC
78. The components of ______________ are an offer, an acceptance, and a consideration.

A. Estoppel
B. Legal Contract
C. Warranty
D. Representations

ID: MINZOPASSBMXCC2Q14C3D204012022Q8
79. All of the following are considered to be characteristics of insurance contracts, EXCEPT:

A. Aleatory
B. Bilateral
C. Unilateral
D. Conditional

ID: MINZOPASSBMXCC2Q13C3D204012022Q7DC
80. In what type of contract is the insurer the only party making a legally enforceable promise?

A. One-Sided Contract
B. Unilateral Contract
C. Contract of Adhesion
D. Unenforceable Contract

ID: MINZOPASSEMEXC4Q53C4A04052022Q4DC
81. If a parent buys a life insurance policy on a child, the parent is the policy holder. Which insurance agreement below would be appropriate?

A. Third-party ownership
B. Family term rider
C. A buy-sell agreement
D. An irrevocable beneficiary

ID: MINZOPASSEMADC3Q76C4C040422Q2DC
82. What is the similarity between a life settlement transaction and a viatical settlement transaction?

A. The insured is about to die
B. The policy is about to end
C. A third party pays less than the face value of a life insurance policy
D. The policy is old

ID: MINZOPASSJDEXGEXQ33C4D104052022Q3DC
83. Annuities are usually purchased by individuals who desire to

A. Create an estate
B. Receive income for life
C. Receive income for retirement
D. Both B & C

ID: MINZOPASSEMADC6Q77C4D2040422Q3DC
84. ABC Corporation employs 75 people. The employer decides to get a group life insurance policy and will pay the entire premium. For this model to work, what percentage of employees must participate?

A. 50%
B. 25%
C. 75%
D. 100%

ID: MINZOPASSEMADC7Q90C4E104042022Q4DC
85. In a defined contribution plan, what is "defined"?

A. The percentage of an employee's salary paid out in life insurance
B. The percentage or quantity of a plan participant's distributions
C. The proportion or amount of the plan's distribution to an employee by the employer
D. The amount or percentage of an employee's contributions to the plan

ID: MINZOPASSESKAC3Q2C4E2040922Q3DC
86. Which statement about nonqualified deferred compensation plans is false?

A. Most deferred compensation plans are unfunded because they are unsecured promises made by an employer
B. Employees can rely on guaranteed future benefits
C. Defers an employee's compensation until an agreed upon future date
D. The employer is not entitled to tax deductions for the deferred compensation until it is disbursed to the employee

ID: MINZOPASSEMADC3Q62C4F1040222Q3DC
87. In Life Insurance, the face amount is also known as

I. The cash surrender value
II. The limit of liability
III. The cash value
IV. The Death Benefit

A. II
B. I
C. II & IV
D. III

ID: MINZOPASSEMEXC4Q55C4F204052022Q4DC
88. The owner and beneficiary on a Key Person Life Insurance policy can be referred to as whom?

A. The employer
B. The key employee is the owner, and the employer is the beneficiary
C. The key employee
D. The owner is the employer, and the beneficiary is the key employee

ID: MINZOPASSEMEXC4Q59C4F2B04052022Q5DC
89. The following are associated with the business uses of life insurance, EXCEPT

A. Buy-sell agreements
B. Executive Bonus
C. Funding against the company's general financial loss
D. Key Person Insurance

ID: MINZOPASSEMADC7Q91C4H104052022Q3DC
90. What tax penalty result from an annuitant taking money out of their annuity before they turn 59 1/2?

A. A 15 percent tax penalty is added to the tax-deferred component of the withdrawal
B. A 10% tax penalty is added to the total withdrawal
C. There is a tax and a ten percent penalty on the withdrawal that represents earnings
D. Tax on the cost basis, plus a 10% penalty on the tax-deferred portion of the Withdrawal.

ID: MINZOPASSEMADC7Q82C4H204042022Q12DC
91. When is it permissible for an employer to deduct premiums paid for an employee's life insurance benefit from their taxes?

A. An employer can never deduct premiums paid for a life insurance benefit for an employee
B. As long as the policy does not provide a direct profit to the company, it is acceptable
C. If the business does not receive more than half of the death benefit
D. Employers can always deduct the premiums they spend for a life insurance benefit for their employees.

ID: MINZOPASSJDEXGEXQ44C4H304052022Q3DC
92. If the amount of premium paid exceeds the amount that would have provided paid-up insurance in ___________years, then a life insurance policy automatically becomes a modified endowment contract (MEC).

A. 7
B. 4
C. 2
D. Before the policy endows

ID: MINZOPASSESXCSEQ1C5A1040622Q5DC
93. The Commissioner of Insurance issues what kind of license to permit a deceased producer's representative to provide service to existing policyholders?

A. Temporary license
B. Interim license
C. Deceased provider license
D. Short-term license

ID: MINNZOPASSJDADC14Q18C5A2022Q2DC
94. Regarding examining records in The District, the Mayor must:

A. Examine every insurer at least once every five years
B. Examine every insurer in the District at least once every three years
C. Examine every insurer at least once every two years
D. There is no mandatory examination period for insurers

ID: MINZOPASSESXCSEXQ9C5A3040622Q2DC
95. What must be done by the Commissioner before the hearing for the suspension or revocation of a producer's license?

A. Notify the National Association of Insurance Commissioners (NAIC)
B. Provide the producer written notice and pay expenses related to the producer attending the hearing
C. Provide the producer written notice
D. Provide the producer's insurer written notice

ID: MINZOPASSESXCSEQ34C5B1040722Q7DC
96. A domestic insurance firm must __________.

A. Own property in The District
B. Only write insurance on risks that occur in the District of Columbia
C. Be organized under Washington DC insurance laws
D. Be a member of the fraternal order of insurance companies

ID: MINZOPASSJDADC1Q31C5B204012022Q3DC
97. Transferring part or all of the financial risk of loss from one insurance company to another is best described as

A. FDIC Insurance
B. Reinsurance
C. Third party insurance
D. None of the above

ID: MINZOPASSJDADC1Q27C5B304012022Q1DC
98. Which company creates, sells, and issues insurance policies?

A. Insurance Brokers
B. Producer Agency
C. Insurers
D. None of the above

ID: MINZOPASSJDEXGEXQ92C5C104062022Q7DC
99. To get a nonresident license in this state, a producer must

A. Find an agency in the state and represent it
B. Pass the state exam for nonresidents and fulfil their continuing education requirements
C. Apply and pay the necessary fee
D. Cancel their license in their state of residence

ID: MINZOPASSJDXCSEXQ34C5C204072022Q8DC
100. On what basis can a license be denied, suspended, or revoked by the Commissioner?

A. Making child support payments
B. Not meeting quarterly sales quota
C. Replacing an existing policy
D. If found guilty of misrepresentation in obtaining an insurance license

ID: MINZOPASSJDKAC23Q35C5C304122022Q9DC
101. The mayor appoints the Commissioner of Insurance, who is in charge of the DC Department of Insurance, for a_____ year term.

A. 5
B. 4
C. 2
D. 3

ID: MINZOPASSEMEXC5Q67C5C404052022Q2DC
102. ___________is a payment to a producer for selling an insurance contract or policy.

A. Premium
B. Bonus
C. Finder's Fee
D. Commission

ID: MINZOPASSJDXCSEXQ2C5C104062022Q8DC
103. When an insurance agent changes their address, the commissioner must be notified within how many days?

A. 30
B. 15
C. 40
D. 7

ID: MINZOPASSESXCSEQ10C5C6040622Q2DC
104. What is the required frequency for renewing an insurance producer's license in Washington, D.C.?

A. Every two years
B. Every three years
C. Every five years
D. Every year

ID: MINZOPASSJDXCSEXQ35C5D104072022Q6DC
105. Which of the following is an example of false advertising?

A. A producer spends over $10 on marketing gifts for a client
B. An insurer advertising in a magazine
C. Statement that is guaranteed to be true
D. An insurer exaggerating its dividends in an online advertisement

ID: MINZOPASSEMEXSEXQ80C5D204052022Q10DC
106. All of the following are true regarding rebates, EXCEPT

A. Dividends are not rebates
B. Rebating is anything of value offered as an inducement to purchase an insurance policy
C. Rebates are only allowed if it is written in the policy
D. Rebates are only allowed if it's in the customer's best interest

ID: MINZOPASSJDADC2Q40C5D304012022Q3DC
107. Several days after completing the application, Hiroto remembers that he may have incorrectly stated on his application that he is not on any medication. Which of the following should Hiroto do?

A. Nothing because it was a harmless mistake
B. Nothing because the application was already completed
C. Changes can only be done within 24 hours after completing the application
D. Make sure the insurer or his producer has the correct information by contacting them

ID: MINZOPASSJDKAC23Q22C5D404122022Q12DC
108. Unfair trade practices include all of the following, EXCEPT:

A. Offering special dividends not specified in the insurance contract
B. Making disparaging remarks about an insurer's financial situation
C. Licensed agents receiving commissions
D. Rebating

ID: MINZOPASSEMEXC5D504052022Q1DC
109. Limiting insurance coverage based on marital status is usually illegal, except when?

A. Never
B. More than three divorces in five years
C. More than three divorces in 10 years
D. Applying for group life insurance policies

ID: MINZOPASSEMEXSEXQ66C5D604052022Q7DC
110. The type of misrepresentation that persuades an insured to terminate, lapse, or transfer from one policy to another that is not best for them is known as?

A. False advertising
B. Twisting
C. Defamation
D. Rebating

ID: MINZOPASSBMC5D708052022Q1DC

111. Which of the following is not a penalty for engaging in unfair trade practices in The District of Columbia?

A. Cease and Desist order
B. Civil penalty of up to $1,000 for each violation
C. The commissioner may suspend, revoke, or decline to renew the producer’s license
D. The commissioner may to suspend, revoke, or refuse to renew a producer's licence in addition to imposing a civil penalty of no more than $20,000.

ID: MINZOPASSJDXCC8Q38C5D804112022Q11DC

112. Which of the following is not an unfair trade practice?

A. Rebating
B. Twisting
C. Misrepresentation
D. Representation

ID: MINZOPASSESKAC3Q44C5E041522Q9DC

113. Under which one of the following scenarios would an agent be liable for errors and omissions?

A. The agent communicates with the insurer that she believes the applicant is lying about her health history
B. The agent forgets to reply to multiple client texts and phone calls for one month.
C. The agent does not inform the client that his policy will lapse on December 31st due To nonpayment of premium
D. The agent tells the client that by purchasing life insurance, she is buying shares in the insurance company and that she will receive guaranteed quarterly dividend payments

ID: MINZOPASSBMC5F08052022Q4DC
114. In The District, insurers are prohibited from asking a proposed insured about which one of the following?

I. Sexual identity
II. Sexual orientation
III. Sexual expression
IV. Marital status

A. IV
B. I, II, III & IV
C. I, II, & III
D. II

ID: MINZOPASSJDXCSEXQ16C5G04062022Q7DC
115. In the District, the Life and Health Insurance Guaranty Association is

A. Funded by insurance companies through assessments
B. A for-profit corporation that assists in underwriting limited line insurance
C. Provides optional membership for all domestic insurers
D. Funded by state and federal government

ID: MINZOPASSJDXCSEXQ38C6A104072022Q11DC
116. What is the grace period for an individual life insurance policy in The District of Columbia?

A. 60 days
B. 31 days
C. 30 days
D. 45 days

ID: MINZOPASSEMEXC6Q88C6A204052022Q1DC
117. Shanequa's life insurance policy lapsed one year ago. Which insurance provision allows her to reactivate her policy within three years by submitting evidence of insurability and a new application?

A. Contestable clause
B. Waiver of premium
C. Grace period
D. Reinstatement provision

ID: MINZOPASSJDXCSEXQ10C6B104052022Q21DC
118. In the District of Columbia, a life insurance policy loan interest rate cannot exceed _________.

A. 17%
B. 15%
C. 8%
D. 12%

ID: MINZOPASSJDADC4Q8C6B204022022Q1DC
119. Each state's spendthrift clause shields life insurance benefits from which of the following claims?

A. Only contingent beneficiaries
B. Creditors of any beneficiary
C. Only Creditors of the insured
D. Only Primary beneficiaries

ID: MINZOPASSXCC3Q21C6C104022022Q1DC
120. Which provision allows the policyowner to change a term life policy to a permanent policy without providing proof of good health?

A. Conversion
B. Twisting
C. Even Exchange
D. Adjustable

ID: MINZOPASSJDADC5Q14C6D104042022Q1DC
121. Premium dollars are used to purchase accumulation units during the accumulation phase of a__________ annuity.

A. Variable
B. Deferred
C. Fixed
D. Immediate

ID: MINZOPASSTAXCC10Q10C6E104112022Q21DC
122. What is a retirement plan that distributes a portion of the company's net income to qualified employees?

A. Profit-sharing plan
B. Conversion plan
C. 401(k) Plans
D. IRA

ID: MINZOPASSEMADC6Q59C6F04042022Q1DC
123. Who receives the benefits from a credit life policy?

A. The borrower
B. Both the creditor and the borrower
C. Both the creditor and the borrower only if the insurer approves
D. The creditor

ID: MINZOPASSJDEXGEXQ95C6F04062022QDC
124. The life insurance policy designed to pay off any outstanding credit or loan debt upon the borrower's death is what?

A. Debtor life
B. Credit death insurance
C. Borrower's limit of liability
D. Credit life

ID: MINZOPASSBMC5A310222022Q5

125. Match the following required notices and actions with the correct time period required

#		Within 5 days	Within 10 days	Within 15 days	Within 30 days	Within 45 days	Within 90 days	Within 180 days	Within 12 months	Within 2 years	Within 3 years
1	Insurers must notify the commissioner when a field underwriter's appointment is terminated										
2	Insurer must notify commissioner for agent appointment										
3	Insurers must notify an agent in writing at his/her last known address that his appointment has been terminated after notifying the commissioner										
4	The commissioner must inform the insurer after determining that an agent's appointment is ineligible										
5	An agent must appeal a cease-and-desist order										
6	An agent must appeal a suspension or revocation of license in the superior court in DC										
7	An insurer must respond to a reinstatement application or the application will be considered approved										
8	A lapsed producer license can be reinstated without having to retake the licensing exam										
9	A change in residential or business address must be reported to the commissioner										
10	A felony conviction must be reported to commissioner										
11	A change of name must be reported to the commissioner										
12	An administrative action taken against a producer in another state must be reported to the commissioner										
13	Agent license expires on the last day of the agent's birth month										
14	Variable life insurance policies may be reinstated										
15	Life insurance policies may be reinstated										
16	Temporary producer licenses expire										
17	An agent relocating to DC must apply for a DC resident license without having to take DC's licensing exam										
18	The commissioner must provide this minimum number of days written notice for a hearing										
19	The commissioner must review an agent's appointment										
20	Insurers must provide approved claim forms after receiving notice of a claim										
21	Commissioner must send written notice to subjects of a hearing at least 10 days prior but no later than ____days										

District of Columbia Simulated Exam 3 Answers

ID: MINZOPASSBMXCC3Q28C1A104022022Q3DC
1. Correct Answer: D
A Whole Life insurance policy provides permanent life insurance with premiums payable for life. However, the insured can pay off the entire policy early, just like a mortgage.

ID: MINZOPASSEMEXSEXQ4C1A204052022Q4DC
2. Correct answer: C
A type of whole life insurance that lets you prepay for the complete amount of your coverage for 20 years is called 20-pay limited pay life insurance. Remember that whole life has both a savings component (cash value) and an insurance component.

Term insurance has no savings component and is for a specified term (number of years).

ID: MINZOPASSESEXC2Q21C1B040422Q5DC
3. Correct answer: D
When you hear Universal or Variable, think of FLEXIBILITY. Universal life and variable universal life policies both have a flexible premium. The policyowner can increase or decrease the premium if there is enough money in their cash value.

ID: MINZOPASSEMADC3Q79C1B204042022Q13DC
4. Correct Answer: D
All options about the death benefit for variable whole life are true.
NOTE: The death benefits for variable whole life are recalculated annually, NOT monthly.

ID: MINZOPASSEMADC3Q88C1B304042022Q19DC
5. Correct answer: A
The cash value and overall policy performance (ex, death benefit amount) depend on the performance of the linked stock market indexes.

ID: MINZOPASSBMC1B4061422Q3DC
6. Correct Answer: D
Interest-sensitive whole-life, also referred to as current assumption whole life, has a minimum guaranteed death benefit—NOT maximum death benefit.

ID: MINZOPASSEMEXSEXQ33C1B204062022Q20DC
7. Correct Answer: C
The correct answer is variable life. Variable life is a type of whole life policy, and whole life is a permanent policy.

There are generally two types of life insurance policies: Term(temporary) and Permanent. Permanent life insurance policies come in various types. Whole life, Universal life, Indexed Universal life, and adjustable life are examples of permanent life insurance policies.

Permanent policies differ from Term policies because permanent policies are meant to last for the life of the insured and have a savings component (cash value) in addition to insurance protection.

ID: MINZOPASSESKAC4Q3C1C041122Q21DC

8. Correct Answer: A

Level term life insurance policy refers to the type of insurance in which the face amount and coverage issued stay unchanged during the policy's life.

Hence, if the insured lives longer than ten years, the policy expires, and benefits are not payable. Term policies do not offer cash values (savings accounts).

ID: MINZOPASSESKAC4Q49C2A4041322Q37DC

9. Correct Answer: D

"Paying off outstanding loans when the borrower prematurely dies" is the correct answer. Decreasing term insurance is usually used when an insured's life insurance needs decrease with time. In this case, final expenses are expected to increase, not decline with time. However, an outstanding loan balance will likely decrease as the borrower makes payments against the loan. Therefore, a decreasing term insurance would best cover an outstanding loan.

ID: MINZOBMC1C3ID060922Q1DC

10. Correct Answer: D

Return of policy term is more expensive than a regular level term policy. All of the other options are true for Return of Premium Term Policies. Return of Premium Term can be attached as a rider to a level term policy, or it can be issued as a standard stand-alone term policy.

ID: MINNZOPASSJDEXGEXQ15C1C104052022Q8DC

11. Correct answer: D

A type of term life insurance wherein future insurability is guaranteed for a certain number of years is called annual renewable term insurance (ART). The policyholder may renew annually within the specified time frame without having to reapply or undergo another medical examination to confirm eligibility. Because of the insured's increased age, the rates typically rise when it is renewed.

ID: MINZOPASSESXCC3Q40C1C040522Q15DC

12. Correct answer: A

Renewable term provides life insurance coverage that can be renewed without any new underwriting. Insurance coverage continues even if the insured's health declines. However, the policyholder's premium will always increase with each renewal at the end of each term.

ID: MINZOPASSESKAC4Q6C1C041122Q23DC

13. Correct Answer: C

Term means temporary protection for a specified number of years. There are many riders available with term insurance. Among them are the renewability and convertibility riders. Renewable contracts have higher premiums than nonrenewable contracts and convertible term policies have higher premiums than nonconvertible term policies. With a convertible rider, the insured can always change their term insurance into a permanent policy without having to provide proof of insurability. On the other hand, a renewability rider allows an insured to renew their term contract within a specified period without having to prove insurability. Remember that the premium will usually increase when a rider is added to an insurance policy.

ID: MINNZOPASSJDADC5Q22C1D104042022Q18DC

14. CORRECT ANSWER: B

This question asks for two things: the type of annuity and the type of benefit payment. In this case, the correct answer is Single Premium Fixed Immediate Annuity.
Single Premium, because payment was made only once in June.
Fixed because the income payments and interest rate are guaranteed.
Immediate because benefit payments began less than one year after the annuity started.
Deferred Annuity: A deferred annuity is one that will start paying out periodic benefits within one year after it is issued.

ID: MINZOPASSESXCC7Q2C1D040622Q34DC

15. Correct Answer: A

Benefit payments from a deferred annuity start one year after the issue date and are made on a periodic basis beginning at a predetermined future date.

ID: MINZOPASSESXCC7Q5C1D040622Q37DC

16. Correct Answer: A

A Fixed Deferred annuity will pay out a fixed amount at a future specified date. This has to be at least one year after it is purchased

ID: MINZOPASSESEXC2Q18C1D040422Q20

17. Correct answer: D

For straight-life policies, the policyowner pays a level annual premium for life or until death, whichever occurs first. Equity-indexed annuity (EIAs) is a type of tax-deferred fixed annuity that credits interest based on the performance of a linked equity index. The most common linked equity index is the S&P 500. It usually guarantees interest rates between 1 and 3%. EIA returns typically have higher interest rates than fixed annuities but lower rates than variable annuities.

Equity Indexed Annuities highlights:

- A type of fixed annuities that are linked to a stock market index (ex: the S&P 500)
- Value is guaranteed by the company
- Interest earned can go up or down but with a minimum guaranteed interest rate
- Interest tied to stock market
- ONLY life insurance license required to sell it
- Money is held in insurer's general account

ID: MINZOPASSPCXCC9Q42C1D304092022Q61DC

18. Correct answer: D

Tax-sheltered annuity (TSA) benefit payments are taxed as regular income in the year they are paid.

ID: MINZOPASSADXCC9Q16C1D2022Q16DC

19. Correct answer: B

The fixed amount option guarantees the annuitant (insured) a fixed payout until the contract value is depleted, regardless of when that occurs. If the annuitant dies before the contract is fully paid out, the remaining benefit is given to the beneficiary.

ID: MINZOPASSPCXCC9Q34C1E04092022Q10DC

20. Correct answer: A

A joint and survivor annuity, which covers two or more individuals, pays out benefits as long as one person lives.

A Joint Life annuity, or First-To-Die Policy, covers two lives. However, unlike Joint and Survivor Annuity, a Joint Life Annuity stops paying benefits when the first annuitant dies and the annuity is automatically ended.

A Survivorship Annuity is an annuity where the annuitant or annuity owner (if different from the annuity owner) opens an annuity for the sole benefit of a survivor. The owner or annuitant does not receive any benefit payments. However, the survivor will receive benefit payments for life or a specified time when the annuitant dies.

ID: MINZOPASSEMADC3Q69C1E2040222Q4DC

21. Correct answer: D

In most circumstances, married couples concerned about estate taxes would benefit from a Last-to-Die (aka Survivorship or second-to-die) policy.

Joint survivorship or last-to-die life insurance policy is a life insurance policy that covers the lives of two persons, usually partners. The death benefit can be paid out only when both individuals pass away.

ID: MINZOPASSEMKA5Q9C2A104122022Q14DC

22. Correct Answer: B

The *waiver of premium* rider ONLY waives the premium payment if the insured becomes disabled and cannot work for longer than 90 days. The policy remains active, and the insurer must pay the full death benefit if the insured dies during this period.

ID: MINZOPASSEMEXSEXQ16C2A204052022Q4DC

23. Correct Answer: A

The correct answer is guaranteed insurability rider.

The guaranteed insurability rider allows policy owners to purchase additional death benefit coverage at specified periods (ex, every five years) without providing evidence of insurability.

Paid-up addition is a nonforfeiture option that only comes into play when the policyowner cancels or forfeits his policy.

ID: MINZOPASSEMKAC5Q8C2A304122022Q4DC

24. Correct Answer: D

When the premium payor passes away or becomes disabled prior to the insured child reaching the age specified in the policy, or until the policy's maturity date, whichever comes first, the payor rider waives the payment.

ID: MINZOPASSEMADC3Q87C2A404042022Q6DC

25. Correct answer: A

Accidental Death is the correct answer.

ID: MINZOPASSEMEXSEXQ6C2A504052022Q3DC

26. Correct answer: D

A term rider provides additional insurance protection for a fixed period.

ID: MINZOPASSESKAC3Q77C2A6041122Q4DC

27. Correct Answer: D

All of the above are correct.

ID: MINZOPASSEMADC3Q71C2A7040222Q1DC

28. Correct answer: D

A long-term care rider allows a chronically ill person to receive an advance payment of the death benefit for covered long-term care expenses.

More on LTC (Long Term Care):

- If the insured qualifies for long-term care benefits as stated in the rider, such as the inability to perform two out of six activities of daily living, the rider pays up to 100 percent of the policy benefits.

ID: MINZOPASSEMKA5Q7C2A804122022Q3DC

29. Correct Answer: D

The correct answer is $64,000. If an insured has this rider attached to their policy and dies, the beneficiary will receive the death benefit plus the total premiums paid up until the insured's death. In this case, Frank died five years after the policy's effective date, and his annual premium was $800. Therefore, it'll be death benefit ($60,000) + return of premium ($800/year X 5 years) = $64,000.

ID: MINZOPASSBMC2A9061922Q1DC

30. Correct Answer: D

All of the other riders are disability riders except accelerated death benefit rider.

ID: MINZOPASSEMKAC5Q18C2A104122022Q15DC

31. Correct Answer: C

The death benefit will be reduced by the corresponding percentage drop in the consumer Price index. A decrease in the CPI does not result in a decrease in the death benefit. The COLA rider ONLY increases the death benefit.

ID: MINZOPASSJDADC2Q42C5C104012022Q42

32. Correct answer: C

Although the agent's report and completed application are submitted to the insurer, the agent's report does not form a part of THE ENTIRE CONTRACT because it is a confidential report meant only to be seen by the insurer.

Note, a life insurance application is not confidential because a copy of the application (parts I and II) forms part of THE ENTIRE CONTRACT and will be delivered to the policyowner after the policy is issued.

ID: MINZOPASSESXCC3Q43C2B2040522Q3DC
33. Correct Answer: D
The basic promise to pay the benefits specified in the policy upon proof of claim is known as the insuring agreement.

ID: MINZOPASSEMXCPC11Q54C2B304072022Q4DC
34. Correct Answer: B
10 days is the required free look period for life insurance policies. The free look period is when a policy can be returned to the insurer for a full refund of any paid premiums.

ID: MINZOPASSESXCC3Q57C2B4040622Q1DC
35. Correct answer: B
The consideration clause states that the applicant must complete the application and pay the initial premium to be CONSIDERED for the insurance policy by the insurance company.

More on Consideration Clause:

- The amount and premium payment mode are included in the consideration clause
- The exchange of something value is called consideration
- It is one of the four elements of a LEGAL contract
- The insurer's consideration is approving and issuing the policy and agreeing to pay future claims

ID: MINZOPASSESXCC3Q56C2B5040622Q3DC
36. Correct Answer: C
This is a provision within insurance policies that explains all the policy owner's rights and responsibilities.

ID: MINZOPASSJDEXGEXQ24C2B604052022Q7DC
37. Correct answer: B
Once an annuity beneficiary has been named, any benefits paid upon the annuitant's death will go directly to the named beneficiary. The annuitant is considered the *primary* beneficiary for annuities because they are the one entitled to receive the annuity benefits. The annuity beneficiary is considered *secondary* because they only receive benefits when the annuitant dies.

ID: MINZOPASSESXCC4Q61C2B6040622Q10DC
38. Correct Answer: A
A revocable beneficiary is one who can be changed at any time by the policy owner without proof of the beneficiary's death or approval.

ID: MINZOPASSESEXC3Q37C2B6040522Q5DC

39. Correct answer: A

A policy with an irrevocable beneficiary needs written permission from the beneficiary to change and name a new beneficiary.

More on Beneficiaries:

Beneficiary

- A person entitled to policy death benefits after the insured's death. Maybe a person, class of persons (ex, my children), the insured's estate, trust, corporation/business
- It is not a good practice to name minors as life insurance beneficiaries

Beneficiary designations

- Revocable vs Irrevocable
- Primary vs Contingent

Common disaster clause

- If the insured and primary beneficiary perish in the same accident and there is no proof of who passed away first, it is assumed that the primary beneficiary passed away first. Therefore, the contingent(secondary) beneficiary will be entitled to receive the death benefit. The death benefit will be given to the insured's estate if there isn't a contingent beneficiary. The UNIFORM SIMULTANEOUS DEATH ACT mandates this.

ID: MINZOPASSESEXC3Q43C2B6040522Q6DC

40. Correct answer: D

A trustee or legal guardian receives the benefit on behalf of the minor. Legally speaking, a minor cannot relieve the insurer of any further duties.

ID: MINZOPASSJDADC4Q23C2B604022022Q4DC

41. CORRECT ANSWER: C

Once the insurance owner has designated an irrevocable beneficiary, the beneficiary designation cannot be altered without the irrevocable beneficiary's prior written consent or upon their death. The policy is a vested interest of the irrevocable beneficiary.

ID: MINZOPASSESXCC4Q67C2B6040622Q14DC

42. Correct Answer: A

The less frequent the mode of premium payment, the lower the cost of the premium. However, the more regular the payments, the more they'll cost in total because the insurer has to cover expenses for processing each payment.

ID: MINZOPASSJDKAC23Q8C2B0412202Q33DC

43. Correct Answer: B

The amount of time after the premium is due before the policy lapses due to nonpayment is known as the grace period. The grace period varies depending on the frequency or mode of premium payment.

ID: MINZOPASSJDEXGEXQ37C2B704052022Q11DC

44. Correct answer: C

Since the loan is to be used to pay premiums, the insurer should issue it immediately. The provision that allows this is called the Automatic Premium Loan provision.

ID: MINZOPASSESKAC3Q36C2B7041122Q24DC

45. Correct Answer: A

Gross premium can be calculated by adding the net premium (mortality - interest) to the expense element.

The gross premium is paid by the policyholders and is the amount clients are asked to pay in email and mail correspondence from the insurer.
The net single premium is the single amount needed instantaneously to finance future benefits.

ID: MINZOPASSESXCC3Q58C2B8040622Q4DC

46. Correct Answer: A

The reinstatement provision states that if a policy has lapsed unintentionally due to nonpayment of premium, it can be reinstated within three years of the date it lapsed.

ID: MINZOPASSTAXCC9Q29C2B904092022Q5DC

47. Correct answer: B.

All surrender charges are meant to discourage annuity withdrawals and exchanges. Note that surrender changes are usually highest at the beginning of the contract and gradually decrease annually, usually down to zero after 15 years.

ID: MINZOPASSJDADC4Q18C2B1004022022Q3DC

48. CORRECT ANSWER: B

Extended term is the default nonforfeiture option if no settlement option is selected.

ID: MINZOPASSESEXC3Q42C211040522Q3DC

49. Correct answer: A

Term insurance for a year is purchased with the dividend.
Dividend Options

1. Cash
2. Application to reduce premiums

        a. reduces the following year's premium
3. Accumulation at Interest
    a. insurer keeps dividends in an account that accumulates interest
    b. dividends are not taxable, but interest earned on them is taxable.
4. Paid-Up Additions
    a. used to purchase additional death benefit
5. Paid-Up Option
    a. insurer uses the dividend to pay off the policy early
6. One-Year Term Option
    a. insurer uses the dividend to purchase additional one-year term insurance
    b. The beneficiary will get both the original death benefit and the one-year term death benefit if the insured passes away within the one-year term.

ID: MINZOPASSJDXCC8Q7C2B1204112022Q3DC

50. Correct answer: C

The incontestable clause in a life insurance policy specifies that, unless involving fraud, the insurer cannot contest the validity of the policy after two years.

ID: MINZOPASSEMEXSEXQ26C2C1704052022Q7DC

51. Correct Answer: B

Absolute assignment is the permanent transfer of all ownership rights in a policy. This is an ownership transfer.

The other type of assignment is collateral. This is a temporary transfer of ownership and is usually associated with collateral for a loan.

ID: MINZOPASSESXCC3Q50C2B14040522Q1

52. Correct Answer: C

'Denies claims under the Suicide Clause Policy" is the correct answer.
Under the Suicide Clause, an insurer will NOT pay claims if an insured commits suicide during the period of contestability, which is two years from the date of policy issue. However, all premiums paid will be returned to the beneficiary.

ID: MINZOPASSESXCC11Q1C2B15040722Q3DC

53. Correct Answer: A

This clause permits the insurance company to recalculate benefits and premiums based on the applicant's true age or gender in the event that the applicant misrepresents their age or gender on the policy.

Under the misstatement of age provision, if an insured's age is misstated on the insurance application, the beneficiary will only receive the death benefit that the insured's premium would have purchased at the correct age. For example, if the insured had been paying a $50 monthly premium for a $100,000 coverage based on the misstated age of 30 and it is later discovered that her correct age at application was 35, then her beneficiary may only receive $70,000 if that is how much a $50 monthly premium would have been able to purchase at the correct age of 35.

The incontestability clause does not apply. Gender and age are not considered material for the insurance policy that is being issued.

ID: MINZOPASSJDADC4Q15C2B1604022022Q3DC

54. CORRECT ANSWER: C

If the policy owner does not choose a settlement option while still alive, the beneficiary may do so at the time of claim.

ID: MINZOPASSESEXC3Q34C2B17040422Q3DC

55. Correct answer: A

A required provision known as an "accelerated death benefit" (ADB) permits the insurer to pay all or a portion of the death benefit under a policy EARLY. This rider is activated when the insured experiences any of the following:

- terminal illness
- inability to perform an activity of daily living (ADLs)
- confinement to a LTC facility
- organ transplant
- any other conditions approved by the DOI (department of insurance)

Note: accelerated death benefit payments cannot be taxed.

ID: MINZOPASSBMC2C207262022Q9DC

56. Correct answer: A

With the Status Clause, any death that occurs during the course of active-duty military service is not covered. With this clause, it does not matter whether or not the insured's death was directly caused by military service or war, as long as the insured's status at the time of death was *active-duty military service.* With the Results Clause, ONLY death due to war or military service is excluded. If the insured does not pass away as a direct result of a war or military duty, the insurer is nonetheless required by the Results Clause to pay the death benefit. For instance, even if you are actively serving in the military on active duty, the insurance company will still pay the death benefit if you are killed in a car accident while spending time with your family.

ID: MINZOPASSESEXC3Q36C2C040522Q2DC

57. Correct answer: D

Exclusions are risking an insurance policy will not cover. The three most common exclusions from life insurance policies are aviation, hazardous occupations, and war & military service.

- Aviation
    - Covers a fare-paying passenger, a pilot, or crew on a regular commercial airline, but EXCLUDEs coverage or charges noncommercial pilots more
- Hazardous Occupation/Hobbies
    - The insured may pay a greater premium or have deaths from that career or hobby excluded.
- War or Military Service
    - STATUS Clause
        - excludes ALL cause of death while the insured is on active duty
    - RESULTS Clause
        - ONLY excludes death when the insured is killed as a result of war

Note: Suicide is a stand-alone standard provision even though it is an exclusion.

ID: MINZOPASSBMC2C307262022Q7DC

58. Correct Answer: A

If an insured dies due to a hazardous occupation or hobby, the insurer will not pay claims because this is a common exclusion on life insurance policies. The other two other standard exclusions are war and aviation. Exclusions are a common feature of life insurance policies where the insurer explicitly states certain risks that will not be covered.

ID: MINZOPASSESEXC1Q1C3A1040422Q3DC

59. Correct answer: C

The application must have all appropriate and authorized signatures before reaching the insurer.

More on Required Signatures:

- The agent and the proposed insured (including the applicant/policyholder if different from the proposed insured) MUST sign the application before submitting it to the insurer.

Note: The ONLY time the proposed insured CANNOT or is not allowed to sign the application will be if the proposed insured is a minor/juvenile. In this case, a parent/guardian must sign for the MINOR.

ID: MINZOPASSESXCC5Q76C3A2040522Q5DC

60. Correct Answer: C

Any changes made to the application should be initialled by the applicant. When accepting an application, the agent must verify that all changes on the application are initialed by the applicant.

ID: MINZOPASSESXCC5Q89C3A3040622Q3DC

61. Correct Answer: C

An incomplete application is automatically returned to the applicant through the producer.

ID: MINZOPASSBMXCC2Q7C3A404012022Q3DC

62. Correct Answer: C

Statements made by the applicant that they best believe to be accurate are known as representations.

Other LEGAL terms:

- Misrepresentation
  - Insurance policy can be canceled if misrepresentation is MATERIAL
- Concealment
  - Intentionally withholding information
- Fraud
  - Intentional misrepresentation with the intention of cheating or receiving something of value
- Warranty
  - Statements on application GUARANTEED to be true

ID: MINZOPASSESXCC5Q80C3A504022Q3DC

63. Correct Answer: B

Send the application to the insurance company without paying the first premium. An application submitted to a producer without an initial premium payment is called a trial application. In this case, the producer should submit the trial application to the insurance company. However, the policy will only be issued after the insurance company receives the first premium.

ID: MINZOPASSEMADC7Q93C3A604042022Q1DC

64. CORRECT ANSWER: A

The exchange of an annuity policy for any type of life insurance policy is prohibited by IRC section 1035.

ID: MINZOPASSJDEXGEXQ18C3A704052022Q3DC

65. Correct answer: B

- Policy summary
  - Helps consumers evaluate the suitability of a recommended product
  - Usually provided with every life insurance policy. With a policy summary, there is never any doubt on the part of the policy owner about the details of their policy

- A shortened version or summary of a life insurance policy. A policy summary gives information regarding the coverage limitations, the total premiums that will be charged, and other important information.

ID: MINZOPASSESXCC5Q87C3A8040622Q2DC
66. Correct answer: D
The USA Patriot Act was enacted in 2001.

ID: MINZOPASSBMC3A907282022Q3DC
67. Correct answer: D
The right answer is "all of the above."

The privacy notice must explain the following:

- How the consumer's information is used
- What data is gathered about the consumer
- How the consumer's information is protected
- Where and how that information is shared

ID: MINZOPASSBMXCC2Q11C3B104012022Q3DC
68. Correct Answer: C
Insurable interest is a relationship that must exist at the beginning of the contract (or at the time of application) and not at time of loss.

Insurable interest means a relationship that exists with the insured in which a person stands to suffer emotional or financial loss if the insured dies.

Test Alert: An individual has an UNLIMITED insurable interest in themselves

ID: MINZOPASSEMKAC2Q8C3B204112022Q3DC
69. Correct answer: C
If an applicant's credit rating is bad, the insurer could interpret this to mean that the applicant could be unlikely to make premium payments. Therefore, insurers may anticipate loss of money if the applicant is approved.

As a result, insurers usually obtain inspection reports from reporting agencies on applicants who apply for high amounts of life insurance.

ID: MINZOPASSBMXCC1Q1C3B304012022Q3DC

70. Correct Answer: C

The Fair Credit Reporting Act, a Federal law, mandates that individuals be informed if a credit reporting agency is investigating them.

More on Investigative Consumer Reports:

- Report containing information about an applicant's lifestyle, financial capacity, and character
- The applicant is entitled to a copy of this report.

ID: MINZOPASSJDADC1Q21C3B404012022Q3DC

71. Correct answer: C

Marital status is not a factor evaluated in underwriting.

ID: MINZOPASSBMXC2Q17C3B504022022Q3DC

72. Correct Answer: C

Due to fraudulent abuses brought forth by STOLI, many states have banned STOLI policies for lack of insurable interest. One legal purpose to engage into a contract is to protect an insurable interest.

ID: MINZOPASSJDEXGEXQ47C3C104052022Q3

73. Correct Answer: A

The policy is considered delivered if or when it is handed over in person or mailed to the policy owner. Any other means, like passing through the policy owner's neighbor or family, is not considered delivered.

ID: MINZOPASSESEXC1Q2C3C2040422Q3DC

74. Correct answer: B

Explaining policy provisions, exclusions, riders, and factors that influence ratings and collecting due premiums are all the responsibilities of a producer. The producer must also ensure the applicant signs the application before submission.

Another name for a producer is a FIELD UNDERWRITER. These are some of the responsibilities of the FIELD UNDERWRITER:

- Deliver the policy
- Obtain any required signatures
- Solicit insurance
- Collect the initial premium
- Issue any receipt, if applicable
- Actively work to prevent adverse selection

The AGENT'S REPORT

- Allows the agents to exercise his/her field underwriting role
- Allows the agent to confidentially report their observations about the proposed insured to the insurer
- Is attached to the application, but is NOT considered a part of the application (NOT part of the ENTIRE CONTRACT)

ID: MINZOPASSEMEXSEXQ8C3D104052022Q9DC

75. Correct answer: C

An insurance contract consists of a legal purpose, competent parties, consideration, and agreement (offer and acceptance). These are the four elements of any LEGAL contract, not just insurance.

Note, the UNIQUE features of insurance contracts are:

- Adhesion
- Aleatory
- Unilateral
- Conditional
- Personal (not for life insurance, but insurance in general)

ID: MINZOPASSESEXC1Q9C3D1040422Q8DC

76. Correct answer: B

A legal contract requires that the parties be of legal age, mentally competent, and free from the effects of alcohol or illegal drugs.

The four (4) elements of a legal contract [test alert] are:

- **C**onsideration
- **L**egal purpose
- **A**greement (offer and acceptance)
- **C**ompetent parties

ID: MINZOPASSESEXC1Q7C3D2040422Q12DC

77. Correct answer: A

The four major elements of an insurance contract that make it legally binding are *agreement* (offer and acceptance), *consideration*, *competent parties*, and *legal purpose.*
A counteroffer is not required.

ID: MINZOPASSBMXCC2Q10C3D104012022Q5DC

78. Correct Answer: B

The elements of a legal contract are legal purpose, legal purpose, agreement (Offer and acceptance), and consideration.
Estoppel is the legal name for preventing a person or company from reclaiming a waived right.

ID: MINZOPASSBMXCC2Q14C3D204012022Q8DC

79. Correct Answer: B

Bilateral is not a special feature of insurance contracts. *Unilateral*, *aleatory*, *conditional,* and *adhesion* are all characteristics of insurance contracts.

ID: MINZOPASSBMXCC2Q13C3D204012022Q7DC

80. Correct Answer: B

In a unilateral contract, only one party (the insurer) makes an enforceable promise.

ID: MINZOPASSEMEXC4Q53C4A04052022Q4DC

81. Correct answer: A

When the insured is not the contract owner, it can be termed third-party ownership. This is mostly used for business or minor children, where employers or parents are the policy owners.

Test Alert:

The insurance contract is ALWAYS between the policyowner and the insurer, even in the case of third-party ownership. The signatories to the insurance contract are the policyowner, producer, insured (if different from the applicant/policy owner), and the insurer. However, the insurance contract has only two parties: The applicant/policy owner and the insurer.

ID: MINZOPASSEMADC3Q76C4C04042022Q2DC

82. Correct answer: C

Because a life settlement entail selling an existing life insurance policy to someone different (third party) for more than the cash surrender value but less than the death benefit, it is comparable to a viatical settlement. One distinction between the two is that a life settlement does not require the insured to be terminally ill. A policyowner might sell their policy because they cannot afford their premium due to a job loss or just want to acquire a different policy. Unlike that, a viatical settlement can only be made for terminally ill clients.

ID: MINZOPASSJDEXGEXQ33C4D104052022Q3DC

83. Correct answer: D

An insurance firm will offer an annuity, which is a long-term investment meant to help protect the annuitant against the possibility of outliving their income. The purchase payments made by the annuitant (what they contribute) are transformed into recurring payments through annuitization, which can last a lifetime. This serves as a retirement plan as well...

ID: MINZOPASSEMADC6Q77C4D2040422Q3DC

84. CORRECT ANSWER: D

The question refers to a Noncontributory Group Insurance Plan, which requires 100% participation. All 75 employees must be covered because the employer pays ALL the premiums.

ID: MINZOPASSEMADC7Q90C4E104042022Q4DC

85. CORRECT ANSWER: D

The employee determines how much of their wages to contribute to each payroll cycle under a defined contribution plan. Before calculating income tax, the employer deducts that amount from the employee's compensation and remits it to the plan's custodian for the employee's benefit.

ID: MINZOPASSESKAC3Q2C4E2040922Q3DC

86. Correct Answer: B

Employees should not rely on *guaranteed* future benefits for deferred compensation plans because most nonqualified deferred plans are not funded. Usually, the employer funds its liabilities using a system of meeting costs on an as-they-arise basis (pay-as-you-go).

ID: MINZOPASSEMADC3Q62C4F1040222Q3DC

87. Correct answer: C

The specified death benefit is referred to as the insurer's limit of liability, and it is the maximum amount the policy will pay out in the case of the insured's death. The Death Benefit is another name for the face amount.

The Face Amount is the limit of liability because it is the maximum amount the policy will pay out to the beneficiary in the case of a claim. That amount, unlike the Cash Value, cannot be borrowed from. Loans are taken from the policy's cash surrender value, not the policy proceeds or death benefit.

ID: MINZOPASSEMEXC4Q55C4F204052022Q4DC

88. Correct answer: A

The business, usually the employer, is the applicant, owner, premium payer, and beneficiary in the key person coverage.

More on Key Person Insurance:

- The employee is the INSURED
- Premium is NOT tax-deductible
- Employer receives death benefit Tax FREE

ID: MINZOPASSEMEXC4Q59C4F2B04052022Q5DC

89. Correct answer: C

Businesses can use life insurance to:

- Compensate their executives or owners using EXECUTIVE BONUS PLANS
- Fund the business in case one of the owner(s) dies with BUY-SELL AGREEMENTS
- Pay to replace and continue the business after the premature death of key employees with KEY EMPLOYEE INSURANCE

ID: MINZOPASSEMADC7Q91C4H104052022Q3DC
90. CORRECT ANSWER: C
The withdrawal, which reflects earnings, will be taxed, as well as a 10% tax penalty.

ID: MINZOPASSEMADC7Q82C4H204042022Q12
91. CORRECT ANSWER: B
The life insurance premiums can be deducted by a business, provided that the insurance death benefit is not payable to the employer in the event of an employee's death.

ID: MINZOPASSJDEXGEXQ44C4H304052022Q3DC
92. Correct answer: A
The seven-pay test establishes whether the entire premium paid into a life insurance policy over the first seven years exceeds what is necessary for the policy to be considered paid up in that period of time. When more premiums are paid into an insurance than were required to be paid throughout that seven-year period, the policy becomes a MEC. The entire tax benefit of life insurance is forfeited by MECs.

ID: MINZOPASSESXCSEQ1C5A1040622Q5DC
93. Correct Answer: A
A temporary license may be granted by the Commissioner of Insurance. They may issue a temporary license to a deceased producer's representative to provide service to existing policyholders. A temporary license may not exceed **180** days.

The following people may receive a temporary license from the commissioner:

- The surviving spouse of a deceased licensed producer
- The court-appointed personal representative of a deceased, mentally or physically disabled licensed insurance producer
- An employee of a company holding a license as an insurance producer in the event that the license holder passes away or develops a physical or mental disability
- The designee of a licensed insurance producer going on active-duty military service
- Any other person that the insurance commissioner determines that it will be in the public's best interest to issue a temporary producer license to

ID: MINNZOPASSJDADC14Q18C5A2022Q2DC
94. Correct Answer: A
The Mayor must examine every insurer at least once every five years.

ID: MINZOPASSESXCSEQ9C5A3040622Q2DC

95. Correct Answer: C

Before convening a hearing that could result in a producer's license being suspended or revoked, the Commissioner must notify the producer in writing at least **ten days** before the hearing.

Before canceling or suspending a license, the Commissioner must hold a hearing and allow licensees to present evidence on their behalf via a written notice. Anyone whose license has been revoked has **30 days** to appeal the Commissioner's decision. Unless the Commissioner specifies otherwise, a person whose license to do business as an agent or broker has been revoked or whose application for reinstatement has been denied must wait **three years** from the revocation date or rejection before applying for reinstatement.

ID: MINZOPASSESXCSEQ34C5B1040722Q7DC

96. Correct Answer: C

A domestic insurance company is defined as one that is incorporated and founded in the District of Columbia. It is also organized under Washington, DC, insurance laws.

ID: MINZOPASSJDADC1Q31C5B204012022Q3DC

97. Correct answer: B

Insurers utilize reinsurance to mitigate their direct loss exposure for specific risks.

ID: MINZOPASSJDADC1Q27C5B304012022Q1DC

98. Correct answer: C

Insurance policies and contracts are issued by insurers.

Insurance producers sell insurance policies to the general public on behalf of the insurance company.

Insurance brokers are licensed insurance representatives who market the insurance policies of different insurance companies. Legally, the broker is considered a representative of the insured and NOT the insurer.

Producers are the opposite. Unlike brokers, producers represent the insurer.

ID: MINZOPASSJDEXGEXQ92C5C104062022Q7DC

99. Correct answer: C

To get a nonresident license, a producer must apply for the license and pay any required fees.

ID: MINZOPASSJDXCSEXQ34C5C204072022Q8DC

100. Correct Answer: D

A license may be denied, suspended, or revoked by the Commissioner if they find a producer guilty of misrepresentation in obtaining their license.

ID: MINZOPASSJDKAC23Q35C5C304122022Q9DC
101. Correct Answer: B
The mayor appoints the commissioner for a 4-year term.

ID: MINZOPASSEMEXC5Q67C5C404052022Q2DC
102. Correct answer: D
Most insurance producers are usually compensated with commissions. A commission is a percentage of the client's premium the insurer pays the producer for selling an insurance policy.

Note: Some producers, who are employees of an insurance company instead of independent agents, are paid a salary instead of a commission.

ID: MINZOPASSJDXCSEXQ2C5C104062022Q8DC
103. Correct Answer: A
An insurance producer MUST notify the Commissioner within **30** days of a change of their residential or business address.

Other Important Timelines for producers:

- A producer who moves to this state MUST apply within **90** days of establishing legal residence to become a resident licensee
- Insurers that terminate the contract, appointment, or employment with producers MUST notify the Commissioner within **30** days after the effective date of the termination.
    - The insurance company must mail a copy of the notification to the insurance producer at their last known address within **15** days of notifying the commissioner.
- Insurers must also notify the Commissioner within **30** days when they appoint producers. After receiving the notification, the commissioner must verify within **ten** days that the insurance producer is eligible for an appointment.

ID: MINZOPASSESXCSEQ10C5C6040622Q2DC
104. Correct Answer: A
Every two years, on the final day of the producer's birth month, their license expires. An insurance producer's license must be renewed every two years(biennially).

ID: MINZOPASSJDXCSEXQ35C5D104072022Q6DC
105. Correct Answer: D
False advertising is false advertising meant to mislead customers. It is illegal. An insurer exaggerating its dividends in an online advertisement is an example of false advertising.

ID: MINZOPASSEMEXSEXQ80C5D204052022Q10DC

106. Correct Answer: D

Rebates not expressly written in the policy are NEVER allowed.

ID: MINZOPASSJDADC2Q40C5D304012022Q3DC

107. Correct answer: D

Before approving a person for insurance, the insurer must receive the most up-to-date information. Changes can be made to the application any time before the policy is issued.

ID: MINZOPASSJDKAC23Q22C5D404122022Q12DC

108. Correct Answer: C

Below is the list of unfair trade practices:

- Rebating
- Twisting
- Misrepresentation
- Unfair Discrimination
- Defamation
- False advertising
- Unfair claims practice
- Unfair claims settlement practice
- Boycott, Coercion, or Intimidation

ID: MINZOPASSEMEXC5D504052022Q1DC

109. Correct answer: A

Insurance coverage can NEVER be denied based on sex or marital status. However, marital status may be considered to determine eligibility for dependent benefits.

ID: MINZOPASSEMEXSEXQ66C5D604052022Q7DC

110. Correct Answer: B

The correct answer is twisting.

Rebating offers inducements (something of value) not found in the insurance policy as an incentive to buy insurance.

Note: Twisting, Rebating, False Advertising, and Defamation are all unfair trade practices and are illegal in this state.

ID: MINZOPASSBMC5D708052022Q1DC

111. Correct answer: D

Engaging in an unfair trade practice is unlawful in The District of Columbia.

The penalty for engaging in unfair trade practices are:

- The commissioner may issue a *cease-and-desist* order
- The commissioner may issue a fine of up to $1,000 for each violation if the producer does not comply with the *cease-and-desist* order
- The commissioner may suspend, revoke, or decline to renew the producer's license
- The violator may be prosecuted in the Superior Court of The District of Columbia
- The commissioner may impose a civil penalty not to exceed $5,000 in place of or in addition to suspending, revoking or refusing to renew a producer's license.

ID: MINZOPASSJDXCC8Q38C5D804112022Q11DC

112. Correct answer: D

Representation is not an unfair trade practice.

ID: MINZOPASSESKAC3Q44C5E041522Q9DC

113. Correct answer: D

Anytime a producer commits an illegal act, he/she could be liable for errors and omissions. Telling a client that purchasing life insurance is like buying shares of a company and stating that dividends are guaranteed is considered a misrepresentation and is illegal. Errors and omissions insurance (E&O) is professional liability insurance that protects insurance producers from client lawsuits. Errors and omissions insurance often covers court costs and any settlements up to the amount specified in the insurance contract.

ID: MINZOPASSBMC5F08052022Q4DC

114. Correct answer: C

Insurers are prohibited from asking about the sexual identity, sexual orientation, or sexual expression of an applicant. Furthermore, it is illegal in this state to make underwriting decisions based on sexual identity, sexual orientation, or sexual expression. On the other hand, insurers can ask about marital status, but they cannot base their underwriting decision on that.

ID: MINZOPASSJDXCSEXQ16C5G04062022Q7DC

115. Correct Answer: A

The District of Columbia's Life and Health Insurance Guaranty Association protects policy owners and beneficiaries when an insurer becomes insolvent. Membership in this association is a requirement for all <u>*domestic*</u> insurers in The District.
It is funded through members' financial assessments and is a nonprofit organization. The maximum amount that it may pay for any claim is $300,000.

ID: MINZOPASSJDXCSEXQ38C6A104072022Q11DC

116. Correct Answer: C

The grace period is the length of time after the premium is due before the policy lapses for nonpayment. The grace period varies depending on the frequency or mode of premium payment. However, the grace period for individual life insurance policies in The District is **30 days.**

ID: MINZOPASSEMEXC6Q88C6A204052022Q1DC

117. Correct answer: D

In the District of Columbia, the REINSTATEMENT provision allows a lapsed policy to be reinstated within three years by paying outstanding premiums with interest, proving insurability, submitting a new application, and repaying any outstanding loans and interest.

Note: For Variable Life policies, reinstatement must occur within **two years** of policy lapse.

ID: MINZOPASSJDXCSEXQ10C6B104052022Q7DC

118. Correct Answer: C

- A policy loan may be made in a cash value life insurance policy when there is sufficient cash value to borrow from
- For most policies, cash value must be made available to borrow against after three years
- The insurer may defer granting a loan for up to 6 months
- The maximum fixed interest rate for a policy loan in The District is 8%
- The policy loan amount cannot exceed the available cash surrender value

ID: MINZOPASSJDADC4Q8C6B204022022Q1DC

119. CORRECT ANSWER: B

Spendthrift laws forbid a beneficiary's creditors from claiming benefits before they are received. This clause protects the recipient only when the benefits are paid under a settlement option and the proceeds are kept by the insurance company, not in the case of lump sum payment.

Spendthrift Clause

- The beneficiary's right to assign their stake in the policy funds is limited by the Spendthrift Clause.

ID: MINZOPASSXCC3Q21C6C104022022Q1DC

120. Correct Answer: A

For Life insurance policies, the conversion provision allows the policyowner to convert a term insurance policy to a permanent life insurance policy without showing evidence of insurability.

ID: MINZOPASSJDADC5Q14C6D104042022Q1DC

121. CORRECT ANSWER: A

In a variable annuity, the value of annuities is measured in units rather than dollars. The more money you pay in, the more units you'll get. Annuitization converts accumulation units to annuity units, and the income given depends on the annuity unit value.

Variable Annuity

The Securities and Exchange Commission (SEC), Financial Industry Regulatory Authority (FINRA), and state insurance departments regulate variable annuities. Annuity payments and cash values fluctuate based on the investment performance of the separate account established by the contract owner. Instead of dollars, payments are made in units.

ID: MINZOPASSTAXCC10Q10C6E104112022Q21

122. Correct answer: A

A profit-sharing plan distributes a percentage of a company's net income to qualified employees. Unlike 401(k), IRA, and other qualified retirement plans, employees cannot contribute to a profit-sharing plan. The employer only contributes to the profit-sharing plan when it makes a profit.

ID: MINZOPASSEMADC6Q59C6F04042022Q1DC

123. CORRECT ANSWER: D

Credit life insurance is a type of group life insurance owned by the creditor and exclusively benefits the creditor in the event of the borrower's death. It can be issued as a single premium type of coverage with a decreasing term for a short-term obligation, such as a loan to purchase household appliances.

ID: MINZOPASSJDEXGEXQ95C6F04062022Q2DC

124. Correct Answer: D

Credit life insurance is a policy designed to pay off a borrower's outstanding debts if the borrower dies. The face value of a credit life insurance policy decreases proportionately with the outstanding loan amount as the loan is paid off over time until both reach zero value.

ID: MINZOPASSBMC5A310222022Q5

125. Match the following required notices and actions with the correct time period required

#		Within 5 days	Within 10 days	Within 15 days	Within 30 days	Within 45 days	Within 90 days	Within 180 days	Within 12 months	Within 2 years	Within 3 years
1	Insurers must notify the commissioner when a field underwriter's appointment is terminated				X						
2	Insurer must notify commissioner for agent appointment				X						
3	Insurers must notify an agent in writing at his/her last known address that his appointment has been terminated after notifying the commissioner			X							
4	The commissioner must inform the insurer after determining that an agent's appointment is ineligible	X									
5	An agent must appeal a cease-and-desist order			X							
6	An agent must appeal a suspension or revocation of license in the superior court in DC				X						
7	An insurer must respond to a reinstatement application or the application will be considered approved					X					
8	A lapsed producer license can be reinstated without having to retake the licensing exam								X		
9	A change in residential or business address must be reported to the commissioner				X						
10	A felony conviction must be reported to commissioner				X						
11	A change of name must be reported to the commissioner				X						
12	An administrative action taken against a producer in another state must be reported to the commissioner				X						
13	Agent license expires on the last day of the agent's birth month									X	
14	Variable life insurance policies may be reinstated									X	
15	Life insurance policies may be reinstated										X
16	Temporary producer licenses expires							X			
17	An agent relocating to DC must apply for a DC resident license without having to take DC's licensing exam						X				
18	The commissioner must provide this minimum number of days written notice for a hearing		X								
19	The commissioner must review an agent's appointment		X								
20	Insurers must provide approved claim forms after receiving notice of a claim			X							
21	Commissioner must send written notice to subjects of a hearing at least 10 days prior but no later than ____days				X						

District of Columbia Simulated Exam 4 Questions

ID: MINZOPASSEMADC3Q74C1A1040222Q4DC
1. As the cash value grows in a traditional whole life insurance contract, the net amount at risk ____________, but the death benefit of the policy stays the same.

A. Decreases
B. Varies
C. Increases
D. Remains the same

ID: MINZOPASSESXCC3Q34C1A2040522Q5DC
2. Tyler, a 36-year-old guy, is thinking of purchasing a whole life insurance policy in order to quickly grow cash value. What policy aligns with his intentions?

A. Life Paid-Up at 70
B. Term Insurance
C. 10-pay Life
D. Life paid-up at 100

ID: MINZOPASSESEXC2Q29C1B040422Q7DC
3. Partial surrenders and withdrawals are allowed under which kind of policies?

A. Universal Life
B. 30-pay life
C. Variable whole life
D. Whole life

ID: MINZOPASSJDEXGEXQ5C1B04052022Q10DC
4. Who takes the investment risk in a variable life insurance policy?

A. The insured
B. The reinsurer
C. The insurer
D. The policyholder

ID: MINZOPASSESKAC4Q4C1B041122Q25DC

5. Which one of the following statements about Variable Universal Life Insurance is INACCURATE?

A. The named beneficiary is paid the death benefit
B. The cash account value is guaranteed
C. Has a savings account from which the insured can make withdrawals or take out loans
D. It offers flexible premium payments, and the death benefit fluctuates based on the Performance of the separate account

ID: MINZOPASSESKAC4Q23C1A1041322Q27DC

6. What happens with interest-sensitive whole life insurance policies?

A. The cash value fluctuates according to interest rates
B. The policy pays guaranteed quarterly dividends
C. Guaranteed 5% interest rate
D. The policy owner bears the investment risk

ID: MINZOPASSESXCC3Q39C1B040522Q17DC

7. These statements about equity-indexed life insurance policies are true, except

A. The premiums can be lowered or raised according to the performance of the selected investment portfolio
B. A minimum interest rate is guaranteed
C. Cash Value performance is based on equity indexes such as the S&P 500 or Dow Jones
D. The cash value will match the index if the gain exceeds the minimum rate of return specified in the policy.

ID: MINZOPASSESKAC4Q5C1C041122Q22DC

8. Lisa owns a term life insurance plan in which the amount of coverage remains the same throughout the life of the term. Which of the following categories of term life insurance does Lisa own?

A. Individual
B. Increasing
C. Decreasing
D. Level

ID: MINZOPASSESKAC4Q67C2A4041322Q44DC

9. Robell just secured a $250,000 mortgage for her dream home in the suburbs of Los Angeles. She's thinking of getting a life insurance policy to ensure that the mortgage gets paid off in the event of her death. What type of life insurance would you recommend to Robell?

A. Decreasing term
B. Variable life
C. Level term
D. Universal life

ID: MINZOPASSESEXC2Q30C1C040422Q7DC

10. Which option is best associated with an Annually Renewable Term (ART)?

A. It requires proof of insurability with each renewal
B. The premium and death benefit are not affected by the insured's age
C. It's a level term policy
D. It provides an annually decreasing death benefit

ID: MINZOPASSEMADC3Q63C1C2040222Q1DC

11. Which of the following is not a term life insurance feature?

A. Lower premium
B. Pure protection
C. Cash value
D. Temporary coverage

ID: MINZOPASSESKAC4Q80C2A4041322Q45DC

12. Which of the following statements of a contract with a one-year renewable term is TRUE?

A. It is renewable with a decreased premium due to the insured's *attained* age
B. It cannot be renewed more than two times
C. Its premium increases yearly based on the insured's health
D. It is renewable with an increase in premium due to the insured's *attained* age

ID: MINZOPASSESKAC4Q6C1C041122Q23DC
13. Which of the following statements about term insurance is ACCURATE?

A. Cannot be renewed
B. Cannot be converted to a permanent policy
C. Term insurance contracts provide coverage for only a temporary time
D. Jessy and Sarah are 25 years old and have term policies with the same face amounts. Jessy's contract is convertible, and Sarah's contract cannot be renewed. Therefore, Sarah will pay a higher premium than Jessy.

ID: MINZOPASSTAXCC9Q57C1D104112022Q76DC
14. Richard bought an annuity for $2,000,000 from his divorce settlement. No further payments are allowed, and the income stream will begin in 5 years. This type of contract is known as a ___________.

A. Single Premium Deferred Annuity
B. Single Premium Immediate Annuity
C. Single Premium Deferred Lump-sum Annuity
D. Single Premium Immediate Lump-sum Annuity

ID: MINZOPASSTAXCC9Q59C1D204112022Q77DC
15. Many deferred annuity contracts have the surrender charge waived if the following condition(s) are met:

A. When the annuitant dies, becomes incapacitated, or dies
B. The interest rate falls below the assumed interest rate (AIR)
C. The Annuitant has been unemployed for over one year
D. The annuity is canceled within the first six months

ID: MINZOPASSADXCC9Q17C1D304092022Q17DC
16. How is a variable annuity different from a fixed annuity?

A. The insurer bears the investment risk
B. The payout period lasts for life
C. Need only a life insurance license to sell it
D. The owner(purchaser) bears the investment risk

ID: MINZOPASSESEXC2Q24C1D040422Q25DC
17. Which of the following is a reason equity-indexed annuity is considered to be a fixed annuity?

A. Because it has a guaranteed minimum interest rate
B. It is not bound to an index
C. It has a fixed rate
D. It has a separate account

ID: MINZOPASSEMEXSEXQ53C2B604072022Q19DC
18. Who will receive the annuity benefits if an annuitant dies during the accumulation period?

A. The annuitant's estate
B. The annuitant's next of kin
C. The annuity owner
D. The beneficiary

ID: MINZOPASSESEXC2Q16C1D040422Q19DC
19. Princess won a $20,000,000 Jackpot and was told she would receive a monthly check each month for the next 20 years. What type of annuity product will make this possible?

A. Immediate annuity
B. Deferred interest annuity
C. Variable annuity
D. Deferred annuity

ID: MINZOPASSESKAC4Q21C1E041222Q14DC
20. Oliver and Karen are both husband and wife. To ensure the same amount of life insurance protection is provided in case either of them dies, they must consider paying for one of the following plans?

A. Joint Life
B. Family income
C. Children Protection
D. Family Protection

ID: MINZOPASSTAXCC9Q63C1E204112022Q13DC

21. Which annuity would be the best option in a scenario where a retired couple wants to get the most out of their combined life savings and have it paid to them until they both die?

A. Life with Refund
B. Joint and Survivor
C. Joint Life
D. Life Income Period Certain

ID: MINZOPASSEMKA5Q22C2A104122022Q16DC

22. The insured must be _______________ for a waiver of premium rider to become effective.

A. Chronically or critically ill
B. Unemployed for more than one year
C. Totally disabled for at least 90 days
D. Partially disabled for at least 180 days

ID: MINZOPASSESXCC3Q45C2A2040522Q5DC

23. Which of these statements contradicts the features of a guaranteed insurability rider?

A. Coverage can be added at specific events (like the birth of a child, marriage, etc)
B. When this rider is exercised, evidence of insurability is required
C. Evidence of insurability is not needed when the policy owner wants to renew their policy or increase coverage
D. Only available for policies that have been in force for at least three years

ID: MINZOPASSEMKAC5Q23C2A304122022Q5DC

24. Generally, the payor benefit rider is used for

A. Whole life policies
B. Juvenile insurance policies
C. Family Income policies
D. Accidental Death and Dismemberment policies

ID: MINZOPASSEMEXSEXQ39C2A404062022Q7DC

25. Xuan is insured on a $1,000,000 life insurance policy with a triple indemnity rider. Unfortunately, Xuan was killed in a car accident on Interstate 95 one year after his policy was issued. According to the police report, Xuan was at fault for the accident because he was driving drunk. The triple indemnity rider in the policy specifies that the death must not be caused by the insured. In this case, what will Xuan's beneficiary receive?

A. $1,000,000
B. $500,000
C. $0
D. $3,000,000

ID: MINZOPASSEMKAC5Q11C2A504122022Q4DC

26. Which statement about a *spousal* rider is true?

A. Additional premium is added to the regular premium for this rider, and it is a type of *Other Insured* rider
B. This rider usually consists of level term life insurance. It expires at a given age or date, or when the covered person passes away
C. Allows the spouse to convert it to a permanent policy before the rider expires or when the insured dies
D. All of the above

ID: MINZOPASSEMKAC5Q27C2A504122022Q5DC

27. Which policy adds term insurance for a spouse and children to a whole life insurance policy?

A) Joint and Survivor
B) Household Protection Rider
C) A family Term Income Rider
D) A family Term Rider

ID: MINZOPASSJDEXGEXQ2C2A704052022Q2DC

28. How does the long-term care(LTC) rider affect death benefits of a life insurance policy after LTC benefits have been paid to the insured?

A. Triples the death benefit
B. The death benefit is reduced
C. There is no impact on the death benefit
D. Increases the death benefit by the paid LTC benefit amount

ID: MINZOPASSEMADC3Q73C2A8040222Q1DC
29. If an insured dies when an increasing term rider is still in force, the beneficiary will receive the death benefit amount plus the total premiums paid. Your client wants to know the name of this rider attached to their policy. What should you tell your client?

A. Guarantee Cash Addition Rider
B. Increasing Term Rider
C. Return of Premium Rider
D. Waiver of Premium Rider

ID: MINZOPASSBMC2A9061922Q1DC
30. All of the following are disability riders, except

A. Waiver of Premium
B. Disability Income Benefit
C. Payor Benefit
D. Accelerated Death Benefit

ID: MINZOPASSEMKAC5Q15C2A204122022Q12DC
31. All of the following about the standard *cost-of-living*(COLA) rider are true, except

A. The yearly death benefit increases are capped at a specific percentage
B. NEVER increases the death benefit, and there is no additional premium required for increases in the death benefit associated with this rider
C. The rider works by attaching an increasing term rider to the policy
D. Typically automatically increases the death benefit when the consumer price index increases

ID: MINZOPASSBMADC4Q26C2B104102022Q8DC

32. Match the policy provisions with the correct description

		Payment of claims	Consideration Clause	Reinstatemen	Insuring Clause	Grace Period	Suicide Clause	Entire Contrac	Mode of Premium Payment
	Policy owner can reactivate their policy, usually within 3 years, if certain conditions are met								
2	Time period after the premium is due but before the policy lapses Death benefit is paid during this period if the insured dies								
3	If the insured takes his life(suicide) within two years of the policy's issuance, no death benefit is given All premiums paid, though, will be reimbursed in full.								
4	Exchange of value. The Insured pays the premium, and the insurer promises to pay future claims								
5	Identifies the parties to the insurance contract. Specifies the risk that is insured and the benefit that will be paid when a claim is filed								
6	The frequency of premium payments								
7	Claims will be paid immediately or within 60 days after proof of claim is received. If the claim is paid later than after 60 days, interest must be paid.								
8	Riders, Policy, amendments, and application copy								

ID: MINZOPASSEMADC3Q62C4F1040222Q3DC
33. In Life Insurance, the face amount is also known as

I. The cash surrender value
II. The limit of liability
III. The cash value
IV. The Death Benefit

A. II
B. I
C. II & IV
D. III

ID: MINZOPASSEMXCPC11Q63C2B304072022Q5DC
34. At least _______ days is an individual life insurance plan's free look or right-to-examine period.

A. 60
B. 30
C.10
D. 15

ID: MINZOPASSESXCC3Q57C2B4040622Q1
35. What relevant detail is included in the Consideration Clause of a life insurance contract?

A. The offer and acceptance
B. States that the policyowner must complete the application and pay the initial premium
C. The absolute assignment
D. The frequency of application

ID: MINZOPASSJDADC4Q11C2B50402022Q1DC
36. In a policy, the____________enables the owner to designate a beneficiary, select a payout or settlement option, and borrow from the policy.

A. Incontestable Clause
B. Insuring Clause
C. Assignment Clause
D. Ownership Provision

ID: MINZOPASSEMEXSEXQ27C2B604052022Q9DC

37. When a life insurance policy was issued, the policyholder designated a primary and a contingent beneficiary. Ten years later, both the insured and the primary beneficiary died in the same boat accident, and it was impossible to determine who died first. According to the Uniform Simultaneous Death Benefits Act, which of the following should receive the death benefit ?

A. The tertiary beneficiary
B. The contingent beneficiary
C. The primary beneficiary's estate
D. The primary beneficiary's designated next of kin

ID: MINZOPASSESXCC472C2B6040622Q17DC

38. Which of the following beneficiaries can be changed WITHOUT the consent of the beneficiary?

A. Primary
B. Replaceable
C. Revocable
D. Irrevocable

ID: MINZOPASSESEXC3Q37C2B6040522Q5DC

39. Under which circumstance can an irrevocable beneficiary be changed?

A. With the written permission of the beneficiary
B. The owner can change the beneficiary anytime they please
C. Beneficiary can NEVER be changed under any circumstance
D. The beneficiary cannot be changed for at least five years

ID: MINZOPASSJDADC4Q6C2B604022022Q1DC

40. Which of the following does a contingent beneficiary have the right to?

A. Prevent the policyholder from borrowing against the cash value of the policy
B. If the principal beneficiary is a minor child, receive the death benefit
C. The death benefit when the primary beneficiary is unavailable
D. The primary beneficiary will get a portion of the death benefit

ID: MINZOPASSJDADC4Q7C2B604022022Q2DC

41. Which of the below statements describes a possible problem with beneficiary "class" designations?

A. They are meant to make it possible for people who are not identified to share the proceeds of insurance policies
B. They are ambiguous beneficiary descriptions that could lead to a court having to decide who will or will not receive the policy proceeds
C. They indicate who can file a claim on the policy's proceeds
D. They make it impossible to name contingent beneficiaries

ID: MINZOPASSESXCC4Q70C2B6040622Q15DC

42. Gerald decides to pay premiums every month on his Whole Life Insurance Policy. What should he expect as a result of this mode of premium payment?

A. The gross premium will be LOWER on a monthly payment mode than an annual premium mode
B. The cash value for a life insurance policy paid monthly will accumulate FASTER than one paid annually
C. The gross premium will be HIGHER on a monthly payment mode than an ANNUAL payment mode
D. The death benefit of a life insurance policy paid monthly will be HIGHER than one paid on annually

ID: MINZOPASSEMEXSEXQ37C1D404062022Q16DC

43. A policyholder fails to pay the $100 premium due on his Variable Universal Life Policy after the grace period passed, but the policy remains in force. What policy provision made this possible?

A. Grace Period
B. Nonforfeiture Option
C. Automatic premium loan
D. Both A & B

ID: MINZOPASSEMEXSEXQ54C2B704072022Q17DC

44. When is the automatic premium loan provision activated?

A. 30 days before policy surrender
B. When the grace period expires
C. 7 days before the dividend period
D. 30 days before selecting a nonforfeiture option

ID: MINZOPASSESEXC2Q27C2B7040422Q10DC
45. Which policy contains the LEAST expensive premium during its first year?

A. Variable life Term
B. Decreasing term
C. Increasing Term
D. Annually Renewable Term

ID: MINZOPASSJDADC4Q4C2B1204022022Q2DC
46. What is the principal benefit of reinstating a life insurance policy to the policyholder?

A. A new contestability period cannot be started by the insurer
B. The benefits of the original policy, including the original premium, are still available to the policy owner
C. All outstanding policy loans are forgiven, and the entire cash value of the policy is reinstated
D. If the insured is under the age of 40, no proof of insurability is necessary

ID: MINZOPASSEMKAC6Q19C2B904122022Q6DC
47. How may the owner of a whole life insurance policy obtain the policy's cash value while the policyholder is still living without terminating the policy?

A. Through cash withdrawal
B. Through policy loan
C. Through cash dividend
D. Through cash surrender

ID: MINZOPASSESEXC3Q32C2B10040422Q4DC
48. Under this nonforfeiture option, the insurer pays the surrender value and has no more obligations to the policy owner. Which nonforfeiture option is this?

A. Cash surrender
B. Paid-up options
C. Reduced paid-up
D. Extended term

ID: MINZOPASSJDEXGEXQ7C2B1104052022Q4DC
49. Which of the following options uses dividends to reduce the following year's premiums?

A. Reduction of premium
B. Dividend payout
C. Increased premium
D. Annually Renewed

ID: MINZOPASSJDXCC8Q16C2B1204112022Q4DC
50. After ________ of coverage, a life insurance policy becomes incontestable.

A. 2 years
B. 180 days
C. 3 years
D. 12 Months

ID: MINZOPASSJDEXGEXQ11C2B1304052022Q1DC
51. Using one's life insurance policy as collateral for a loan is known as what?

A. Absolute assignment
B. A unilateral agreement
C. A collateral assignment
D. Aleatory contract

ID: MINZOPASSESXCC3Q55C2B14040522Q2DC
52. What is the purpose of the Suicide Clause in life insurance?

A. Discourage applicants from purchasing policy while contemplating suicide
B. Decline applicants contemplating suicide
C. Prevent the insurance company from ever paying a claim as a result of suicide
D. Mandates that the insurer ALWAYS pay the death benefit in cases of the insured's suicide

ID: MINZOPASSESXCPC11Q3C2B15040722Q4DC

53. If Sara's age was misstated on her life insurance policy, what would be required under the Misstatement of Age provision regarding her death benefit?

A. The insurer must pay an amount the premiums would have purchased at the correct age
B. The insurer must reduce the death benefit by 50%
C. No death benefit will be paid
D. A 25% reduction in the death benefit will occur

ID: MINZOPASSESEXC3Q38C2B16040522Q4DC

54. John is troubled and wants a policy that will pay a portion of the proceeds to his surviving spouse annually and the principal be paid to his children when they reach age 21; which of the following life policies should he go for?

A. Fixed amount option
B. Life income with period certain
C. Fixed amount
D. Interest only option

ID: MINZOPASSESEXC3Q40C2B17040522Q4DC

55. At what point can an insured tap into the accelerated death benefit provision?

A. When the insured has a terminal illness
B. When the beneficiary becomes disabled
C. When the beneficiary becomes terminally ill
D. When the insured is incarcerated

ID: MINZOPASSJDEXGEXQ8C2C04052022Q4DC

56. When dealing with life insurance policies, which of these options is NOT a standard Exclusion?

A. Aviation
B. War and military service
C. Disability
D. Hazardous Occupation

ID: MINZOPASSBMC2C207262022Q8DC

57. If an insured dies while flying a plane as a private pilot or working as a crew member on a private flight, the insurer will

A. Pay claims only after the contestability period
B. Pay claims
C. Not pay claims
D. Pay claims only if the policy had a double indemnity rider

ID: MINZOPASSESEXC3Q36C2C040522Q2DC

58. The clause that denies death benefit if death was caused by war is_____________.

A. Result or war clause
B. Aviation
C. Hazardous occupation
D. Exclusions

ID: MINZOPASSJDEXGEXQ52C3A104052022Q5DC

59. The following signatures are required in a life insurance application, EXCEPT

A. Beneficiary
B. The applicant/owner if different from the insured
C. The insured
D. The producer

ID: MINZOPASSEMEXSEXQ43C3A2040522Q6DC

60. For an insurance application that requires some changes, a producer may do all the following except

A. State the reason for the change on the application
B. Draw a line through the original answer, write the correct answer, and have the applicant initial the change
C. Erase the incorrect answer and write the correct answer
D. Discard the application and complete a new one from scratch

ID: MINZOPASSEMEXSEXQ38C3D304062022Q4DC

61. ABC Insurance Company issued a policy based on an application from Sayed that had unanswered questions. Which of the following is TRUE?

A. ABC insurance company may deny coverage later because Sayed's application contained missing information
B. By issuing the policy, ABC Insurer waived its rights to have the questions answered
C. The policy will be voided within two years due to the incontestability provision
D. The policy will be canceled after two years due to the incontestability provision

ID: MINZOPASSBMXCC2Q9C3A404012022Q4DC

62. Which of these is considered a statement guaranteed to be true in every respect?

A. Estoppel
B. Warranty
C. Guarantee
D. Representation

ID: MINZOPASSESXCC5Q90C3A504022Q5DC

63. Daisy applies for a non-medical insurance policy to be accepted for coverage on the same day. Immediate coverage will take effect when the producer collects a signed application and _______________.

A. The initial premium
B. Medical Information Bureau Report
C. A signed, notarized statement of good health
D. Forward it immediately to the insurer

ID: MINZOPASSEMADC7Q93C3A604042022Q1

64. The following are permitted in Section 1035 Exchange transactions, Except

A. An annuity is traded for a Whole Life Insurance Policy
B. An annuity contract is traded for another
C. A Whole Life Insurance Policy is traded for a Universal Life Insurance Policy
D. A Variable Universal Life Policy is exchanged for an Equity-Indexed Annuity

ID: MINZOPASSJDEXGEXQ40C3A704052022Q4DC
65. Which of the following will NOT be included in the buyer's guide?

A. Comparison of policies with different insurers and their costs
B. Details on how to choose the amount and type of insurance
C. Specific information about the policy
D. Basic information regarding life insurance policies

ID: MINZOPASSEMXCPC11Q46C3A804072022Q4DC
66. The anti-money laundering provisions of the USA Patriot Act require insurance companies to report any cash payment received that is greater than _____________.

A. $5,000
B. $40,000
C. $50,000
D. $10,000

ID: MINZOPASSBMC3A907282022Q4DC
67. According to the Gramm-Leach-Bliley Act (GLBA), which information must be included in a financial institution's privacy notice?

I. How the consumer's information is used
II. What information is gathered regarding the customer
III. How the consumer's information is protected
IV. Where and how that information is shared

A. I, II, III, & IV
B. I, II, & III only
C. IV only
D. III & IV only

ID: MINZOPASSESEXC1Q12C3B1040422Q4DC
68. Insurable interest must exist during which period in a life insurance policy?

A. Time of policy delivery
B. Time of proof of loss
C. Change in beneficiary
D. Time of application

ID: MINZOPASSEMKAC2Q14C3B204112022Q5DC
69. A medical report required on an applicant is performed by ______________.

A. An examining physician or paramedic
B. The producer
C. The insurer's underwriting department
D. Only the applicant's personal physician

ID: MINZOPASSJDEXGEXQ27C3B304052022Q5DC
70. What is the purpose of the Fair Credit Reporting Act?

A. It protects consumers against the circulation of inaccurate financial and personal information.
B. Guarantees coverage for all applicants over the age of 50
C. Mandates that a copy of the investigative report reaches the consumer in ALL circumstances
D. Protects the insurer from a substandard rating

ID: MINZOPASSJDADC1Q22C3B404012022Q4DC
71. Kwame decides to assume responsibility for a loss. What risk management technique is Kwame using?

A. Retention
B. Reduction
C. Transfer
D. Avoidance

ID: MINZOPASSBMXC2Q19C3B504022022QDC
72. Which of the following arrangements allows one to circumvent the laws of insurable interest?

A. Concealment
B. Investor-Originated Life Insurance
C. Contract of adhesion
D. Fraud

ID: MINZOPASSEMEXSEXQ20C3C104052022Q4DC
73. When does acceptance usually occur in an insurance policy?

A. When the insured submits the insurance application
B. When the agent delivers the policy
C. When the application gets approved by the insurer
D. When the insurance company receives the application

ID: MINZOPASSESEXC1Q14C3C2040422Q4DC
74. Any of the following things may be obtained when delivering a policy, EXCEPT

A. Delivery receipt
B. Statement of good health
C. Conditional receipt
D. Premium payment

ID: MINZOPASSESADC1Q12C3D1033122Q2DC
75. The following are elements of a legal contract, except

I. Indemnity
II. Legal Purpose
III. Competent Parties
IV. Consideration

A. I & IV
B. I
C. III & I
D. II, III, IV

ID: MINZOPASSJDADC1Q23C3D104012022Q4DC
76. Which of the following is NOT a required component of any legal contract?

A. Offer and Acceptance
B. Indemnity
C. Competent Parties
D. Legal Purpose

ID: MINZOPASSESEXC1Q7C3D2040422Q12DC
77. __________is NOT an important element of an insurance contract.

A. Counteroffer
B. Agreement
C. Consideration
D. Legal Purpose

ID: MINZOPASSBMXCC2Q10C3D104012022Q5DC
78. The components of ______________ are an offer, an acceptance, and a consideration.

A. Estoppel
B. Legal Contract
C. Warranty
D. Representations

ID: MINZOPASSJDADC1Q18C3D204012022Q3DC
79. What is a conditional contract?

A. A false statement on an insurance application
B. Only one party, the insurance company, is legally bound to the contract
C. Both parties must do certain things to make the contract legally binding
D. False statement on an insurance application

ID: MINZOPASSBMXCC2Q14C3D204012022Q8DC
80. Which of the following is not considered an attribute of insurance contracts?

A. Aleatory
B. Bilateral
C. Unilateral
D. Conditional

ID: MINZOPASSBMXCC2Q20C3D204022022Q9
81. Regarding a policy of adhesion, only one party can write or modify the policy. Who is entitled to this right?

A. The insurer
B. The applicant
C. The Policy owner
D. The agent

ID: MINZOPASSESEXC1Q5C3D2040422Q11DC
82. Which contract enables claims to be paid if a proposed insured makes premium payments on a new policy but dies and the policy is approved?

A. Unilateral
B. Adhesion
C. Personal
D. Conditional

ID: MINZOPASSJDEXGEXQ59C4A04052022Q5DC
83. Jonas bought a life insurance policy on his 16-year-old son Jeremi. Jonas is the policy owner, and Jeremi is the insured. This is known as ______________.

A. Insurable ownership
B. Third-party ownership
C. Family rider
D. Status clause

ID: MINZOPASSEMADC3Q76C4C040422Q2DC
84. The similarity between a life settlement transaction and a viatical settlement transaction is that

A. The insured is about to die
B. The policy is about to end
C. A third party pays less than the face value of a life insurance policy
D. The policy is old

ID: MINZOPASSESXCC6Q91C4D1040622Q4DC
85. Precious recently retired at age 59 1/2 from her company. Her employer's group life insurance policy can be:

A. Converted to an individual permanent insurance policy at an individual rate
B. Converted into a group-rate individual permanent policy
C. Discontinued and NOT converted
D. Continued at a group rate

ID: MINZOPASSEMADC6Q54C4D2040422Q4DC
86. An employee controls which of the following in a group life insurance plan?

A. Mode of premium payments
B. The master contract
C. Choosing the insurer
D. Choosing the beneficiary

ID: MINZOPASSEMADC7Q92C4E104042022Q5DC
87. Which of these is a qualified retirement plan designed specifically for unincorporated self-employed people?

A. 403(b) Plan
B. Keogh Plan
C. IRA
D. Roth IRA

ID: MINZOPASSESKAC3Q9C4E2040922Q4DC
88. Which of the following describes an executive bonus plan?

A. 401(k) plan for executives only
B. The employer is the premium payer on a permanent life insurance policy that the worker owns
C. An employee is the owner, premium payer, and beneficiary
D. Owned by the employer

ID: MINZOPASSEMADC6Q60C4F104042022Q4DC
89. The most common face amount for industrial life insurance is ____________.

A. $10,000
B. Up to $50,000
C. $1,000 or less
D. $50,000 to $100,000

ID: MINZOPASSESXC10Q28C4D2040622Q6DC

90. What is the exception to what a third-party owner can be in a key employee life insurance policy?

A. Insured
B. Applicant
C. Payor
D. Owner

ID: MINZOPASSESKAC3Q1C4F2B040922Q7DC

91. Which of the following options below is not a business use of life insurance contracts?

A. Workers compensation
B. Buy-sell agreement
C. Key-person protection
D. Deferred compensation

ID: MINZOPASSEMADC7Q88C4H104052022Q4DC

92. A Roth IRA is unique for which of the following reasons?

A. Nondeductible Contributions and Nontaxable Distributions
B. Tax Deductible Contributions and Nontaxable Distributions
C. Tax Deductible Contributions and Taxable Distributions
D. Nondeductible Contributions and Taxable Distributions

ID: MINZOPASSESXCC10Q29C4H2040622Q16DC

93. In the employees' group life insurance policy, the premiums paid by the employer for his employees are ________________.

A. Taxable income to the employee
B. Tax-deductible to the employer
C. Tax-deductible to the employee
D. None of the above

ID: MINZOPASSEMADC7Q82C4H304042022Q13DC
94. Which statement is false regarding a Modified Endowment Contract (MEC)?

A. If a policy is categorized as a MEC, the owner has seven years to request a premium refund and have the MEC designation removed
B. A MEC is a policy that fails to meet the 7-pay requirements
C. Distributions from a MEC made before the age of 59 1/2 are subject to a 10% penalty in addition to taxes.
D. LIFO is the tax treatment for distributions from a MEC

ID: MINZOPASSJDXCSEXQ4C5A104062022Q4DC
95. What is the required minimum frequency for the commissioner to examine domestic insurers?

A. Every year
B. Every ten years
C. Every four years
D. Every five years

ID: MINNZOPASSJDADC14Q34C5A2022Q3DC
96. All of the following must be disclosed in the disclosure of charges against separate accounts, except ________________.

A. Guarantee charges for mortality and expenses
B. Expenses related to administration and investment management
C. No tax charged
D. Expenses for accidental insurance benefits

ID: MINZOPASSEMEXSEXQ71C5A3404052022Q4DC
97. The Commissioner must notify all interested parties about the place, time, and purpose of a hearing within how many days of the scheduled hearing?

A. 3 days
B. 7 days
C. 10 days
D. 30 days

ID: MINZOPASSBMADC1Q3C5B1033122Q1DC
98. Which of the following describes an insurer that is registered under the laws of a different state in the United States?

A. Domestic
B. Alien
C. Authorized
D. Foreign

ID: MINZOPASSBMADC1Q1C5B2033122Q1DC
99. An insurer that is owned by its policyholders is known as a____________insurer.

A. Fraternal Benefit Society
B. Mutual
C. Stock
D. Reciprocal

ID: MINZOPASSEMEXC5Q62C5B304052022Q2DC
100. Regarding a Certificate of Authority, which of the options below is NOT true?

A. It is ONLY issued to Life Insurance Policyholders in the District of Columbia
B. The commissioner has the authority to suspend or revoke a Certificate of Authority
C. It is issued by the state Department of Insurance
D. It is equivalent to a licence for insurance

ID: MINZOPASSJDADC2Q42C5C104012022Q42DC
101. Which one of the following statements about life insurance applications is not correct?

A. The producer attaches an agent's report to the completed life insurance application and forwards it to the insurer
B. Life insurance applications are usually divided into two sections: Medical History and General Information
C. The agent's report forms a part of THE ENTIRE CONTRACT
D. The application contains identifying information about the insured

ID: MINZOPASSJDADC1Q8C5C2033122Q1DC
102. To work in the insurance industry, a prohibited person must first obtain a(n):

A. A felony conviction waiver
B. 1033 Consent to Work Waiver
C. A pardon by the state's insurance commissioner
D. A prohibited person can never conduct insurance business

ID: MINZOPASSBMADC1Q5C5C3033122Q1DC
103. Based on the public's perception of an agent's actions, which of the following authorities does the public believe the agent has?

A. Authorized
B. Implied
C. Apparent
D. Express

ID: MINZOPASSEMEXC5Q70C5C404052022Q3DC
104. Commissions can be shared or split by producers on which of the following grounds?

A. A written agreement between the producers
B. Under no circumstances is it legal for producers to share commission.
C. ONLY if the insured is aware of it and agrees to it in writing
D. Each party has the appropriate license for that specific line of insurance.

ID: MINZOPASSJDADC14Q19C5C504052022Q2DC
105. Which of the following statements about policyholder reports is correct?

A. On the policy's anniversary date, an insurer must mail an annual report to each policyholder
B. Within 30 days of the end of each quarter, an insurer must mail a quarterly report to each policyholder
C. Each policyholder must get a monthly report from the insurer
D. Within 30 days of the policy's anniversary; an insurer must send an annual report to each policyholder

ID: MINZOPASSJDADC14Q26C5C604052022Q1DC
106. If a producer's license has lapsed for _________ year(s), they can apply for reinstatement without having to pass a written exam.

A. 3
B. 1
C. 2
D. 5

ID: MINZOPASSJDEXGEXQ84C5B104052022Q1DC
107. Which of the following actions does not constitute false advertising?

A. Making it clear that dividends are not guaranteed
B. Misrepresenting the policy's terms
C. Persuading an insured to abolish an existing policy with false details of the new policy
D. Representing a policy of insurance as a share of stock

ID: MINZOPASSJDEXGEXQ93C5D204062022Q3DC
108. Which of the following statements best defines the unfair trade practice of rebating?

A. Offering an inducement with something of value not specified in the policy
B. Making false statements about someone engaged in the insurance business
C. Selling cheap policies at high prices
D. Making statements that misrepresent an insurance policy to induce an insured to replace the policy

ID: MINZOPASSEMADC1Q14C5D3033122Q1DC
109. What is a misrepresentation?

A. Unequal exchange of value
B. Only one party, the insurance company, is legally bound to the contract
C. Both parties must do certain things to make the contract legally binding
D. False statement on an insurance application

ID: MINZOPASSEMEXC5Q71C5D404052022Q1DC
110. What is a term for the act of making false statements regarding an insurer's financial situation with the intention of injuring anyone who engages in the insurance business?

A. Rebating
B. Defamation
C. Slander
D. Misrepresentation

ID: MINZOPASSJDXCSEXQ27C5D504062022Q3DC
111. Which of the following describes the practice of unfair discrimination?

A. Requiring a loan applicant to obtain insurance from a specific provider in order to receive loan approval
B. An insurance company that charges different premiums for insureds in the same risk classification
C. Inducing the sale of insurance by providing a valuable benefit
D. Refusing to share commission with a proposed insured

ID: MINZOPASSESXCSEQ14C5D6040622Q5DC
112. The act of replacing a current life insurance policy with a new policy based on deception is known as ____________________.

A. Twisting
B. Coercion
C. Sliding
D. Rebating

ID: MINZOPASSEMKAC2Q4C5D704112022Q1DC
113. If a consumer report is obtained using false pretenses, what is the maximum penalty?

A. Imprisonment for one year, $7,000 fine, or both
B. Imprisonment for five years, $7,500 fine, or both
C. Imprisonment for two years, $10,000 fine, or both
D. Imprisonment for one year, $5,000 fine, or both

ID: MINZOPASSEMEXC5Q65C5D804052022Q1DC
114. An unfair claims settlement would be which of the options below?

A. Not telling the insured anything about arbitration
B. requesting a signed proof of loss statement from the insured following their verbal request of the claim to the insurer
C. Failing to respond or deny claims settlement within a reasonable time of completing the proof of loss statements
D. Delaying a claim settlement for 30 days so the insurance company can investigate

ID: MINZOPASSBMADC1Q6C5E033122Q1DC
115. An individual with a financial or ethical trust relationship with another individual/entity is known as:

A. Adjuster
B. Fiduciary
C. Producer
D. Accountant

ID: MINZOPASSBMC5F08052022Q2DC
116. Within how many years are insurers permitted to contest a policy after it has been issued if the insured intentionally did not disclose that they had AIDS at the time of application, if the insurer was not permitted to test for AIDs at the time of application, renewal or amendment?

A. 1
B. 2
C. 3
D. 5

ID: MINZOPASSJDADC14Q2C5G04052022Q1DC
117. Which of these statements about the Life and Disability Insurance Guaranty Association is untrue?

A. An insurer can choose to join the association as a member
B. In no situation will the association be responsible for more than $300,000 in total for any single individual.
C. It protects policyholders against financial loss when an insurer goes bankrupt
D. The association requires all insurers allowed to transact life and health insurance in The District to be members

ID: MINZOPASSEMEXC6Q85C6A104052022Q2DC
118. ________ is the grace period for scheduled premium payments on a variable life insurance policy

A. 10 days.
B. 30 days.
C. 31 days.
D. 60 days.

ID: MINZOPASSJDEXGEXQ75C6A20405202Q2DC
119. All of the following must be done by the insured when reinstating a life insurance policy, EXCEPT

A. Refund all outstanding debt, including interest
B. Prepay the premium for the following year
C. Pay back premiums
D. Pay any interest owed on overdue premium

ID: MINZOPASSJDADC4Q19C6B104022022Q1DC
120. Failure to repay a loan or the interest on a loan will result in canceling a life insurance policy in which of the following instances?

A. If interest rates rise by more than 5% in a single year
B. After the loan defaults for over four years
C. Following a 30-day written notice from the insurance that the loan is due
D. If the total amount owed matches or exceeds the cash value of the insurance Policy

ID: MINZOPASSJDADC14Q3C6B204052022Q2DC
121. Which of the following statements about benefits in The District protected from creditors is untrue?

A. A creditor can reclaim a debt from proceeds pledged as security for the debt by the insured
B. The proceeds of a life insurance policy are shielded from claims by creditors
C. Transferring a policy is not invalid in any circumstance
D. A creditor must not retrieve a debt from proceeds offered as collateral for the obligation by the insured

ID: MINZOPASSEMEXC4Q52C6C104052022Q3DC
122. Upon termination of a group life plan, which insured employees would qualify for individual insurance with the same coverage conversion?

A. Employees insured under the plan for at least five years
B. Those who have worked in the company for at least three years
C. Employees with dependents
D. Those with no history of claims

ID: MINZOPASSJDEXGEXQ82C6D104052022Q7DC
123. In a variable annuity contract, which one of the following statements will most likely be included?

A. Payments do not guarantee a fixed dollar amount
B. Payments from the policy are always fixed
C. Death benefits are not guaranteed
D. Dividends are always guaranteed

ID: MINZOPASSBMXCC3Q33C6E04022022Q3DC
124. Gabbie owns a life insurance policy. Her policy's cash value fluctuates based on the performance of the S&P 500. Gabbie is the policy owner of which policy?

A. Variable Universal life
B. Variable whole life
C. Variable term life
D. Endowment

ID: MINZOPASSEMADC14Q13C6F04052022Q3DC
125. Which of the following assertions about credit life, accident, and health insurance in The District is correct?

A. Credit Life/Accident and Health restrictions apply to loans with a term of less than five years.
B. Term or whole life policies are available for group credit life insurance
C. Individual credit life insurance policies can be whole life or term
D. Credit Life/Accident and Health restrictions apply to loans with a term of less than ten years.

ID: MINZOPASSJDADC14Q8C6G04052022Q1DC

126. If the insured fails to make premium payments in The District, they will be eligible for nonforfeiture benefits and cash surrender values after _________ years.

A. 1
B. 5
C. 3
D. 2

District of Columbia Simulated Exam 4 Answers

ID: MINZOPASSEMADC3Q74C1A1040222Q4DC

1. Correct answer: A

The net amount at risk drops as the cash value rises, while the face amount of the insurance remains the same.

Net Amount is the amount left over after all deductions are made.

ID: MINZOPASSESXCC3Q34C1A2040522Q5DC

2. Correct Answer: C

10-pay life is the shortest pay period in this scenario. The lesser the number of payments or duration of payment, the faster the cash value grows.

ID: MINZOPASSESEXC2Q29C1B040422Q7DC

3. Correct answer: A

"Flexible Premium Adjustable Life" policies are another name for universal life insurance policies.

More on Universal Life (UL) Insurance Policies:

- Universal life policies are FLEXIBLE because they offer flexible premiums and flexible death benefits. With universal life policies, the policy owner can adjust the minimum premium, target premium, or skip premium payments. In addition, the policy owner can also do partial surrender and withdrawal
- Have two components: Insurance and cash value (aka cash account)
- The insurance component is Annually Renewable Term (ART)
- Two death benefit options:
    - Option A (level)
    - Option B (increasing)

ID: MINZOPASSJDEXGEXQ5C1B04052022Q10DC

4. Correct answer: D

A variable life is a whole life policy with benefits that tends to change based on market conditions, and policy owners/holders bear all the risk of investment.

ID: MINZOPASSESKAC4Q4C1B041122Q25DC

5. Correct Answer: B

Even though variable universal life (VUL) policies permit the owner to control the investment, a minimum cash value is rarely guaranteed. The face amount and the policy cash value vary based on the investment performance of the separate accounts.

Therefore, most VULs state that the death benefits will not fall below a certain minimum. The cash value in VULs is NEVER guaranteed, and VULs are considered security products. For these two reasons, individuals need a securities license and a life insurance license to sell VULs.

ID: MINZOPASSESKAC4Q23C1A1041322Q27DC

6. Correct Answer: A

Whole life contracts that are Interest-sensitive do not pay dividends. Remember that dividends are NEVER guaranteed. The cash value rises and falls in accordance with interest rates.

ID: MINZOPASSESXCC3Q39C1B040522Q17DC

7. Correct Answer: A

The premium cannot be lowered or raised because it is fixed.

Accumulated cash values are tied to a stock market index in an Equity Indexed Life Insurance policy.

ID: MINZOPASSESKAC4Q5C1C041122Q22DC

8. Correct Answer: D

For the whole length of the policy, the death benefit (face amount) for level term life insurance stays the same.

ID: MINZOPASSESKAC4Q67C2A4041322Q44DC

9. Correct Answer: A

"Decreasing term" is the correct answer. A decreasing term insurance policy provides insurance protection for decreasing insurance needs. Robell's outstanding home loan would decrease annually as she makes regular payments. Therefore, a decreasing term is ideal for Robell.

ID: MINZOPASSESEXC2Q30C1C040422Q7DC

10. Correct answer: C

Annually Renewable Term (ART) provides the lowest insurance cost. ART is a type of level term insurance.

More on Term Insurance:

- Temporary insurance
- Provides PURE DEATH PROTECTION
- No additional living benefits or cash value
- 3 types are level, increasing & decreasing
- Level term is the most common type
- Annually Renewable Term (ART) is a level term insurance
    - Premium increases annually
    - May be guaranteed to be renewed every year without proof of insurability

- Decreasing Term
    - Usually used for mortgage or other types of death for protection against premature death
- Return of Premium (ROP)
    - Is a type of Increasing Term Policy
    - Full premium is paid in addition to death benefit if the insured dies within a specified period or outlives the term policy

ID: MINZOPASSEMADC3Q63C1C2040222Q1

11. Correct answer: C

Term life insurance has no cash value. It has a fixed premium, provides temporary coverage, and is frequently called pure protection.

- Term Life Insurance provides a pure death benefit type because it does not accumulate cash value
- Term Life Insurance provides coverage for a limited period specified in the contract.

Some features of Term Life Insurance

- Annually Renewable Term
    - Premium is increased yearly, and death benefit remains level
- Renewable Term
    - Allows the policy owner to renew the policy at the anniversary date of the policy without providing proof of insurability
- Convertible Term
    - Allows the policy owner of a term life insurance to convert it to a permanent life insurance policy without proof of insurability

ID: MINZOPASSESKAC4Q80C2A4041322Q45DC

12. Correct Answer: D

The policy is renewable with an increase in premium due to the insured's *attained* age.

ID: MINZOPASSESKAC4Q6C1C041122Q23

13. Correct Answer: C

Term means temporary protection for a specified number of years. There are many riders available with term insurance. Among them are the renewability and convertibility riders. Renewable contracts have higher premiums than nonrenewable contracts, and convertible term policies have higher premiums than nonconvertible term policies. With a convertible rider, the insured can always change their term insurance into a permanent policy without having to provide proof of insurability. On the other hand, a renewability rider allows an insured to renew their term contract within a specified period without having to prove insurability. Remember that the premium will usually increase when a rider is added to an insurance policy.

ID: MINZOPASSTAXCC9Q57C1D104112022Q76DC

14. Correct answer: A

Because only one payment is necessary, this annuity contract is considered a single *premium.* The income stream does not begin until five years after the contract is signed; hence, it is called *Deferred.* Deferred annuities start benefit payments AFTER 12 months of the annuity's issue date.

ID: MINZOPASSTAXCC9Q59C1D204112022Q77DC

15. Correct answer: A

When the annuitant passes away, gets disabled, or becomes incapacitated, the surrender charge is usually waived under deferred annuity contracts.

ID: MINZOPASSADXCC9Q17C1D304092022Q17DC

16. Correct answer: D

With a variable annuity, the buyer(owner) bears all investment risks.

In a variable annuity, the value of annuities is measured in units rather than dollars. The more money you put in, the more units you'll get. Annuitization converts accumulation units to annuity units, and the income given depends on the annuity unit value.

More on Variable Annuity:

- Variable annuities are regulated by the Financial Industry Regulatory Authority (FINRA), the Securities and Exchange Commission (SEC), and state insurance departments. Annuity payments and cash values fluctuate based on the investment performance of the separate account established by the contract owner. Instead of dollars, payments are made in annuity units
- Individuals need both a life insurance license and a securities license to sell
- Benefit payments fluctuate based on the performance of the *separate* account

ID: MINZOPASSESEXC2Q24C1D040422Q25DC

17. Correct answer: A

Fixed annuities and equity-indexed annuities (EIA) both guarantee a minimum interest rate. However, EIAs usually earn a higher minimum interest rate than fixed annuities.

ID: MINZOPASSEMEXSEXQ53C2B604072022Q19DC

18. Correct Answer: D

The beneficiary will receive the annuity benefits when the annuitant dies during the accumulation period.

Note that the annuitant and annuity owner may be the same person. The accumulation period is when the annuitant is paying into the annuity.

This period begins when the annuitant makes the first deposit/payment and ends when the annuitant starts receiving benefits. Immediate Annuities do not have an accumulation period; only Deferred Annuities Do.

ID: MINZOPASSESEXC2Q16C1D040422Q19DC
19. Correct answer: A
For this arrangement, a 20-year fixed period distribution, annuities purchased with a single lump sum payment will do just fine.

ANNUITIES:
- Insurance product that provides income for a fixed number of years or life
- Protects the annuity owner against outliving their money
- Opposite of life insurance
- Liquidates an estate

Parties to an annuity contract:
- Owner
    - Can be a corporation, trust, or natural person
    - Has all ownership rights
- Annuitant
    - First in line to receive benefits and is the insured
    - Must be a natural person. CANNOT be a corporation or trust
- Owner & annuitant may be different
- Beneficiary
    - receives the benefits if the annuitant dies

Premium Payment options
- Single premium Vs periodic(flexible) premium

Benefit Payout options
- Immediate VS Deferred

Interest Rate Options
- Fixed Vs. Variable Vs Indexed

Settle Options
- Life Income (Pure, Life with No Refund, or Straight Life)
- Life Income with Refund (Cash Refund or Installment)
- Joint Life Annuity
- Joint & Survivor Annuity

ID: MINZOPASSESKAC4Q21C1E041222Q14DC

20. Correct Answer: A

Two persons are covered under a joint life insurance policy. This policy pays the death benefit upon the death of the first insured. The other advantage of this is that the survivor has the opportunity to buy a single individual policy without submitting proof of insurability.

ID: MINZOPASSTAXCC9Q63C1E204112022Q13DC

21. Correct answer: B

In a joint and survivor annuity, two or more lives are covered, lasting as long as one of them lives.

ID: MINZOPASSEMKA5Q22C2A104122022Q16DC

22. Correct Answer: C

"Totally disabled for at least 90 days" is the correct answer.

ID: MINZOPASSESXCC3Q45C2A2040522Q5DC

23. Correct Answer: B

With a guaranteed insurability rider, a policyholder can renew or add more coverage without having to provide proof of insurability.

ID: MINZOPASSEMKAC5Q23C2A304122022Q5DC

24. Correct Answer: B

"Juvenile insurance policies" is the correct answer. Because a parent or guardian owns juvenile policies, the *payor* rider is usually added to keep the policy in force if the payor (usually the parent) becomes disabled or dies.

ID: MINZOPASSEMEXSEXQ39C2A404062022Q7DC

25. Correct answer: A

In this case, Xuan's beneficiary will only receive the ORIGINAL death benefit and not the triple indemnity (death benefit multiplied by 3) because Xuan caused his death. His triple indemnity rider explicitly excludes coverage if he is the cause or contributed to his death in any manner.

Note: If the accident were not Xuan's fault, then his beneficiary would have received $3,000,000 instead of $1,000,000

ID: MINZOPASSEMKAC5Q11C2A504122022Q4DC

26. Correct Answer: D

Everything mentioned above is true. Note that this rider DOES NOT usually last as long as the base/original insurance policy coverage.

ID: MINZOPASSEMKAC5Q27C2A504122022Q5DC

27. Correct Answer: D

"A family Term rider" is the correct answer. This is one of the many types of *other insured* riders.

ID: MINZOPASSJDEXGEXQ2C2A704052022Q2DC

28. Correct answer: B

Paying out LTC benefits to the insured will reduce the death benefit of the original policy.

ID: MINZOPASSEMADC3Q73C2A8040222Q1DC

29. Correct answer: C

If the insured dies during the term, the beneficiary receives the death benefit of the insurance policy and the total premiums paid.

More on Riders:

Return of Cash Value (The Early Cash Value Rider)

- Added to IUL to eliminate or reduce the policy's Surrender Charge in the first 1 to 5 years. This allows the policyowner to obtain higher cash liquidity in the first five years.

Waiver of Premium

- If an insured person becomes totally handicapped/disabled, the insurer will waive premiums for the period of the disability, or until the policy expires, whichever occurs first. The insured must be disabled for at least 3-6 months to be eligible for the waiver(90 days - 6 months). During the waiting time, the policyowner must continue to pay premiums, but once eligible, the waiver is retroactive to the beginning of the disability.

ID: MINZOPASSBMC2A9061922Q1DC

30. Correct Answer: D

All of the other riders are disability riders except accelerated death benefit rider.

ID: MINZOPASSEMKAC5Q15C2A204122022Q12DC

31. Correct Answer: B

"NEVER increases the death benefit, and no additional premium is required for increases in the death benefit associated with this rider" is the correct answer. The cost-of-living rider, also called the cost-of-living (COLA) adjustment rider, increases the death benefit annually in accordance with a specified linked consumer price index. Note, however, that the policy's premium will also increase when the death benefit is increased.

ID: MINZOPASSBMADC4Q26C2B104102022Q8DC

32. Match the policy provisions with the correct description

		Payment of claims	Consideration Clause	Reinstatement	Insuring Clause	Grace Period	Suicide Clause	Entire Contract	Mode of Premium Payment
	Policy owner can reactivate their policy, usually within 3 years, if certain conditions are met			X					
2	Time period after the premium is due but before the policy lapses. Death benefit is paid during this period if the insured dies					X			
3	If the insured takes his life (suicide) within two years of the policy's issuance, no death benefit is given. All premiums paid, though, will be reimbursed in full						X		
4	Exchange of value. The Insured pays the premium, and the insurer promises to pay future claims		X						
5	Identifies the parties to the insurance contract. Specifies the insured risk and the benefit that will be paid when a claim is filed				X				
6	The frequency of premium payments								X
7	Claims will be paid immediately or within 60 days after proof of claim is received. If the claim is paid later than after 60 days, interest must be paid.	X							
8	Riders, Policy, amendments, and application copy							X	

ID: MINZOPASSEMADC3Q62C4F1040222Q3DC

33. Correct answer: C

The specified death benefit is referred to as the insurer's limit of liability, and it is the maximum amount the policy will pay out in the case of the insured's death. The Death Benefit is another name for the face amount.

The Face Amount is the limit of liability because it is the maximum amount the policy will pay out to the beneficiary in the case of a claim. That amount, unlike the Cash Value, cannot be borrowed from. Only the cash value gives out loans, not the policy proceeds.

ID: MINZOPASSEMXCPC11Q63C2B304072022Q5DC

34. Correct Answer: C

Life insurance policies sold in this state must provide a minimum free-look period of 10 days that begins on the date of policy delivery.

This gives the policyowner time to determine whether or not to keep the policy.
All premiums must be reimbursed if the policyowner decides within the ten-day free-look period not to keep the policy.

ID: MINZOPASSESXCC3Q57C2B4040622Q1DC

35. Correct answer: B

The consideration clause states that the applicant must complete the application and pay the initial premium to be CONSIDERED for the insurance policy by the insurance company.

More on Consideration Clause:

- The amount and premium payment mode are included in the consideration clause
- Consideration is the exchange of something of value
- It is one of the four elements of a LEGAL contract
- The insurer's consideration is approving and issuing the policy and agreeing to pay future claims

ID: MINZOPASSJDADC4Q11C2B50402022Q1DC

36. CORRECT ANSWER: D

The policy owner's ownership rights are a standard contract provision that permits them to do all these and more.

Ownership provision

- The policyowner has complete control over the policy, including the ability to identify or replace revocable beneficiaries, assign the policy, and make any policy-related choices
- The owner bears the additional responsibility of covering the premiums.
- All rights in the policy are retained by the Policy Owner.

ID: MINZOPASSEMEXSEXQ27C2B604052022Q9DC

37. Correct Answer: B

The correct answer is the contingent beneficiary. The primary beneficiary is assumed to die first under the Uniform Simultaneous Death Benefits Act if both the insured and the primary beneficiary pass away in the same accident. The funds will be awarded to the contingent beneficiary. This is done to protect the contingent beneficiary. The death benefit will go to the insured's estate if there is no contingent beneficiary.

ID: MINZOPASSESXCC472C2B6040622Q17DC

38. Correct Answer: C

Revocable beneficiaries are those who can be changed at any moment by the policy owner without the beneficiary's consent or proof of death.

ID: MINZOPASSESEXC3Q37C2B6040522Q5DC

39. Correct answer: A

A policy with an irrevocable beneficiary needs the written permission of the beneficiary or the death of the beneficiary to change and name a new beneficiary.

ID: MINZOPASSJDADC4Q6C2B604022022Q1

40. CORRECT ANSWER: C

A contingent beneficiary has no claim to the policy benefit if there is a surviving primary beneficiary. The death benefit is not shared between contingent and primary beneficiaries. In a life insurance policy, only an irrevocable primary beneficiary has the authority to interfere with some of the owner's rights.

BENEFICIARY PROVISIONS:

Types of Beneficiaries

- Revocable
    - A policyowner can change a revocable beneficiary at any time
- Irrevocable
    - An irrevocable beneficiary cannot be changed unless they die or give written approval
    - When an irrevocable beneficiary is selected, the owner of the insurance cannot make changes to the coverage or benefits without the beneficiary's approval
    - There is a vested interest in the policy for the irrevocable beneficiary

Succession of Beneficiary

- Primary Beneficiary
    - When the insured dies, the primary beneficiary is the first to receive the death benefit
- Contingent or Secondary Beneficiary
    - The secondary beneficiary gets the death benefit only if no primary beneficiary survives the insured's death.

If the primary and contingent beneficiaries pass away before the insured, the policy proceeds are paid to the tertiary beneficiary. When there is no surviving designated beneficiary at the time of the insured's death, the benefits will be paid to the policyowner if they are alive or to the insured's estate if the policyowner is deceased.

ID: MINZOPASSJDADC4Q7C2B604022022Q2DC

41. CORRECT ANSWER: B

The purpose of beneficiary class designations is to provide benefits to a class of anonymous individuals; nevertheless, they may cause problems if it is unclear who is being designated as a beneficiary. "All my children" does not specify which children are included-- those from a previous marriage, those from this one, or both. Similarly, "My minor children" ignores the notion that children will grow up to be adults and, as a result, may accidentally omit a child.

Beneficiary Designation

- A beneficiary designation is usually chosen at the time of application. Whether or not the insured is alive when the insurer receives the notice, a change of beneficiary takes effect on the day the request was signed by the owner.
- Individual/Named — This is a fairly common designation. The beneficiary is identified by name, such as Susan Myers (sister) or Jesse Preston (wife)

Here are more examples:

- Per Capita
    - If a named beneficiary predeceases the insured, this designation will pay all surviving beneficiaries equally.
    - If an insured chooses their three children as beneficiaries and one of them dies before the insured, the payout will be split equally among the remaining specified beneficiaries.
- Per Stirpes
    - This provision will give a deceased beneficiary's portion to the beneficiary's heirs if the insured passes away before the beneficiary.
    - If the insured outlives all other beneficiaries, the estate may be the third beneficiary.
    - A trust is used when the funds are to be sent in accordance with the insured's specified wishes and a recipient, such as minor children, does not have direct access to the death benefits.
- Minors
    - If minors are specified as beneficiaries without trust, the assets are deposited in a settlement option (held with interest) with the insurer acting as trustee.
- To cover an obligation, a creditor is designated via assignment or specified on an application. The creditor can be the named beneficiary or the assignee for a collateral assignment

ID: MINZOPASSESXCC4Q70C2B6040622Q15DC

42. Correct Answer: C

The premium cost will increase as the policy owner pays more frequently. The more frequent the mode of payment, the more costly the premium.

ID: MINZOPASSEMEXSEXQ37C1D404062022Q16DC

43. Correct Answer: C

The automatic premium loan provision makes this possible. With the automatic premium loan provision, the insurer uses the policy's cash value to pay the overdue premium.

Think about the automatic premium loan provision as a bank overdraft protection. The policy owner will eventually have to repay or subtract it from the death benefit when the insured dies. This feature comes standard on permanent life insurance policies at no additional cost.

ID: MINZOPASSEMEXSEXQ54C2B704072022Q17DC

44. Correct Answer: B

The automatic premium loan provision is activated at the end of the grace period. Automatic premium loan occurs when the insurer automatically uses money in the policy's cash value to pay an overdue premium. This provision has now become standard in most permanent life insurance policies.

ID: MINZOPASSESEXC2Q27C2B7040422Q10DC

45. Correct answer: D

For annually renewable terms, the death benefit is level throughout, but the premium increases each year as the insured's attained age increases.

The annually renewable term (ART) is the most basic type of term insurance. Most group life insurance is written as an annually renewal term.

<u>More on Types of Term Insurance:</u>

Note: Only the face amount is subject to change during the term, not the premium. The premium only changes when renewing or converting the term policy based on the ATTAINED age. Attained age is the applicant's age at the time of application.

Decreasing Term

- Death benefit decreases
- Premium remains constant throughout the life of the policy

Level term

- The premium and death benefit are level.

Increasing term

- The death benefit increases
- Premium remains the same

ID: MINZOPASSJDADC4Q4C2B1204022022Q2DC

46. CORRECT ANSWER: B

Reinstatement brings the policy back to its original state as if it had never expired. Even if the insurance is reactivated at a later age, the insurer will only require the initial issue premium.

Reinstatement clause states:

- If a policy has lapsed accidentally for three years due to nonpayment, the owner can reactivate it
- The insured must produce proof of insurability to be reinstated
- All retroactive premiums, including interest, must be paid by the owner from the date of lapse
- A new incontestability period begins upon reinstatement

ID: MINZOPASSEMKAC6Q19C2B904122022Q6

47. Correct Answer: B

Whole life insurance policy owners can take policy loans from their policy without surrendering(canceling) the policy. Remember that the loan will still have to be repaid.The loan amount will be deducted from the death benefit proceeds before being distributed to the beneficiary if it is not repaid and the insured passes away.

Whole life policies *do not* allow cash withdrawal. Cash surrendering the policy will result in its cancellation.

ID: MINZOPASSESEXC3Q32C2B10040422Q4

48. Correct answer: A

The contract is terminated when the cash surrender value is paid.

More on NONFORFEITURE (Guaranteed) OPTIONS:

- For permanent life insurance policies ONLY
- Required by state law
- 3 types (Acronym = REC)

Reduced paid-up insurance

- Insurer uses the cash value as a single premium to purchase a completely PAID-UP permanent policy
- The death benefit under the new policy will be reduced
- The new policy remains in force until death or maturity (age 100)

Extended Term

- For the SAME Death Benefit, the insurer converts the policy to term insurance using the cash value of the policy.

- The new term policy will last for as long as the available cash value is able to purchase
- This is the **DEFAULT** nonforfeiture option if no nonforfeiture option is selected

Cash

- Surrenders/cancels the policy and the policy owner receives the cash surrender value
- Policies surrendered for cash value cannot be reinstated
- The insurer charges a surrender fee when the policy is surrendered for the cash value

NOTE: The insurer will AUTOMATICALLY select the Extended-term option if the policyowner cancels the original policy without selecting a nonforfeiture option.

ID: MINZOPASSJDEXGEXQ7C2B1104052022Q4DC
49. Correct answer: A
The reduction of premium option allows dividends to reduce the following year's premium.

The dividend options are (Mnemonic is CARPPO)

- Cash
- Reduction of premium
- Accumulation at interest
- Paid up additions
- Paid-Up Option
- One-Year Term Option

ID: MINZOPASSJDXCC8Q16C2B1204112022Q4DC
50. Correct answer: A
There is a two-year contestability term for life insurance policies. After two years of coverage, a life insurance policy becomes incontestable and cannot be canceled except for fraud and nonpayment of premiums.

Incontestability Clause

- If the insurer discovers evidence of a material misrepresentation or fraud during the first two years of a life insurance policy, they can contest the claim and cancel the contract.
- A material misstatement in The District is one in which the insurer, having to know the true information, would not have issued the policy.
- Once the policy is in effect for two years from the date of issue, it becomes incontestable with the exception of fraud and nonpayment of premiums.

ID: MINZOPASSJDEXGEXQ11C2B1304052022Q1DC
51. Correct answer: C
Collateral assignment temporarily transfers ownership of one's life insurance policy. This is mostly done with credits and loans.

ID: MINZOPASSESXCC3Q55C2B14040522Q2DC

52. Correct answer: A

The suicide clause is there to discourage people who are actively considering suicide from buying an insurance policy. If the insured commits suicide during the contestability period, which is the first two years of the policy, no death benefit will be paid.

ID: MINZOPASSESXCPC11Q3C2B15040722Q4DC

53. Correct Answer: A

The insured must repay the amount that, at the correct age, the premiums would have purchased.

Under the misstatement of age provision, if an insured's age is misstated on the insurance application, the beneficiary will only receive the death benefit that the insured's premium would have purchased at the correct age. For example, if the insured had been paying a $50 monthly premium for a $100,000 coverage based on the misstated age of 30 and it is later discovered that her correct age at the time of application was 35, then her beneficiary may only receive $70,000 if that is how much a $50 monthly premium would have been able to purchase at the correct age of 35.

ID: MINZOPASSESEXC3Q38C2B16040522Q4DC

54. Correct answer: D

When the insurance company keeps the proceeds and pays interest to the beneficiary regularly, this provision is termed an interest-only option.

ID: MINZOPASSESEXC3Q40C2B17040522Q4DC

55. Correct answer: A

In circumstances of disability, terminal sickness, or severe illness as specified by their contract, the insured may receive a portion of the death benefit under the accelerated death benefit provision.

ID: MINZOPASSJDEXGEXQ8C2C04052022Q4DC

56. Correct answer: C

Policies for life insurance do not have disability as a standard exclusion.

ID: MINZOPASSBMC2C207262022Q8DC

57. Correct Answer: C

Exclusions are a common feature of life insurance policies where the insurer explicitly states certain risks that will not be covered. Aviation is one of the exclusions in life insurance policies. The aviation exclusion excludes coverage only for test pilots, military pilots and crew, and private pilots. **Note: This exclusion does not apply to insureds who are fare-paying passengers on a regularly scheduled commercial airline or commercial airline pilots or crew.**

Note: If an insurer covers a pilot, the pilot's premium will usually be much higher than the standard premium charged for the same risk.

ID: MINZOPASSESEXC3Q36C2C040522Q2DC

58. Correct answer: D

Exclusions are risks that an insurance policy does not cover. The three most common exclusions found in life insurance policies are aviation, hazardous occupations, and war & military service.

- Aviation
    - Excludes coverage only for test pilots, military pilots and crew, and private pilots
    - This exclusion does not apply to insureds who are fare-paying airline passengers on a regularly scheduled commercial airline or commercial airline pilots or crew.
- Hazardous Occupation/Hobbies
    - Death from a specific occupation/hobby may be excluded or the insured pays a higher premium
- War or Military Service
    - STATUS Clause
        - When the insured is on active duty, ALL causes of death are excluded.
    - RESULTS Clause
        - ONLY excludes death when the insured is killed as a result of war

Note: Suicide is a stand-alone standard provision even though it is an exclusion.

ID: MINZOPASSJDEXGEXQ52C3A104052022Q5DC

59. Correct Answer: A

In a life insurance contract, the signatures that are needed and essential are the agent, the Insured (if different from the owner), and the policy owner. The beneficiary is never a signatory to a life insurance contract.

ID: MINZOPASSEMEXSEXQ43C3A2040522Q6DC

60. Correct Answer: C

A producer may correct an insurance application after it has been completed under certain circumstances. The applicant must, however, initial the corrections or changes. Instead of erasing the incorrect answer, the correct thing to do is draw a line through the incorrect answer, make the correction, and have the insured initial the change.

On the exam, when given a choice between the applicant making changes and initialing the application versus discarding it and starting a new application, the MOST correct answer is always discarding the original application and completing a new application.

ID: MINZOPASSEMEXSEXQ38C3D304062022Q4DC

61. Correct answer: B

Insurers waive their right to have the applicant answer the questions after the policy is issued with an incomplete application. The policy cannot be voided at any time due to the insurer's failure to do their due diligence by not ensuring all the questions were answered.

ID: MINZOPASSBMXCC2Q9C3A404012022Q4DC

62. Correct Answer: B

A warranty is a statement that is GUARANTEED to be true.

ID: MINZOPASSESXCC5Q90C3A504022Q5DC

63. Correct Answer: A

Insurance coverage begins when the application is signed, and the producer receives the initial premium in a non-medical insurance policy.

ID: MINZOPASSEMADC7Q93C3A604042022Q1DC

64. CORRECT ANSWER: A

The exchange of an annuity policy for any type of life insurance policy is prohibited by IRC (Internal Revenue Code) Section 1035.

ID: MINZOPASSJDEXGEXQ40C3A704052022Q4DC

65. Correct answer: C

The buyer's guide, often called the consumer guide, is a general brochure intended for anyone considering applying for or buying insurance. It includes essential policy information needed to compare insurance policies from different insurance companies. It does NOT give specific details on a policy.

ID: MINZOPASSEMXCPC11Q46C3A804072022Q4DC

66. Correct Answer: D

USA Patriot Act:

- The purpose of the USA Patriot Act is to detect and prevent terrorism. It also seeks to prevent money laundering used to fund terrorism and other criminal activities. It requires insurers to report suspicious activities.

Suspicious activities:

- Showing greater interest in the early termination features of a product rather than its potential performance
- Fake identification or reluctance to provide identification
- Maximum borrowing against a policy almost immediately after purchasing it
- Receipt of any cash payment greater than $10,000

- Purchase of insurance that the customer does not need
- Requests to have surrender value or other benefits paid to an unrelated person

ID: MINZOPASSBMC3A907282022Q4DC
67. Correct answer: A
According to the Gramm-Leach-Bliley Act (GLBA), the privacy notice must explain the following:
- How the consumer's information is used
- What data is gathered about the consumer
- How the consumer's information is protected
- Where and how that information is shared

ID: MINZOPASSESEXC1Q12C3B1040422Q4DC
68. Correct answer: D
Insurable interest, in life insurance must exist at the time of application.

By law, insurers must decline an insurance application if no insurable interest exists between the insured and the applicant/policyowner.

Individuals do not have to prove an insurable interest in themselves because it is assumed that they have an unlimited insurable interest in themselves.

ID: MINZOPASSEMKAC2Q14C3B204112022Q5DC
69. Correct answer: A
Medical reports are usually required when the application for insurance coverage exceeds a certain face amount.
Any paramedic or examining physician the insurance company selects may complete a medical report. The medical report's expense is covered by the insurance.

ID: MINZOPASSJDEXGEXQ27C3B304052022Q5DC
70. Correct Answer: A
The FCRA gives people the right to be told if information in their credit file is used against them to deny their application for credit, employment, or insurance. Additionally, the FCRA grants individuals the ability to obtain and seek access to all of the consumer reporting agency's data on them (file disclosure).

ID: MINZOPASSJDADC1Q22C3B404012022Q4DC
71. Correct answer: A
Taking on the risk of loss is known as risk retention.

The five types of risk management techniques are (STARR):

- **S**haring
- **T**ransfer
- **A**voidance
- **R**eduction
- **R**eduction

ID: MINZOPASSBMXC2Q19C3B504022022Q4DC

72. Correct Answer: B

Investor-owned life insurance (IOLI) and stranger-owned life insurance (STOLI) are used to bypass state insurable interest laws. The investor(stranger) purchases the insured's policy and is responsible for paying premiums. The investor then collects the death benefit from the insurance company when the insured dies.

ID: MINZOPASSEMEXSEXQ20C3C104052022Q4DC

73. Correct Answer: C

Acceptance in an insurance application occurs when an insurance company approves the application. The insured's offer is the application and initial premium, and the insurer's acceptance is approving the application. All legal contracts must have an agreement, which means there must be an offer and acceptance.

ID: MINZOPASSESEXC1Q14C3C2040422Q4DC

74. Correct answer: C

For a policy to be issued, premiums must be collected. The premium must be received before the insurance policy takes effect. If the premium is not collected during the application, then a statement of good health from the applicant and the initial premium are needed at the time of policy delivery. The field underwriter issues the conditional receipt at the time of application, NOT during policy delivery. Conditional receipt MUST be issued anytime the initial premium is received with the application.

ID: MINZOPASSESADC1Q12C3D103312022Q2DC

75. Correct answer: B

A legal contract does not include indemnity.

A contract is an arrangement whereby two or more parties agree to carry out a certain action in return for something of value, or "consideration."

A legal contract consists of four components.

1. Competent Parties
    a. All parties to a contract, including the insurer and policyowner, must meet the legal competence to enter into a contract
2. Legal Purpose

   a. All parties to a contract must enter into it for a legal reason. A legal contract cannot violate existing laws
3. Agreement
   a. One party must make and transmit to the other party an offer, which the other party must accept or reject
4. Consideration
   a. Each of the contracting parties' exchanges something of value called *consideration*. The consideration for the applicant is the first premium and the application in exchange for the insurer's consideration, which is issuing the policy and agreeing to pay future claims.

ID: MINZOPASSJDADC1Q23C3D104012022Q4DC
76. Correct answer: B
Consideration, agreement (offer and acceptance), legal purpose and competent parties are the four essential components of a legal contract.
There is no element of a legal contract called indemnity.

ID: MINZOPASSESEXC1Q7C3D2040422Q12DC
77. Correct answer: A
The four major elements of an insurance contract that make it legally binding are *agreement* (offer and acceptance), *consideration*, *competent parties*, and *legal purpose*.
A counteroffer is not required.

ID: MINZOPASSBMXCC2Q10C3D104012022Q5DC
78. Correct Answer: B
The elements of a legal contract are legal purpose, legal purpose, agreement (Offer and acceptance), and consideration.
Estoppel: the legal name for preventing a person/company from reclaiming a right already waived.

ID: MINZOPASSJDADC1Q18C3D204012022Q3DC
79. Correct Answer: C
Both parties must perform specific duties to make the contract legally enforceable.

ID: MINZOPASSBMXCC2Q14C3D204012022Q8DC
80. Correct Answer: B
Bilateral is not a special feature of insurance contracts. *Unilateral*, *aleatory*, *conditional,* and *adhesion* are all characteristics of insurance contracts.

ID: MINZOPASSBMXCC2Q20C3D204022022Q9DC

81. Correct Answer: A

A policy of adhesion describes a policy written by the insurer and presented to the applicant or policy owner, leaving no room for negotiation.

ID: MINZOPASSESEXC1Q5C3D2040422Q11DC

82. Correct answer: D

In a conditional contract, the insurer and the policy owner agree on certain conditions for the contract to be executed successfully.

Four Unique Characteristics of Insurance Contracts [test alert]:

1. Adhesion
    a. Take-it-or-leave-it
2. Aleatory
    a. Unequal exchange of value
3. Unilateral
    a. ONLY one party, the insurer, is legally bound to enforce the contract
4. Conditional
    a. Before the contract is executed, certain conditions must be fulfilled by both parties.

ID: MINZOPASSJDEXGEXQ59C4A04052022Q5DC

83. Correct Answer: B

A policy in which the insured and the owner are two different individuals is known as a third-party insurance policy.

ID: MINZOPASSEMADC3Q76C4C04042022Q2DC

84. Correct answer: C

Life settlement have to do with the sale of an existing life insurance policy to someone different (third party) for an amount that is more than the cash surrender value but smaller than the death benefit. This makes it similar to a viatical settlement. One distinction is that a life settlement does not require the insured to be terminally ill. A policyowner might sell their policy because they cannot afford their premium due to a job loss or just want to acquire a different policy. Unlike that, a viatical settlement can only be made for terminally ill clients.

ID: MINZOPASSESXCC6Q91C4D1040622Q4DC

85. Correct answer: A

The insured in this case may convert, at individual rates, to a permanent policy.

ID: MINZOPASSEMADC6Q54C4D2040422Q4DC

86. CORRECT ANSWER: D

In group life insurance, the plan provider, usually the employer, has complete control over all aspects of coverage and cost. However, the member, typically the employee, chooses the beneficiary.

In a group life Insurance policy, the group's sponsor receives the Master Policy, and the employees receive a Certificate of Insurance.

The policy is not under the employee's control. Yet, when they leave the company, they still have the right to choose the beneficiary and convert the group policy to an individual policy.

ID: MINZOPASSEMADC7Q92C4E104042022Q5DC

87. CORRECT ANSWER: B.

The Keogh Plan is the answer.

Keogh or HR-10 plans:

- For self-employed individuals like doctors, farmers, lawyers, or other sole- -proprietors.
- Possibly defined benefit or defined contribution plans.
    - Defined contribution Keoghs can only contribute a maximum of $49,000 annually.
    - defined benefit Keoghs receive a maximum of $195,000 in benefits annually.
    - Dividends and interest are tax-deferred, and contributions are tax deductible.

ID: MINZOPASSESKAC3Q9C4E2040922Q4DC

88. Correct Answer: B

The worker is the policyholder for executive bonus plans (162 plans), not the employer. The employer is the premium payer on a permanent life insurance policy that the worker owns.

ID: MINZOPASSEMADC6Q60C4F104042022Q4DC

89. CORRECT ANSWER: C

Premiums are usually paid to an agent weekly or monthly in cash. The death benefit is generally available in $1,000 or less increments. Some states limit the amount of life insurance coverage to $10,000 per person.

ID: MINZOPASSESXC10Q28C4D2040622Q6DC

90. Correct Answer: A

The insured in a key employee insurance policy is the key employee. The applicant, owner, and beneficiary is the business.

ID: MINZOPASSESKAC3Q1C4F2B040922Q7DC

91. Correct Answer: A

Life insurance is not used for workers' compensation, nor is it a business use of life insurance.

Life insurance can be used for the following purposes by businesses:

- Buy-sell agreements
  - Two types
    - Cross-purchase
    - Entity plan
- Key-person(employee) insurance
- Deferred compensation
  - Ex: Executive bonus plans

ID: MINZOPASSEMADC7Q88C4H104052022Q4DC

92. CORRECT ANSWER: A

After-tax (nondeductible) funds are used to contribute to Roth retirement plans. Distributions, including all gains, are tax-free under existing tax law.

ID: MINZOPASSESXCC10Q29C4H2040622Q16DC

93. Correct Answer: B

"tax-deductible to the employer" is correct.
An employer's premium for his employees' life insurance is usually deductible to the business.

ID: MINZOPASSEMADC7Q82C4H304042022Q13DC

94. CORRECT ANSWER: A

A policy that fails the 7-Pay Test will be categorized as a Modified Endowment Contract for the duration of the contract. Once it has become an MEC, a policy cannot be reversed.

ID: MINZOPASSJDXCSEXQ4C5A104062022Q4DC

95. Correct Answer: D

Although the commissioner can examine insurers as frequently as they decide, the commissioner must examine or inspect every insurer licensed in The District of Columbia at least once every **five years**.

ID: MINNZOPASSJDADC14Q34C5A2022Q3DC

96. Correct Answer: C

Taxes are imposed on separate accounts, and the tax or tax reserves must be stated in the disclosure.

ID: MINZOPASSEMEXSEXQ71C5A3404052022Q4DC

97. Correct answer: C

10 days is the correct answer.

ID: MINZOPASSBMADC1Q3C5B1033122Q1DC
98. Correct answer: D

A foreign insurer is an insurance company that is governed by the laws of another state other than the state it is doing business in.

Alien insurers are governed under the laws of a different country outside of the United States.

Domestic insurer is an Insurance company that conducts business in a state where it was established.

An authorized or admitted insurer is a certified insurance company, or an insurance company admitted to conduct insurance business in this state.

ID: MINZOPASSBMADC1Q1C5B2033122Q1DC
99. Correct answer: B
A mutual insurance company is owned by its members, often known as policyholders.

A mutual insurance company is a participating company whose members share policy dividends. When and if declared by the directors, policyholders may receive non-taxable dividends as a return of any divisible excess.

ID: MINZOPASSEMEXC5Q62C5B304052022Q2DC
100. Correct answer: A
Insurers must be granted a Certificate of Authority (equivalent to a license) from the Department of Insurance before transacting business in this state. In addition, they must satisfy all state-required financial requirements.

More on Certificate of Authority

- The ONLY insurers not required to acquire a certificate of Authority are licensed Excess and surplus lines brokers
- Insurers with a Certificate of Authority are considered ADMITTED/AUTHORIZED
- Unapproved insurers (insurers that do not have a certificate of authority) are considered UNAUTHORIZED or NONADMITTED

ID: MINZOPASSJDADC2Q42C5C104012022Q42DC

101. Correct answer: C

Although the agent's report and completed application are submitted to the insurer, the agent's report does not form a part of THE ENTIRE CONTRACT because it is a confidential report meant only to be seen by the insurer.

Note, a life insurance application is not confidential because a copy of the application (parts I and II) forms part of THE ENTIRE CONTRACT and will be delivered to the policyowner after the policy is issued.

ID: MINZOPASSJDADC1Q8C5C2033122Q1DC

102. Correct answer: B

A prohibited person convicted of a felony must first apply to the commissioner for a 1033 Waiver for Consent to Work.

ID: MINZOPASSBMADC1Q5C5C3033122Q1DC

103. Correct answer: C

When the agent's actions give the impression that they have power, this is *apparent* authority.

Implied Authority - Although implied power is not expressly stated in the contract, it is essential, reasonable, and customary for the producer to carry out given responsibilities.

Express Authority - The producer's agency contract gives them explicit authority. It contains written information about the producer's ability to transact business on the principal's(insurer's) behalf.

ID: MINZOPASSEMEXC5Q70C5C404052022Q3DC

104. Correct answer: D

In the insurance industry, producers must be appropriately licensed in the line of insurance to be able to receive commissions.

Although uncommon, splitting commission is legal among producers appointed by the same insurer and licensed to sell that specific insurance.

ID: MINZOPASSJDADC14Q19C5C504052022Q2DC

105. Correct Answer: D

An insurer is required to mail an annual report to every policyholder within thirty days of the policy's anniversary.

ID: MINZOPASSJDADC14Q26C5C604052022Q1DC

106. Correct Answer: B

If a producer allows their license to lapse, they can reapply for it within one year of the expiration date without completing a written exam. The producer must, nevertheless, pay a penalty equal to twice the unpaid renewal cost.

ID: MINZOPASSJDEXGEXQ84C5B104052022Q1DC

107. Correct answer: A

Stating that dividends are not guaranteed is an important way to avoid false advertising.

ID: MINZOPASSJDEXGEXQ93C5D204062022Q3DC

108. Correct answer: A

If not specified in the policy, rebating offers an inducement to purchase insurance.

ID: MINZOPASSEMADC1Q14C5D3033122Q1DC

109. Correct Answer: D

A false statement on an insurance application is considered a misrepresentation.

ID: MINZOPASSEMEXC5Q71C5D404052022Q1DC

110. Correct answer: B

Defamation is any false written or oral statement(s) intended to harm anyone (including a producer or insurance company) involved in the insurance business.

Defamation is also any malicious, false information or statement about the financial condition of any company or person.

MISREPRESENTATION is any false statement.

REBATING offers inducement(s) to proposed insureds/applicants to make a sale.

Note: The offer or acceptance of rebates is illegal. Note: offering merchandise, educational materials, or promotional materials that cost LESS THAN $10 are allowed and, therefore, legal.

ID: MINZOPASSJDXCSEXQ27C5D504062022Q3DC

111. Correct Answer: B

Charging different premiums for individuals in the same risk class with the same life expectancy is the unfair trade practice of unfair discrimination. Unfair Discrimination in insurance is illegal in this state.

ID: MINZOPASSESXCSEQ14C5D6040622Q5DC

112. Correct answer: A

Twisting is a deception insurance agents use to persuade policyholders to let their policies lapse to purchase new policies.

ID: MINZOPASSEMKAC2Q4C5D704112022Q1DC

113. Correct answer: D

A fine of $5,000,1 year of imprisonment, or both are the maximum penalties for obtaining consumer reports under false pretenses.

Information gathered by consumer reporting organizations, including credit bureaus, companies that provide medical information, and tenant screening services, is protected by the Fair Credit Reporting Act (FCRA). A consumer report's contents cannot be given to someone without a legitimate need as stated by The Act.

ID: MINZOPASSEMEXC5Q65C5D804052022Q1DC

114. Correct answer: C

If an insurer does not confirm or reject coverage of claims within a reasonable time after completing proof of loss statements, it is guilty of unfair claim settlement.

ID: MINZOPASSBMADC1Q6C5E033122Q1DC

115. Correct answer: B

A fiduciary, in insurance terms, is someone who holds a position of trust with another individual and is accountable for managing that individual's financial affairs.

Responsibilities of the Producer to the Insurer

- A fiduciary manages another person's finances, particularly when it comes to managing premiums for insurance policies.
- Premiums must be kept apart from other monies in a trust account and forwarded to the insurer as soon as possible.

ID: MINZOPASSBMC5F08052022Q2DC

116. Correct Answer: C

The correct answer is three years.

Insurers are permitted to contest a policy for ***three*** years after it has been issued, renewed, or amended if the insured intentionally did not disclose that they had AIDS at the time of application AND the insurer was not permitted to test for AIDs at the time of application, renewal or amendment.

ID: MINZOPASSJDADC14Q2C5G04052022Q1DC

117. Correct Answer: A

The Association requires all insurers doing business in The District to be members. It is not a choice but a requirement.

Life and Health Disability Insurance Guaranty Association

- In the case of insurer impairment or insolvency, the Life and Health Insurance Guaranty Association protects policyholders and beneficiaries.
- The association's responsibility will not go above the following:
    - In no case will the Association be responsible for more than $300,000 in total for any single individual
    - The cost of health insurance is $100,000 in addition to any net cash surrender and withdrawal amounts.
    - Annuity benefits of $300,000, including $100,000 in net cash surrender and withdrawal values
    - $300,000 in life insurance death payouts and $100,000 in net cash surrender and withdrawal values

A few things that won't be covered:

- A policy not guaranteed by the insurer and in which the risk is assumed by the policyholder, contract holder, or certificate holder.
- Unless assumption certificates have been issued and delivered, any reinsurance policy or contract.

ID: MINZOPASSEMEXC6Q85C6A104052022Q2DC

118. Correct answer: B

In a variable life policy, there is a grace period of 30 days after the premium is due for all scheduled premiums.

Other District of Columbia Provisions on Variable Life Insurance Policies:

- A 10 day Free-look period from the date the insured (or policyowner if different from the insured) receives the policy or 45 days from the date of application, whichever occurs LATER
- Reinstatement of the policy within three years of lapse, as long as the insured provides evidence of insurability and submits a written application
- Incontestable by the insurer after two years

ID: MINZOPASSJDEXGEXQ75C6A20405202Q2DC

119. Correct answer: B

When reinstating a life insurance policy, an insured must pay back premiums with interest, if applicable, pay all credits or loans with interest, and show evidence of insurability.

ID: MINZOPASSJDADC4Q19C6B104022022Q1DC

120. CORRECT ANSWER: D

Failure to repay a loan or loan interest does not cancel a policy unless the total amount owed exceeds the insurance policy's cash value.

ID: MINZOPASSJDADC14Q3C6B204052022Q2DC

121. Correct Answer: C

A borrower may collect a debt from proceeds pledged as collateral for the payment by the insured. Transferring a policy could be valid under certain circumstances.

Credit Life/Accident and Health

- Credit Life/Accident and Health restrictions apply to debts and other credit transactions with a term of less than five years
- The period will begin when the debtor is legally committed to the creditor
- Any refunds must be credited as soon as possible
- The complete amount of the debt cannot be charged to a debtor
- All payments must be made either by check or by a draft drawn from the insurance company
- If someone breaks any of these rules, they could pay a fine of $1,000, or spend up to a year in jail, or both..

ID: MINZOPASSEMEXC4Q52C6C104052022Q3DC

122. Correct answer: A

Employees who have been part of the group plan for five years can simply convert to an individual policy with the same coverage when the master plan ends.

Note: An employee or group member who leaves their job has **31** days to convert their group life insurance to an individual policy. However, if the group sponsor terminates a group policy (aka master plan), the participants/employees can ONLY convert it if they have been on the group plan for at least five years.

ID: MINZOPASSJDEXGEXQ82C6D104052022Q7DC

123. Correct Answer: A

The statement " payments do not guarantee fixed dollar amounts" comes up when discussing variable annuity contracts because variable annuity contracts do not guarantee fixed income payments.

ID: MINZOPASSBMXCC3Q33C6E04022022Q3DC

124. Correct Answer: B

In a variable life policy, the cash value fluctuates in accordance with the performance of securities (ex, stocks, mutual funds, etc) of the underlying investments. The correct answer in this scenario is variable universal life and variable whole life. However, since you can only select one answer, the variable whole life is the most correct.

ID: MINZOPASSEMADC14Q13C6F04052022Q3DC

125. Correct Answer: A

Credit life insurance policies for individuals and groups must be term life insurance policies. Credit Life laws apply to loans with a term of less than five years.

ID: MINZOPASSJDADC14Q8C6G04052022Q1DC

126. Correct Answer: C

In the event of premium payment default after three years, the insured will be eligible for nonforfeiture benefits and cash surrender values.

Mandatory Provisions

- The company will award a paid-up nonforfeiture benefit if the insured defaults on a premium payment only after policy premiums for regular insurance have been paid for an entire year and if petitioned no later than **60 days** after the premium due date
- The company will pay a cash surrender value rather than a paid-up nonforfeiture value if the insured defaults on a premium payment for conventional insurance after the policy premiums have been paid for three years and if requested no later than **60 days** after the premium due date
- After 60 days of the defaulted premium due date, a specified paid-up nonforfeiture benefit will automatically take effect unless the policyholder selects another available option
- If the client surrenders the policy during **30 days** of any policy anniversary or the insurance company continues the policy under a paid-up nonforfeiture benefit that became applicable after the policy has been in force for 3 years, the firm will pay the cash surrender value
- The mortality table, interest rate, and method used to determine cash surrender values and paid-up nonforfeiture options must be described or shown in guaranteed policies that allow for unscheduled changes in benefits or premiums.

Minzo Pass National Life Insurance Pre-Licensing Study Guide

Important Definitions

Every profession has unique jargon, and the insurance industry is no different. You will only answer most of the questions on your exam if you understand the key insurance terms.

Insurance
Test Alert: Insurance is *the transfer of risk*. Anytime you obtain insurance, you are transferring the financial risk from you to the insurer. Insurance is the most common method of handling risk. This question is almost guaranteed to be on your exam and is one of the easiest.

Risk
Risk is the uncertainty of loss. Insurance provides certain guarantees of financial wholeness in place of the uncertainty of risk. The insurance company calculates the value of the potential loss in monetary terms and gives you a specified amount of money in case of a loss. For example, when the insured dies, the beneficiary receives a set amount. Although the money will not bring back your loved one, it will help to return you to financial stability or wholeness.

Pure and speculative risks are the two categories of risks. Insurance only covers pure risk. Pure risk consists entirely of the possibility for loss. For example, there is no gain in crashing your vehicle. For this reason, insurance companies will provide automobile coverage.
Test Alert: Insurance ONLY covers pure risk. Speculative risk is a risk with both potential for gain and potential for loss. For example, gambling is an example of a speculative risk because there's a possibility you could win or lose. Insurance companies do not cover speculative risks.

Peril
A peril is a specific event causing a loss. In the case of life insurance, death is the peril because death is the cause of the loss. Note: A loss must occur before a company can pay benefits or claims. Insurance companies only cover uncertainties.

Loss
Loss is a reduction in value. Insurance companies place a financial value on the insured before and after a loss. For example, when you purchase a one-million-dollar life insurance policy, the insurance company will value your life at one million dollars. When you die (your death is the

loss), there will be a reduction in your family's earnings. The insurance company will then pay your family the one-million-dollar benefit to restore them financially.

Hazard

Anything that increases the possibility of a loss happening is considered a hazard. Hazards are just things that make a loss more likely to happen. Remember that hazards do not cause a loss but just *increase* the chance of a loss occurring. The three types of hazards are *Moral*, *Physical,* and *Morale*.

InsurER

An *insurer or principal* is another name for an insurance company. You will likely see the word insur***er*** instead of insurance company on your exam. Do not confuse insur***er*** with insur***ed.*** The person whose life the insurance company is covering is known as the insured. That person must die before the life insurance company can pay out benefits.

InsurED

Insur**ed** is the person whose life the insurance company is covering. That person must die before the life insurance company can pay out benefits.

Producer

Another name for an insurance agent is a producer. A producer is a representative of an insurance company, although the term includes both agents and brokers. On your exam, expect to see the word producer used instead of agent.

Underwriter

An underwriter is an insurance company employee responsible for evaluating insurance applications, rating the applicants, and approving or denying applications.

Beneficiary

A beneficiary is someone who has the right to benefits in the event of a loss. In life insurance, the person who is eligible to get the death benefit in the event that the insured passes away is the beneficiary. Note: The beneficiary and the insur**ed** cannot be the same person or entity for life insurance policies.

Policy Owner or Policy Holder

The life insurance policy's owner. Note: The applicant and policy owners are usually the same person for life insurance policies. The insurance contract is always between the insurer and the policyholder. The policy owner has all the rights of the insurance contract. They have the right to assign beneficiaries, pay premiums, cancel the policy, etc.

Applicant

An applicant is the person or entity that applies for insurance.

Death Benefit

The death benefit is the money the beneficiary of an insurance contract will receive upon the insured's death. It is also called *face amount, policy proceeds, and limit of liability.*

Insurance Policy or Insurance Contract

A legal contract whereby the insurer guarantees payment to the policyholder or beneficiary in the event of a specified loss.

Premium

The amount of money paid to an insurance provider for coverage is called the premium.

Surrender

Surrender is the act of a policy owner canceling an insurance policy earlier than the specified date in the contract.

Attained Age

In insurance, attained age means *current* age.

Cash Value

Cash value is a permanent life insurance policy's savings account. The insurer puts a portion of the premiums for permanent life insurance policies in this savings account.

Exposure

Exposure is simply the risk an insurance company is willing to accept and pay for. Exposure units measure exposure. For example, an insurance company's $200,000 life insurance policy exposure is $200,000. Insurance companies use exposure to calculate premiums.

Indemnity

Indemnification means returning to financial wholeness or a person's financial state before a loss. Insurance is an indemnity contract because it returns the beneficiary to financial wholeness after a covered loss.

Assignment

Assignment is the *transfer* of an insurance policy's ownership rights to an individual or entity.

Claim
A claim is the official payment request from a beneficiary or policy owner to an insurance company for a covered loss. Insurers only pay insurance benefits after they receive a claim.

Insurable Interest
The financial or emotional interest that an applicant or policy owner has in the well-being of the insured. If insurable interest exists, if the insured becomes sick, disabled, or dies, the applicant/policy owner will suffer a financial or emotional loss.

Rider
A rider is an attachment(add-on) to an insurance policy that expands or restricts coverage. An *exclusion* rider is a rider that limits or denies coverage.

Underwriting
Underwriting is how an insurer determines whether to accept or reject an insurance application. The underwriting department determines the insurance premium during the underwriting process.

Surrender
Surrender occurs when a policy owner voluntarily gives up or cancels their insurance policy.

Lapse
A lapse occurs when an insurance policy is canceled or terminated due to nonpayment of premium by the insurer.

Cash Surrender Value
Cash surrender value is the portion of the policy owner's paid premiums available for withdrawal or to take a loan against. Consider the cash surrender value as the policy owner's *available* account balance.

Cash Value
Cash value is the total premiums paid minus the cost of insurance(the insurer's expenses).

Types Of Insurance Policies

There are many life insurance policies. However, the two main types are *term* and *permanent.* Term provides *temporary* insurance protection, while *permanent* provides permanent insurance protection that lasts for the insured's entire life or until age 100, whichever occurs first.

Term insurance coverage is written for a specified time (e.g., 10 or 20 years), has no living benefits like cash value (savings account), and is always cheaper than permanent policies.

On the contrary, permanent policies offer living benefits like cash value, loans, and withdrawals and are more expensive than term insurance.

Whole life, universal life, index, and variable life are the different types of permanent insurance. The most common and oldest type of permanent insurance is whole life. Below are the different types types of whole life policies:

A. Traditional Whole Life Policies

Ordinary Whole Life

Ordinary whole life is the most common type of whole life. Whole life insurance offers fixed-level premium payments that are due at age 100 or upon death (whichever comes first), insurance protection up to age 100, and cash value accumulation up to age 100.

Limited-Pay and Single-Premium Life

Limited-pay insurance policies provide insurance protection for life. Only the duration of premium payment is *limited,* not the duration of insurance coverage. In a limited-pay life contract, the insured pays premiums for a specific time frame, provided the premium payment duration is at least ten years, and the total required premium for the policy is paid by age 65. Single Premium Whole Life pays one lump sum premium to cover you for life. A single premium policy will cost less than premiums paid over multiple years because the insurance company will spend less on the administrative costs of handling many premium payments.

B. Interest/Market-Sensitive/Adjustable Life Products

Universal Life

A Universal Life Policy is also known as an Unbundled Life Policy because the expense charges, the interest earned, and the cost of insurance are available to the policy owner. The hallmark of ALL universal life policies is flexibility. All types of universal life (UL) insurance provide more than one death benefit option as a standard feature. All Universal Life policies allow the policyholder to adjust/change the amount of premium payments when those premium payments are made, as well as the option to make no payments at all. The death benefit can be increased or decreased according to the policy's terms and provisions.

Variable Whole Life

Variable life insurance policies offer a minimum guaranteed death benefit, although the death benefit may fluctuate with the performance of the separate account. Variable Life Insurance has two accounts: the General Account and the Separate Account.

The General Account - The general account is fixed and guaranteed, with a minimum death benefit guaranteed until age 100. The insurer can fund policy loans using the general account for a variable whole life.

Separate Account - The separate account contains funds the insurer invests in its equity securities. The owner can invest the premium in one of several separate accounts. The cash value in the separate account will change depending on market conditions and the separate account's performance, comparable to that of a mutual fund.

The premium is fixed, with a guaranteed minimum death benefit for variable life policies.

Note: A person must hold both a securities licence and a life insurance licence in order to sell variable life insurance.

Variable Universal Life (VUL)

Both universal and variable universal life policies have a flexible premium and death benefit. The policyholder can increase or decrease the premium and the death benefit at any time. Remember, to increase the death benefit, the insured must show evidence of insurability if they did not purchase the guaranteed insurability rider.

Even though variable universal life (VUL) policies permit the owner to control the investment, a minimum cash value is rarely guaranteed. The face amount and the policy cash value vary based on the investment performance of the separate accounts.

Therefore, most VULs state that the death benefits will not fall below a certain minimum in their policies. The cash value in VULs is never guaranteed, and VULs are considered securities products. For these two reasons, individuals need a securities license and an insurance license to sell VULs.

Interest-Sensitive Whole Life

Another name for *current assumption whole life* is interest-sensitive whole life. With this type of policy, the insurance company can either change the premiums or adjust the interest rate that it credits to the cash value based on the current interest rates on the market.

More on interest-sensitive whole life:

- Has guaranteed minimum death benefit
- The death benefit may increase if the cash value grows based on higher interest rates

- Higher current interest rates result in
  - reduced premium or
  - The cash value increases very quickly
- Note: the policy could mature before age 100 if the cash value matures before age 100. For this reason, the insurer usually will automatically increase the death benefit to prevent early endowment. When this happens, it is generally called a corridor.

Indexed Life

Indexed life insurance, of which universal life is the only kind, is an insurance policy that offers a minimum guaranteed interest rate. The cash value is connected to an index of the stock market. Indexed life is similar to *indexed* annuities because indexed annuities offer a minimum guaranteed interest rate. Still, the credited interest rate may be higher depending on the interest rate of the linked stock market index, like the S&P 500. Indexed insurance products are better than regular insurance products at protecting against inflation, except variable products, because they provide relatively higher interest rates.

C. Term Life

There are several types of term insurance. Some types of term insurance are *level, decreasing,* and *increasing*. Note: When an individual wants life insurance for a limited number of years at a low cost, term insurance will be the best option.

Level

A level term refers to the type of insurance in which the face amount and premium stay *unchanged(level)* during the policy's duration. Term(temporary) insurance is always cheaper than permanent life insurance because it does not have a cash value attached.

Decreasing

A decreasing term insurance policy provides insurance protection for decreasing insurance needs. Throughout the term of the policy, the premium stays the same, but the death benefit reduces in accordance with a specified schedule. People typically use decreasing term insurance when an insured's life insurance needs decrease with time. Decreasing term insurance is generally used to cover outstanding loans.

Increasing

An increasing term insurance policy provides insurance protection for increasing insurance needs. Throughout the duration of the coverage, the premium stays the same, but the death benefit *increases* according to a specified schedule. Increasing term insurance automatically increases life insurance coverage, and insurers rarely issue it as a stand-alone policy. Instead, insurers typically use it as a rider(e.g., return of premium rider and the rider for cost of living).

Annually Renewable

A type of level term life insurance that ensures future insurability for a number of years is called annual renewable term insurance (ART). The policyholder can renew yearly during the stated period without reapplying or proving insurability. The premium for ART will increase every time an insured renews it due to the insured's increased age.

Special Features(Riders) of Term Insurance

Renewable

Renewable term provides life insurance coverage, which policyholders can renew without any new underwriting. Insurance coverage continues even if the insured's health declines. However, the policyholder's premium will always increase with each renewal at the end of each term.

Convertible

With a convertible rider, the insured can convert their term insurance into a permanent policy without having to provide proof of insurability. On the other hand, a renewability rider allows an insured to renew their term contract within a specified period without proving insurability. Remember that the premium usually increases when the insured adds a rider to an insurance policy.

Return of Premium

The Return of Premium(ROP) is an increasing term policy. The cost is more expensive than that of level term insurance. If the insured suddenly dies within a specified period, the entire premium is paid in addition to the death benefit. However, if the insured outlives the policy, then the insured will receive a full refund of all paid premiums. Applicants may add the ROP as a rider to a level term policy.

D. Annuities

Overview

For the lifetime of the annuitant or for a specified period of time, annuities provide a stream of income. Unlike life insurance, people usually use annuities to save for retirement. Protection against untimely or premature death is the main objective of life insurance, NOT annuities.

Important definitions:

<u>Annuitant</u>—an annuitant is the insured and primary beneficiary of an annuity contract. This is the person whose life the annuity contract is based. Unlike life insurance, the insured(annuitant) and primary beneficiary are the same person.

Contract owner—Like a life insurance policy owner, the annuity contract owner owns an annuity. This person applies for the annuity contract, pays the premium, and has all ownership rights.

Beneficiary—The person entitled to receive benefits after the annuitant dies. This person is the secondary beneficiary because the annuitant is the primary beneficiary.

Single vs Flexible Premium Annuities

Contract owners use one lump sum payment for single premium deferred annuities. After this, the annuity immediately becomes annuitized, and the premium payment stops. A flexible premium annuity, by definition, adds more principal value at any moment before the contract's annuitization. A Single Premium Immediate Annuity ("SPIA") starts payments to the annuitant within one month of policy issue; SPIAs must begin payments within one year of policy issue.

Premiums paid regularly into the contract are known as flexible/periodic premiums. A flexible premium is the most common type of periodic premium.

Flexible-Premium—The contract owner can make flexible contributions as often as they want and in whatever amount. On the other hand, most insurers have minimum and maximum amounts that they will accept.

Immediate vs Deferred Annuities

An immediate annuity must start providing income WITHIN a year (12 months) of the first premium payment.

Deferred Annuity -A deferred annuity will begin paying out benefits on a regular basis one year (12 months) after the issue date, starting at a specified future date.

Fixed vs Variable Annuities

Fixed annuities provide a guaranteed income for the rest of a person's life, preventing the annuitant from outliving their money.

An annuity that is subject to fluctuations in account value due to the performance of an underlying security product is known as a variable annuity.

More on Variable Annuities:

- Regulated by FINRA, the SEC, and state insurance departments
- Payments for annuities vary according to how well the separate account performs.
- Cash value varies according to how well the separate account performs.
- Payments are based on UNITS, not dollars
- It may act as a hedge against inflation due to higher returns
- The owner bears the investment risk
- To sell it, you must have both an insurance licence and a securities licence.

- The applicant must be given a prospectus(unlike a buyer's guide for life insurance) during or before the sale

For exam purposes, remember to learn all the features of variable annuities and remember that fixed annuities will be the exact opposite.

Indexed

An equities-indexed annuity is linked to a stock index, such as the S&P 500, but offers a guaranteed minimum interest rate. The annuitant can outperform the inflation rate by receiving at least 5 % guaranteed interest rates. Equity-indexed annuities usually provide a higher rate of return than fixed-index annuities.

Accumulation and Annuity Periods

There are two phases for annuities: the accumulation/pay-in phase and the annuitization/payout/liquidation/distribution phase.

The accumulation period is when the annuitant is paying into the annuity. This period begins when the annuitant makes the first deposit/payment and ends when the annuitant starts to receive benefits. Immediate Annuities do not have an accumulation period; only Deferred Annuities do. The Annuity payout/annuitization/liquidation/distribution phase is when the accumulated funds in the annuity start to pay out to the annuitant. During the liquidation phase of an annuity, an annuitant usually gets benefit payments at regular intervals.

Payout (Settlement) Options

The insurer has no way of knowing how long the annuitant will live. In addition, the annuity contract is for the annuitant's benefit. For these two reasons, a life-only option provides the largest possible payment out of the four options listed. Due to the increased risk of paying more than the principal value at the time of annuitization, the insurance company may choose to pay an amount that is calculated by the annuitant's expected lifespan.

Below is the list of different life settlement options for annuities:

Life Income (Pure or Straight Life)

- The insurer pays annuity benefits for as long as the annuitant lives, and payments stop when the annuitant dies.

Life Income Period Certain

- Annuity payments are made for the rest of one's life or a predetermined period, whichever comes first.

Life Income with Refund (Cash Refund or Installment)

- The annuitant receives benefit payments for their entire life. If an annuitant does not receive the total paid premiums (not the growth) at their death, the insurer will refund the balance to the beneficiary as a lump sum, cash, or installment refund.

Joint Life Annuity

- This type of annuity pays out to two or more named annuitants while alive. The benefits cease with the death of the first annuitant.

Joint & Survivor Annuity

- This type of annuity pays out to two annuitants (in one payment) while they are alive. Survivor benefits continue after the original annuitant dies, paying the entire amount or reducing it to 2/3 or 1/2 of the survivor's income until the survivor dies.

E. Combination Plans and Variations

Joint life (first to die)

A permanent life insurance policy that covers two or more insureds—typically a husband and wife—is called a joint life policy. The insurer uses the average age of both insureds to determine the premium amount. This policy pays death benefits when one of the insureds dies.
Another name for Joint Life is the First To Die Policy.

Unlike Joint Life, joint survivorship policies pay death benefits ONLY when the last insured on the policy dies.
These are other names for joint survivorship policies:

- Second-To-Die
- Joint And Survivor Policy
- Survivorship Life Policy
- Last To Die Policy

Survivorship life (second-to-die)

Joint survivorship or last-to-die life insurance Policy is a life insurance policy that covers the lives of two persons, usually partners. The death benefit is only paid out once both individuals pass away.

Joint Survivorship Life (Last to Die)

- ➔ whole life policy covers two or more lives, and the insurer pays the death benefit when the last insured dies
- ➔ The insurer uses the average age of both insureds to determine the premium
- ➔ lower premium than two separate policies
- ➔ Typically used to provide a lump sum death benefit to pay estate taxes when the second insured dies.

Joint and Survivor Annuities pay all co-annuitants(co-insureds) for life. For a Joint and 100% Survivor Annuity, the other annuitant (usually the surviving spouse) will continue to receive 100% of the annuity benefits when a co-annuitant (usually the spouse) dies. For a Joint and 75% Survivor

Annuity, the insurer will reduce the surviving spouse's monthly benefit payments to 75% of the original amount upon the death of the co-annuitant(spouse).

POLICY OPTIONS, RIDERS, EXCLUSIONS, AND PROVISIONS

A. Policy Riders

Overview:

A rider is an optional add-on or attachment to a standard insurance policy. Usually, the premium will increase when an applicant or policyholder adds a rider to an insurance policy.

Waiver of Premium

An insured person who is disabled receives a monthly income through a disability income rider, also known as a waiver of premium rider. The income is usually expressed as a percentage of the death benefit and in dollars per $1,000 death benefit payment. When an insured is disabled, a waiver of premium rider allows them to avoid paying premiums. Money received as income under a disability income rider has no immediate effect on the death benefit.

Waiver of Monthly Deduction

This rider waives the expense charges and the deduction of the monthly cost of insurance associated with a universal life insurance policy. This waiver requires the insured to be *totally disabled* continuously for six months before benefit payments begin.

Guaranteed Insurability

The guaranteed insurability rider is the type of rider that allows an individual to have additional coverage in the future at specified dates WITHOUT having to prove insurability. By their nature, riders never come standard because they are add-ons to a life insurance policy. Adding rider(s) to a life insurance policy increases the premium.

Payor Benefit

A payor benefit rider waives the monthly premium in the event that the payor—typically the parent—dies or becomes totally disabled on a juvenile policy (individual policyholder under the age of 18). Premiums will resume when ownership of the policy is transferred to the child, usually at age 21 or 25.

Accidental Death Benefit (Double Indemnity)

An accidental death rider pays double or triple the face amount if the insured dies from an accident within 90 days after an accident. This rider does not cover death caused by accidental death. The accidental death benefit rider is the cheapest way to purchase additional coverage for a fixed period. Another name for the accidental death benefit rider is the *double indemnity* rider.

Accidental Death and Dismemberment

Unlike the accidental death benefit rider, this rider pays benefits for accidental death <u>*or*</u> dismemberment. It pays the principal sum for the loss of both legs and loss of vision in both eyes, hands, or arms. It pays the principal sum (100% of the face value) of the rider when the insured dies from an accident or double dismemberment. It pays the capital sum (50% of the face value) for accidental single dismemberment.

Term Riders

A term rider provides additional insurance protection for a fixed period.
When added to a permanent life policy, the term rider is called the <u>*base insured*</u> rider.

Other Insureds

This rider provides insurance coverage for additional individual(s) on the original policy. For example, instead of a father purchasing separate insurance for his children, he may add a *children rider* to his policy to provide insurance coverage for his children under his policy. *Children, family, child*, and *spousal riders* are <u>other insured riders</u>. *Other Insureds rider* allows multiple people to be insured under the same insurance policy, usually for a fraction of the cost of purchasing separate policies.

Long-Term Care (LTC)

A long-term care rider allows a chronically ill person unable to perform two out of six activities of daily living(eating, bathing, walking, toileting, etc.) to receive an advance death benefit payment for covered long-term care expenses.
If the insured qualifies for long-term care benefits as stated in the rider, the rider pays up to 100 percent of the death benefits in daily or monthly payments for non-hospital expenses.

Return of Premium (ROP)

The ROP is a rider that can be attached to term policies. The ROP rider returns a portion or all of the paid premium at the end of a term policy if the insured outlives the term coverage. Remember that this term policy is usually more expensive than a standard level term policy for the same age and face amount.

Disability

Disability riders pay the insured benefits regularly (ex, monthly or quarterly) if the insured becomes disabled. *Waiver of premiums, disability income benefits, and payor benefits* are all disability riders. Note that disability benefits will NOT affect the death benefit.

Cost of Living

The Cost-of-Living rider automatically increases monthly benefits after the onset of a disability (therefore giving additional death benefits) as the Consumer Price Index (PCI) increases and protects the insured against inflation. The CPI is the most common consumer price index used with this rider. The cost-of-living rider is also called the cost-of-living adjustment (COLA) rider. For example, if the CPI increases by 3% this year, the death benefit will automatically increase by 3% if this rider is attached to that policy. This rider increases the death benefit annually following a specified linked consumer price index. Note, however, that the policy's premium will increase anytime the death benefit increases.

B. Policy Provisions and Options

Overview

Provisions are parts of an insurance policy that outline specific benefits, conditions, or other essential features. The National Association of Insurance Commissioners (NAIC) created standard life insurance provisions. Life insurance policies sold in every state must include these standard provisions. The standard provisions are:

1. Entire Contract
2. Insuring Clause
3. Free Look
4. Consideration Clause
5. Grace Period
6. Owner's Rights
7. Assignments
8. Beneficiary Designations
9. Premium Payment
10. Reinstatement
11. Incontestability
12. Misstatement of Age and Gender
13. Settlement/Payment of claims
14. Policy Loans, Withdrawals and Partial Surrenders
15. Suicide clause

Policy options give the policy owner some options in exercising their rights and receiving benefits. The two policy options are ***nonforfeiture*** and ***dividend*** (for participating policies only).

Entire Contract

The ENTIRE CONTRACT provision is the delivered policy, a copy of the signed application, and any attached riders/amendments. Nothing, written or verbal, outside the *entire contract*, is considered a part of the contract. The *entire contract* is a mandatory provision in all life insurance policies.

Insuring Clause
The portion of an insurance policy that describes the risks that the insurer accepts and its commitment to provide benefits. Put another way, this phrase specifies the extent of coverage and identifies the precise risk or risks for which the insurer is responsible. The core of the policy is the insuring provision.

Free Look
During the free look period, policyholders can return their policies to the insurer to get a complete reimbursement of all premiums paid. **Ten (10)** days is the required free look period for life insurance policies in most states. The free look period begins AFTER the policy is delivered. Think of the free look period as the 'refund period.'
Remember to check your state's law supplement for the exact duration of the free look period because this is very likely to be on your exam.

Consideration
The consideration clause states that the applicant must complete the application and pay the initial premium to be CONSIDERED for the insurance policy by the insurer.
More on Consideration Clause:

- It contains the amount and premium payment mode
- Consideration is the exchange of something of value
- It is one of the four elements of a LEGAL contract
- The insurer's *consideration* is approving and issuing the policy and agreeing to pay future claims
- The applicant/policy owner's *consideration* is applying and paying the initial premium

Owner's Rights
The policy owner is the person who owns an insurance policy and, therefore, has all the ownership rights, including access to cash value. The owner is often the same person as the insured for life insurance policies. The policy owner's rights of ownership are a standard provision.
The policyholder has ALL the ownership rights, like paying premiums, naming and changing beneficiaries, canceling/surrendering the policy, and assigning the policy.

Beneficiary Designations
A beneficiary is someone who has all legal rights to benefits in the event of a loss. In life insurance, the person who is eligible to get the death benefit in the event that the insured passes away is the beneficiary. Note: The beneficiary and the insured cannot be the same person or entity for life insurance policies. A beneficiary may be a person, a class of persons (e.g., my children), the insured's estate, trust, or corporation/business.

Insurers require at least one beneficiary on a life insurance application. A change of beneficiary takes effect on the day the change request was signed by the policy owner, whether or not the insured is alive when the insurer receives the notice.

a. Primary vs Contingent Beneficiaries
- When the insured passes away, the primary beneficiary is the first to get the death benefit.
- The secondary beneficiary is entitled to the death benefit if no primary beneficiary survives the insured's death.

b. Revocable vs Irrevocable
- A revocable beneficiary is an individual who can be changed at any time by the policy owner without proof of the beneficiary's death or approval.
- A policy owner cannot change an irrevocable beneficiary unless the beneficiary dies or provides written approval.

c. Common Disaster Clause
- If an insured and primary beneficiary die in the same accident, the primary beneficiary must survive the insured for a certain number of days, usually **90 days**; otherwise, the insurance company will assume that the insured died last and the primary beneficiary died first. This clause ensures that the contingent beneficiary receives the death benefit if the insured and primary beneficiary die in the same accident.
  The contingent beneficiaries will receive the death benefits if the primary beneficiary is unavailable.

d. Minor Beneficiaries

Since minors lack the legal power to release the insurer of additional obligations, a trustee or legal guardian receives the benefit on their behalf.

If minors are the beneficiaries without a trust, the assets are deposited in a settlement option (held with interest) with the insurer. The insurer will act as the trustee until the minor(s) becomes a legal adult. Because of this, naming minors as beneficiaries of life insurance is generally not a smart idea.

e. Designation by Class

Beneficiary class designations benefit a group of nameless individuals, but they might be problematic if there is a need for more clarity about a beneficiary. "All my children" does not specify which children - those from a previous marriage, those from the current marriage, or both. Similarly, "My minor children" ignores that children will grow up to be adults and, as a result, may accidentally omit a child.

f. Individual/Named

Individual/Named is a common designation. The beneficiary is identified by name, such as Susan Myers (sister) or Jessica Preston (wife).

Per Capita vs Per Stirpes
- Per Capita

- If a named beneficiary predeceases the insured, this designation will pay all surviving beneficiaries equally.
- If an insured chooses their three children as beneficiaries and one dies before the insured, the insurer will **equally** share the death benefit among the remaining specified beneficiaries.

- Per Stirpes
    - Per Stirpes, a deceased beneficiary's portion is transferred to the beneficiary's heirs if the insured passes away before the beneficiary.
    - If the insured outlives all other beneficiaries, the insured's estate may be the third beneficiary.
    - A trust is used when the funds are to be transmitted in accordance with the insured's specified wishes and a recipient, such as minor children, does not have direct access to the death benefits.

Premium Payment

The amount of money paid to an insurance provider for coverage is called the premium. Life insurance policies usually specify exactly how much the required premium payment is.

a. Modes

In insurance, mode means frequency. The provision known as the Mode (frequency) of Premium permits the policy owner, or the insured, if they are not the same person, to pay premiums more than once a year.

The modes of premium payment are:

- Single premium (one time) -----accumulates instant cash value
- Annual-----*least expensive* mode of payment
- Biannual-----every six months
- Quarterly----every three months
- Monthly----Most common and *most expensive*

b. Grace Period

The grace period lets you pay your past-due premium without incurring any penalties or losing your insurance coverage. The insurer must pay any claim arising within the grace period, but any unpaid premiums will be subtracted from the claim when paid.

Unless state law states differently, the usual grace period is 30 or 31 days.

Remember to check your state law supplement for your state's grace period because you will likely see it on your exam.

c. Automatic Premium Loan (APL)

The Automatic Premium Loan Provision allows the insured to borrow enough money from a permanent life insurance policy's cash value to prevent it from lapsing. APL only works if sufficient cash value is available. A policy loan may include annual prepayment interest, depending on the arrangement.

d. Level or Flexible

Most life insurance premium payments are fixed. Fixed means that the policy owner pays a specified premium for the duration of the policy until the insured's death, the expiration of the term (for term policies), or the policy's endowment (for permanent policies). The few exceptions to this are adjustable whole life and universal policies.

Reinstatement means reactivating a policy that has lapsed. To reinstate a policy, the policy owner must pay back all premiums from the expired date with interest plus any outstanding loans, fill out the reinstatement application (if the insurer demands it), and submit a statement of good health. The standard reinstatement time frame for most states is **three years.**

Policy Loans, Withdrawals, and Partial Surrenders

Policy loans will not automatically affect a policy's death benefit. However, if there is an existing loan at the time of death, the insurer will deduct the loan amount from the beneficiary's payout.

More on Policy Loan Provisions

- The loan cannot exceed the cash surrender value.
- Refusal to repay a loan or interest will void or terminate the policy when the total amount of the outstanding loan and unpaid interest equals or exceeds the entire cash surrender value.
- The insurer may deny a loan request for up to six months, except for automatic premium loans.
- Policy loans with fixed rates usually have a maximum fixed interest rate of **8%** or less.
    - **Reminder:** check your state law supplement for your state's policy loan interest rate.

Incontestability

Incontestability indicates that the insurance company cannot refuse to pay a death benefit based on the statements made in the original application. In most states, the policy becomes incontestable after <u>**two years**</u>.

The Incontestability Clause states:

- If, during the first two years of the policy, there is evidence of a material misrepresentation or fraud, the insurer has the authority to contest the claim and end the insurance contract.
- The policy will be *incontestable* after it has existed for at <u>least two years</u> from the policy issue date, except for nonpayment of premiums or fraud.

Assignments

An assignment is the <u>transfer</u> of an insurance policy ownership. <u>*Absolute*</u> assignment is the *permanent* transfer of all ownership rights in a policy.

The other type of assignment is *collateral*. A temporary transfer of ownership, known as a collateral assignment, is usually associated with loan collateral.

Suicide Clause

The suicide clause dissuades people who are seriously considering suicide from getting life insurance coverage.

If the insured commits suicide during the contestability period, which is the first two years, the insurer will not pay the death benefit.

Misstatement of age and gender

If the insured misrepresented their age or gender on the application, the insurance company may recalculate benefits or premiums depending on the applicant's true age or gender. According to the misstatement of age provision, if an insured misstates their age on the insurance application, the beneficiary will only receive the death benefit that the insured's premium would have purchased at the correct age. For example, suppose the insured had been paying a $50 monthly premium for a $100,000 coverage based on the misstated age of 30, and the insurer later discovered that her correct age at application was 35. In that case, her beneficiary may only receive $70,000 if that is how much a $50 monthly premium would have been able to purchase at the correct age of 35.

The incontestability clause does not apply to the misstatement of age and gender. Age and gender are not considered material to an insurance policy.

Accelerated Death Benefits

The accelerated death benefit provision allows an insured to receive a portion or all of their policy's death benefit while still alive in specified circumstances. Terminal illness and long-term care are two conditions that may trigger the payment of accelerated death benefits while the insured is still alive.

Nonforfeiture Options

Insurers include nonforfeiture options in permanent policies. Nonforfeiture options prevent the policyholder from losing all benefits if the policy lapses due to nonpayment of premiums or termination.

The nonforfeiture options are:

- Cash Surrender
    - Upon surrendering the insurance to the insurer, the policy owner will receive the cash surrender value specified in the policy, minus any outstanding loans and accrued interest.
- Reduced Paid-Up

  - A single premium permanent policy with a reduced face amount is purchased using the present cash value. Because no extra premiums are due, this policy is considered paid-up.
- Extended Term
  - The insurer uses the current cash value to purchase a single premium term policy with the same face amount for as long as it will last. If no other option is selected, this option provides the biggest death benefit and is sometimes known as the Default or Automatic Option.

Dividends and Dividend Options (e.g., participating or non-participating)

Dividends are considered a return of premium by the insurance company and are not taxable. When *mutual* insurance companies earn higher than expected profits, they return some excess profits to their policyholders as dividends. ***Dividends are NEVER guaranteed.***

The policyholder chooses which dividend option to use and can change their selection anytime.

The DIVIDEND Options are (Acronym: CARPPO)

- Cash
  - On or near each policy anniversary, the policy owner receives a check for the declared dividends.
- Reduction of Premium
  - The amount that the insured must pay is decreased when dividends are applied to the subsequent premium.
- Accumulation at Interest
  - The insurer keeps the dividends, and they accrue interest
- Paid-up Additions
  - Buys additional permanent insurance coverage with a single premium when the insured reaches a specified age.
  - It generates cash value and dividends as though the paid-up policy was part of the original policy while the insured is alive.
- One Year Term
  - A one-year term policy is purchased with a single premium by using the one-year term dividend option. The insured's attained age achieved is used to determine the premium.
- Paid-up Option
  - Pays off the policy sooner than specified in the policy.

Settlement Options

Settlement means benefit payment. When an insurer receives a life or annuity claim, the insurer will use one of the following settlement (benefit payment) options to pay the benefits to the beneficiary:

Cash (lump-sum) payment

The cash lump sum is the **default settlement** option if the insured did not select a settlement option before their death.

With this settlement option, the insurer pays the beneficiary one lump sum cash benefit.

Life Income

Income is guaranteed for life under this settlement option. The three most common types are:

a. Life-Income Option (straight/pure life)
    i. Provides income for life, but the insurer keeps proceeds if the beneficiary dies before receiving the full benefit.
b. Life income with period certain option
    i. The income is certain or guaranteed within a specified period
    ii. If death occurs during this period, the beneficiary continues receiving the remaining benefit until the period expires
c. Life Income Joint and Survivor
    i. Guarantees income for two or more people.

Interest Only

Only pays the interest to the beneficiary.

Fixed period (aka period certain)

This settlement pays the death benefit over a fixed period—for example, five or ten years.

Fixed amount

d. The insurer regularly pays a portion of the death benefit until all the death benefit is completely paid.

C. Policy Exclusions

Overview

Exclusions are risks that an insurance policy will not cover. The three most common exclusions in life insurance plans are hazardous occupations, aviation, and war & military service. Exclusions are a common feature of life insurance policies where the insurer specifies the risks that it will cover.

War or Military Service

There are two clauses under this exclusion. They are the ***status*** clause and the ***results*** clause.

- STATUS Clause
    - When the insured is on active duty, ALL causes of death are excluded.
- RESULTS Clause
    - ONLY excludes death when the insured is killed as a result of war

Aviation

Covers individuals who are fare-paying passengers or pilots on a regularly scheduled commercial airline, but EXCLUDEs coverage for all other airline travelers or charges more premium. Deaths caused by aviation (ex, as a pilot) are usually not covered by life insurance policies, except as a fare-paying passenger on an airplane or a commercial pilot.

Hazardous Occupations/Hobbies

The insured will have to pay a fairly charged higher premium or have death from a particular occupation or hobby excluded.

Note: Suicide is an exclusion, yet it is a stand-alone provision.

Dangerous Occupation

If an insured dies due to a hazardous occupation or hobby, the insurer will not pay claims because this is a common exclusion in life insurance policies. Exclusions are a common feature of life insurance policies where the insurer explicitly states certain risks it will not cover.

COMPLETING THE APPLICATION, UNDERWRITING, AND DELIVERING THE POLICES

A. Completing The Application

1. Required Signatures

The producer and the applicant must sign the application, and ***the insured*** must be different from the applicant. A guardian must sign the application if the insured is a minor.

The Producer/Agent:

- The producer is the agent who represents the insurance company. The producer is the middleman between the applicant and the insurance company.

The Applicant/policyowner/policyholder:

- The applicant is applying for the policy. They pay the premium, own the policy, and are entitled to change it.

The Insured

- The insured is the person whose life the life insurance policy is based upon. The insured is the individual who must die before the insurer can pay the death benefit.
- Note: The insured's signature is needed if the policy owner differs.

2. Changes In The Application

The applicant must consent to any change or corrections in the application before the agent submits it to the insurer. The applicant MUST initial any change to the application. Any incorrect information should be ***crossed out***, not white-out.

3. Consequences of Incomplete Applications

Once the insurer issues a policy, the contract starts. Therefore, any information left out of the application does not affect the contract. The insurer must ensure the application is fully complete before issuing it. Once the policy is issued, the insurer has waived its right to contest it unless for fraud or material concealment.

4. Warranties and Representations

A warranty is a statement on an insurance application guaranteed to be true. If an insurer discovers a warranty is false, the insurer may cancel the policy.

A representation is a statement on the application that the applicant believes is true to the best of their knowledge. **Test Alert:** Statements on insurance applications are considered *representations.*

5. Collecting the Initial Premium and Issuing The Receipt
Whenever an initial premium payment accompanies an insurance application, the agent must issue a *conditional* receipt to the applicant. The conditional receipt is never issued at policy delivery.

Having the applicant agree to a change in the application by the insurer is considered a counteroffer. The applicant accepts the counteroffer when they accept the change by signing the amendment and paying the required premium.
For a policy to be issued, premiums have to be collected. The policy goes into effect once the insurer receives the initial premium. If the agent does not collect the initial premium with the application, then a statement of good health from the applicant and the initial premium are needed at the time of policy delivery.
The field underwriter issues the conditional receipt at the time of application, NOT during policy delivery. Conditional receipt MUST be issued anytime the initial premium is received with the application.

6. Replacement
Agents should consider the following things when determining whether selling or replacing an annuity contract is suitable for a client:

- Risk tolerance
- Age
- Income
- Current assets
- Retirement goals
- Risk tolerance
- Intended use of the annuity
- Financial goals, needs, and past investment experience
- Surrender charges
- Whether or not the proposed annuitant has an existing annuity

Note: Check your state law guide for state-specific *information* about replacement.

7. Disclosures at Point of Sale (e.g., HIPAA, HIV Consent)
A buyer's guide gives <u>*general*</u> information to help potential life insurance buyers make informed decisions. The buyer's guide includes the following information:

- How to choose a policy and compare the price of various policies
- Comparison of various policies and their benefits

Policy Summary

- A shortened version or summary of a life insurance policy. A policy summary gives information regarding the coverage limitations, guaranteed interest rates, total premiums, and other important information.

- It provides information *specific* to a particular insurance policy. On the contrary, a buyer's guide provides *general* information.
- Helps consumers evaluate the suitability of a recommended product. Usually provided with every single life insurance policy.

8. USA Patriot Act

The USA PATRIOT Act was enacted to stop the financial services sector, in general, and the insurance sector, in particular, from being used as a means of money laundering and terrorism financing. It requires insurers and agents to report suspicious activities.

The following are considered suspicious activities:

- Showing greater interest in the early termination features of an insurance product rather than its potential performance
- Fake identification or reluctance to provide identification
- Maximum borrowing against a policy almost immediately after purchasing it
- Receipt of any cash payment greater than $10,000
- Purchase of insurance that the customer does not need
- Requests to have surrender value or other benefits paid to an unrelated person

9. Gramm-Leach-Bliley Act (GLBA) Privacy

The Gramm-Leach-Bliley Act (GLBA) stipulates that application information remains confidential and should ONLY be used for other purposes or shared with third parties not specified in their financial contract with the consumer's consent. The GLBA is a federal law that requires that consumers receive privacy notice when they enter into a financial relationship with a financial institution (including insurance companies) and every year after that. Thanks to this law, consumers have the option to refuse having their information shared with third parties or used for purposes other than those specified in their contract.

The privacy notice must explain the following:

- How the consumer's information is used
- What data is gathered regarding the consumer
- How is the consumer's information protected
- Where and how is that information shared

B. Underwriting

1. The Agent Report

- Is used by the insurer to underwrite insurance applications
- Allows the agent to exercise their field underwriting role.
- Allows the agent to confidentially report their observations about the proposed insured to the insurer

- Is attached to the application but is NOT considered a part of the application (NOT part of the ENTIRE CONTRACT)

2. Insurable Interest

For the insurance contract to be legal, there must be a relationship between the applicant and the insured at the time of application and policy issue that if the insured becomes sick, disabled, or dies, the applicant will suffer a financial loss or emotional loss.

People's insurable interest in themselves is unlimited. As of the application date, there must be an insurable interest. Legally, an insurance contract must include insurable interest.

3. Medical Information and Consumer Reports

Medical reports are usually required when the application for insurance coverage exceeds a certain face amount.

A medical report can be performed by any paramedic or examining physician the insurer chooses. The medical report's expense is covered by the insurance.

The Medical Information Bureau's (MIB) main goal is to gather and disseminate medical information regarding an applicant's health to its members.

An insurer gathers an inspection report concerning the details of a specific risk.

This report also called a consumer investigative report, details the applicant's finances, morals, character, and other habits. Third-party providers compile this report by interviewing associates, neighbors, and friends. According to the Fair Credit Reporting Act (FCRA), the insurer must notify the applicant and consent to this report.

4. Fair Credit Reporting Act (FCRA)

The Federal Trade Commission Act (FCRA) mandates the reporting agency to investigate disputed information and amend it if it contains errors in order to safeguard the public.

Only those with a legitimate and specific use for an individual's consumer report can receive it. Customers are shielded from the reporting of false personal or financial information by the Fair Credit Reporting Act. Note: The consumer has the right to know what is in the report.

The two reports allowed under the Fair Credit Reporting Act are:

Consumer Reports

Contain information about an applicant's credit, reputation, character, habits, and character.

Third-party reporting companies collect it.

Investigative Consumer Reports (ICRs):

These are similar to consumer reports. The only difference is that the consumer reporting agency gathers information through interviews with friends, neighbors, and others who know the consumer.

Unlike consumer reports, the FCRA mandates that the reporting agencies advise the consumer in writing within **three days** of the report's request.

If requested, the insurer has **five days** to provide the consumer with additional info.

5. Risk classification
Individuals with better than average medical history, physical conditions, habits, and lifestyle are categorized as *preferred* risks. Due to this, they pay much lower premiums than standard risk.

The insurance underwriting department can either DECLINE or ACCEPT the risk when the insurance underwriting department receives an application. If they accept an applicant, that applicant will receive one of the following three ratings:

Standard
- For applicants with an average medical history, physical condition, lifestyle, and habits
- The applicants will pay a normal(standard) premium.

Substandard
- Also called 'rated/premium rated-up.' Underwriters assign the substandard rating to applicants with worse than average medical history, physical condition, lifestyle, and habits
- This category is charged the HIGHEST premium

Preferred
- For applicants with better than average medical history, physical condition, lifestyle, and habits
- Insurers charge this category the LOWEST premium

6. Stranger/Investor-owned Life Insurance (STOLI/IOLI)
With STOLI and IOLI, the insureds sell their mortality to a third party(the investor/stranger) for a lump sum payment.
These two terms describe the act of strangers (e.g., agents, brokers) and investors with no insurable interest in the insured purchasing life insurance from the insured/policy owner with the primary purpose of "cashing in" when the insured dies. Because there is no insurable interest, most states have outlawed this practice.
The third party, usually an investor, will take over the premium payment and be named the beneficiary. Then, when the insured dies, they will receive the death benefit.
Typically, investors pay more for insurance than it is worth in cash but less for its death benefit. Thus, they stand to gain financially from the insured's passing.

C. Delivering the Policy

1. When Coverage Begins
For insurance coverage to be effective, the applicant must first complete all the requirements, including the required medical exam (if required) and paying the initial premium. The insurer will require the initial premium and a statement of good health at the time of policy delivery if the

applicant did not pay the initial premium when they submitted their application. In this case, the effective date of coverage is when *the policy is delivered.*
Suppose the applicant receives a conditional receipt after paying the initial premium at the time of application. In that case, the effective date of coverage will be the *date of application* if the application was approved and the policy issued as is. Remember that the date of application is usually the same as the date the conditional receipt was issued.

2. Explaining the Policy and Its Provisions, Riders, Exclusions, and Ratings to The Client
Explaining policy provisions, exclusions, and riders that influence ratings and collecting due premiums are all the responsibilities of a producer. The producer must also ensure the applicant signs the application before submission.
Another name for a producer is a FIELD UNDERWRITER. These are some of the responsibilities of the FIELD UNDERWRITER:

- Deliver the policy
- Obtain any required signatures
- Solicit insurance
- Collect the initial premium
- Issue any receipt, if applicable
- Actively work to prevent adverse selection

Most insurance companies and some states require agents deliver policies in person. Delivering the policy enables the agent to explain and answer all questions the policyholder may have. In addition to that, it helps build or increase the policyholder's trust in the agent. Agents are encouraged to deliver policies in person unless the agent is physically unable to.
Constructive(legal) delivery is legal. Constructive delivery occurs when the insurer mails the issued policy to the producer for the producer to deliver to the policyholder personally. The policy is *legally* delivered when the insurer mails it to the policyholder. The producer bears the responsibility of providing the client with the insurance policy and securing the delivery receipt. Note that constructive delivery only happens for policies for which the applicant paid the initial premium with the application.
Insurance companies usually send issued policies directly to the producer, not the policyholder, so the agent can deliver them to the clients and offer detailed explanations personally.

D. Contract Law

1. Elements of a Contract
An insurance contract consists of a legal purpose, competent parties, consideration, and agreement (offer and acceptance). These are the four elements of any LEGAL contract, not just insurance
a. Consideration
Consideration means the exchange of value. Each contracting party MUST exchange something of value for the contract to become legal. The applicant's consideration is their first premium and

submitted application, and the insurer's consideration is issuing the policy and agreeing to pay future claims.

b. Agreement (Offer and Acceptance)
One party must make and transmit to the other party an offer, which the other party must accept. Agreement simply means that there must be an *agreement* between the applicant and the insurer for the contract to become legally binding.

c. Competent Parties
All parties to a contract, including the insurer and policy owner, must be legally competent to enter into a contract. To be considered competent, parties to a contract must be of legal age, mentally competent, and free from the influence of alcohol or illegal drugs.

d. Legal purpose
All parties must enter into a contract for a legal reason. A legal contract cannot violate any laws.

2. Unique Aspects of The Insurance Contract

a. Conditional
In a conditional contract, the insurer and the policy owner agree to certain conditions for the contract to be legally enforceable.

b. Unilateral
An agreement in which the insurance company is the only party with legal obligations is known as a unilateral agreement.

c. Adhesion
A contract of adhesion is prepared by one party, the insurer, and presented to the insured/applicant on a "take-it-or-leave-it" basis. The applicant can either accept it or reject it.

d. Aleatory
Aleatory contract is a contract that has an exchange of unequal value. Insurance contracts are aleatory contracts because the insured is paying a small premium in exchange for the insurer's promise to pay a claim bigger than the insured's premiums.

Retirement and Other Insurance Concepts

A. Third-Party Ownership

Third-party ownership occurs when insurance one person owns insures another person's life. The policy owner, insured, and insurer are the three parties involved in third-party ownership.

Examples of Third-Party Ownership

- A business partner purchases insurance on his business partner
- A husband gets his wife an insurance policy
- A wife buys her husband an insurance policy
- A parent purchases a policy for one of their children
- A company purchases a policy for a key employee

B. Life Settlements

A life settlement entails selling an existing life insurance policy to someone different (third party) for an amount that is higher than the cash surrender value but less than the death benefit. It is comparable to a viatical settlement. One distinction is that a life settlement does not require the insured to be terminally ill. A policy owner might sell their policy because they cannot afford their premium due to a job loss or want to acquire a different policy. Unlike that, only terminally ill individuals qualify for a viatical settlement.

C. Group Life Insurance

Overview

Group insurance is written as a single policy covering many people. An individual policy that covers all family members is still considered an individual policy. Under state insurance requirements, a group created only to get insurance is not a valid organization.

The primary benefit of group insurance is that the participant does not need proof of insurability to obtain coverage.

More on Group Life Insurance

- Does not require evidence of insurability
- Group Insurance is an Annually Renewable Term(ART) Insurance
- Conversion Privilege - individuals covered under group plans can convert to an individual policy within **31 days** period

- Open Enrollment Period - the period when eligible employees can enroll under group coverage
- Probationary Period - the period before an open enrollment period.
This period delays immediate coverage.

1. Conversion Privilege

After losing their work or quitting, employees have a 31-day window during which to transfer their group life insurance coverage to an individual policy. During this conversion period, the employee can convert their group life insurance policy to an individual life policy without showing evidence of insurability. The beneficiary will still get the death benefit in the event that the insured passes away during the conversion period.
Remember that the insured's premium will ALWAYS be higher when they convert to an individual policy.

2. Contributory vs. Noncontributory

Non-Contributory Plan

- This is a plan in which employees don't participate in premium payments. With a Non-contributory plan, 100% of eligible employees MUST enroll. A noncontributory group life policy must cover all eligible employees to reduce the effects of adverse selection. The premium is usually paid in full by the employer.

Contributory Plan

- This plan is the direct opposite of a noncontributory plan. Employees participate in premium payments in this plan, which usually requires at least 75% of eligible employees to enroll in this group plan.

D. Retirement Plans

1. Qualified Plans

Qualified retirement plans usually enjoy favorable tax treatment, such as deductible employer premiums, pretax or deductible employee premiums, and penalties waived in some instances. ERISA (The Employee Retirement Income Security Act) is a federal act that does not mandate that companies construct retirement plans, but it does set down fundamental standards for private sector companies that do so.
The IRS requires qualified plans to have a vesting requirement.
Within **90 days** of becoming covered by a qualified plan, new workers must obtain a copy of their plan sponsor's most recent Summary Plan Description.

Note: To comply with ERISA minimum participation standards, qualified retirement plans must allow all employees over age 21 with at least a one-year experience to enroll.

More On ERISA:

- Employee Retirement Income Security Act
- Federal Law
- Does not require that employers establish a retirement plan for their employees
    - But requires that employers who do meet certain minimum standards
- Protects employees and their beneficiaries who are enrolled in employer-sponsored qualified retirement plans and group insurance plans
    - Specifies that employers cannot discriminate in favor of highly paid employees for qualified plans
    - Qualified plans must have a vesting schedule
- Mandates that certain information be shared with plan participants, their beneficiaries, the IRS and the US Department of Labor (DOL)

More on qualified plans:

- Cannot discriminate
- Earnings grow Tax Deferred
- All withdrawals are TAXED
- Approved by the IRS
- Contributions are tax deductible

List of Qualified Retirement Plans:

- IRA
- Roth IRA
- Self-Employed Plans (HR-10 or Keogh Plans)
- Simplified Employee Pension Plans (SEP)
- Savings Incentive Match Plan for Employees (SIMPLE)
- 401(k)
- 403(b) Tax-sheltered Annuities (TSAs)

2. Nonqualified Plans

Nonqualified means that the IRS has not approved the retirement plan. A corporation's owned annuity must be linked to a qualified retirement plan to avoid current income taxation. The Internal Revenue Code has no interest rate ceilings for annuities. Before annuitization, all annuities include a death benefit guarantee, and the annuity's corporate owner will name itself the beneficiary.

Non-Qualified Annuity

- Money that has already been taxed before being added to an annuity is used to fund a nonqualified annuity. Only the earnings are taxable as ordinary income when they are distributed.

Qualified Annuity

- Because a qualifying annuity is funded with pre-tax funds, the contribution may be eligible for a tax deduction, lowering taxable income. Ordinary income taxes apply to the entire distribution from a qualifying annuity.

E. Life Insurance Needs Analysis/Suitability

1. Personal Insurance Needs

Life insurance can be used for personal and business needs.

When a producer uses a *needs approach*, they consider various factors relating to lost future income.

There are two approaches an agent uses to evaluate the need for coverage and the amount of coverage: *Needs Analysis* and the *Human Life Value Approach*.

<u>Need Analysis</u>

- This method assesses whether or not coverage is required in the event of an individual's early death. It always assumes the individual's death is imminent and considers the following considerations when determining the appropriate amount of coverage.
    - Calculate all financial needs resulting from a sudden death, including debts, medical bills, and funeral costs.
    - Ensure that the spouse has a steady source of income for at least ten years
    - Getting rid of a mortgage or other debt
    - Invest in the education of children
    - The agent may include An Emergency Reserve Fund or lump-sum needs in the calculation to cover unexpected expenses that the insured's family may face soon after their death.
    - Any assets available to fulfill financial demands after death are subtracted.

<u>Human Life Value Approach</u>

- This approach just takes into account an individual's economic value in determining the need for life insurance
- Insurance need is calculated with this formula:
    - (applicant's annual income) X (the number of years remaining until retirement)

Below are personal uses of life insurance:

1. Survivor Protection
    a. leave money behind for surviving dependent
2. Estate Conservation
    a. used to pay estate taxes

3. Liquidity
    a. savings account (cash value) and immediate death benefit
4. Estate Creation
    a. Creates an immediate estate in the event that the policyholder passes away
5. Burial expense
    a. used to pay for burial expenses
6. Fund Charities
7. Exemptions from probate & creditors
8. Financial stability for loved ones and peace of mind

2. Business Insurance Needs

Overview

People can use life insurance for business needs. However, life insurance is not used for workers' compensation.

The following are some uses of life insurance for businesses:

- Buy-sell agreements
    - Two types
        - Cross-purchase
        - Entity plan
- Key-person(employee) insurance
- Deferred compensation
    - Ex: Executive bonus plans

a. Key Person

A key person is someone who works directly in sales, production, or customer service, is a member of the management team, and receives a salary that is much higher than that of other employees. The business, usually the employer, is the applicant, owner, premium payer, and beneficiary in the key-person coverage. A key person insurance is a life insurance policy that a business provides for its high-value employees.

The business owner may use the death benefit from the insurance to seek, recruit, and train a replacement.

More on Key Person Insurance:

- The employee is the INSURED
- Premium is NOT tax-deductible
- Employer receives death benefit Tax FREE

b. Buy Sell
Life Insurance provides funding for a buy-sell transaction. It goes by the name "business continuation agreement" as well. It is used to ensure that business ownership is easily transferred upon the death or disability of an owner or partner.
Third-party ownership of life insurance policies is widely utilized in business insurance and estate-planning situations.

Types of buy-sell agreements
Entity Plan
- Under this plan, a business entity agrees to buy the dead owner's share of the company.

A *stock redemption* agreement
- Is an agreement made between a business and its investors. When they pass away, each shareholder promises to sell their shares to the company for the amount, under the terms, and with the conditions specified in the agreement.

Cross-Purchase Plan
- Occurs when business partners buy life insurance on each other. When one of the partners dies, the profits from the policy are used to buy the deceased partner's share of the business from their heirs.

Note that cross-purchase and entity plans are the two types of buy-sell agreements.

F. Social Security Benefits:

The period referred to as blackout is when no Social Security benefits are paid to the spouse who is still alive.
This period begins when the youngest child turns 16 years old and stops when the parent that is alive turns 60 years old or reaches retirement age.
Social security benefits include:
- Surviving spouse
- Surviving children
- Retirement
- Disability
- Death

Disability income benefits are paid after **five months** of total disability in the amount of the primary insurance amount (PIA).
An individual can file for Social Security benefits after being disabled for five months.

Social Security Disability Benefits
- Only available to fully insured workers at the time of disability

- Disability income benefits are paid to the insured individual using PIA [primary insurance amount] after a 5-month waiting period.
- Must be younger than 65
- does not provide benefits for short-term or temporary disability
- Total disability must be expected to persist for a full year or to result in death.
- Benefits may include monthly payments to the worker, child, and spouse.

Remember that Social Security does not provide unemployment benefits.

More on Social Security (SS) Benefits:

Surviving parents
- Benefits begin at 62 & is dependent on the insured child
- For parents who were receiving at least half of their financial support from their deceased working child

Surviving children
- Pay benefits to children up to age 18(or 19 if still in high school)

Surviving spouse
- Pays benefits to surviving spouse with dependent child younger than 16
    - if unmarried, retirement benefits begin at age 60
- **BLACKOUT** Period - time period between when the youngest child turns 16 and when the surviving spouse turns 60

Death Benefit
- Social Security pays a one-time lump sum payment of $255 to the spouse or kids

Retirement Benefits
- Full retirement age (FRA) is up to 67 depending on the year of birth
- As early as age 62, a person may begin receiving benefits.

Disability Benefit
- Must experience total and permanent disability prior to retirement age
- Paid to a disabled worker, spouse, and eligible dependents
- Monthly disability benefits begin after a 5-month waiting period

G. Tax Treatment of Insurance Dividends, Proceeds, and Premiums

1. Individual Life

Taxation excludes policy loans, cash dividends, and cost basis withdrawals. Cost Basis Withdrawal is the withdrawal of all premiums paid into the policy. Cost basis withdrawals are not taxed because they are considered a return of premium. Interest received as part of a death benefit settlement option is subject to ordinary income taxation.

Individual Life Insurance Policies

- Premium is NOT tax-deductible
- Benefits are received tax-free if received in one lump sum
- If the beneficiary is an estate, the benefits may be taxable
- If the policy is sold to a third-party, then benefits may be taxable

2. Group Life

The main advantage of group coverage is that it does not need each group member to provide proof of insurability.

Group Life Policy

- Tax-deductible premiums for employer
- Nontax-deductible premium for employees, but benefits are received income tax-free

3. Modified Endowment Contracts (MECs)

Modified Endowment Contracts (MEC):

- An overfunded life insurance policy according to IRS Guidelines
- Policies that fail the 7-pay test are considered MECs and will lose their tax-advantaged treatment.
- The maximum amount that the policy owner may contribute to the policy in the first seven years following the policy's issuance is limited by the 7-pay test
- For example, if the monthly premium is $100, then the maximum payment allowed in 7 years is ($1,200/year X 7 years) = $8,400. Suppose the insured pays more than $8,400 within the first seven years. In this case, the policy automatically becomes a MEC
- 10% penalty if withdrawn before age 59 ½
- Taxation only occurs when the policy owner receives cash distribution
- When money is taken out of a MEC, last-in-first-out (LIFO) taxes apply.
    - This means that gains are taxed first before cost basis
    - Unlike MECs, withdrawals from life insurance are taxed on a FIFO (first-in-first-out) basis, which means that the policy owner's cost basis(total amount paid into the policy) is received tax-free first.

Washington, DC Life Insurance LAW Supplement

District Of Columbia Laws And Regulations Common To Life, Casualty Insurance, Property, Accident, And Health Insurance

A. Commissioner of Insurance, Securities, And Banking

1. Broad Powers and Duties

The insurance commissioner is responsible for enforcing the District of Columbia insurance laws. The commissioner is appointed by the city mayor. The laws are crafted by the city council.

- The Insurance Commissioner
  - Can at any time order an inspection of an insurer's books and records
  - Issue, suspend, or revoke licenses
  - Issue certificate of authority, etc
  - But CANNOT make alterations to the city's insurance law

Any time insurance management changes, the insurer is required to notify the commissioner within five days. The insurer's management may not be paid commissions for an insurance transaction.

2. Examination of Records

The commissioner shall inspect domestic insurers after every five years. Note that the mayor or the mayor's representative (in this case, the commissioner) may examine domestic insurers as frequently as they choose, but they must do it at least once **every five years**.

During a financial examination of an insurance company, the insurer being examined/investigated is responsible for the cost of the examination.

If the commissioner determines that a producer or insurer violated insurance law(s), they may issue a cease-and-desist order. If, within 15 days of receiving it, the person or entity does not request a hearing, the commissioner will enter a cease-and-desist order as final.

3. Notice of Hearings

Before convening a hearing that could result in a producer's license being suspended or revoked, the Commissioner must notify the producer in writing at least **ten days** before the hearing.

Before canceling or suspending a license, the Commissioner must hold a hearing and allow licensees to present evidence on their behalf via a written notice. If the commissioner revokes a producer's license or insurer's certificate of authority, they have **30 days** to appeal the Commissioner's decision. When the commissioner revokes an agent or broker's license to do business, or if the commissioner denies the reinstatement application, the agent or broker must wait **three years** from the revocation date or rejection before applying for reinstatement.

B. General Insurance Definitions

1. Domestic, Foreign, Alien

- An insurer operating in the USA but registered under the legal system of a nation other than the United States of America is known as an alien insurer.
- Domestic Insurer---an insurer organized under the laws of this city
- Foreign Insurer—an insurer that is doing business in the District of Columbia but was organized or incorporated under the laws of another state.

2. Stock and Mutual Companies

Shareholders own stock insurers, and they offer non-participating policies. On the contrary, policy owners own mutual insurers and issue participating policies.

More on Types of Insurers

1. Stock/Nonparticipating
    - An incorporated insurer owned by shareholders or stockholders
    - Shareholders or stockholders receive STOCK dividends
    - Also called Nonparticipating companies
    - Dividends from insurance companies are taxable
    - **Test Alert: Dividends are NEVER guaranteed**
2. Mutual/Participating
    - An incorporated insurer owned by policyholders
    - Policyowner receives POLICY dividends
    - Dividends are received tax-free because they are considered a *return of some premium.*
    - Also called participating companies
    - Members are called policyholders
    - Members elect the insurer's governing body, including its board of directors.
    - **Test Alert: Dividends are NEVER guaranteed**

3. Certificate of Authority

A certificate of authority permits an insurance company to conduct business in the District of Columbia. Insurers must be granted a Certificate of Authority (equivalent to a license) from the Department of Insurance before transacting business in this state. In addition, they must satisfy all state-required financial requirements.

More on Certificate of Authority

- The ONLY insurers not required to obtain a certificate of authority are licensed excess and surplus lines brokers.
- Insurers with a certificate of authority are called ADMITTED/AUTHORIZED
- Unapproved insurers, insurers that do not have a certificate of authority, are considered UNAUTHORIZED or NONADMITTED

C. Licensing Requirements

1. Producer

In The District, only individuals licensed in a particular line of authority may negotiate, solicit, or sell that line of insurance. In addition to being licensed, an insurer must appoint a producer before representing that insurer.

Other Requirements for Licensing

- A resident insurance producer license is available to anyone who maintains their primary residence and place of business in The District.
- A nonresident insurance producer license is available to those with a primary residence and business outside The District.

Resident producer licensing requirements:

- Pass the examination for the lines of authority for which the person has applied unless exempt
- Be at least eighteen years old
- Pay any fees that are due
- Pass the criminal background check
- Avoid any actions that can result in denial, suspension, or revocation.
- Does not intend to get licensed to write mainly *controlled* business

2. License denial, nonrenewal, suspension or revocation

A prohibited person convicted of a felony must first apply to the commissioner for a *1033 Waiver for Consent to Work.*

The commissioner may suspend, revoke, or deny a producer's license for all the following reasons:

- Providing false information on the insurance producer's license application
- Violating insurance laws and subpoenas
- Violating Washington DC insurance commissioner's orders or the orders of another state's insurance commissioner
- Misappropriating or commingling client funds with personal funds
- Felony conviction

- Purposefully providing false information about the terms of an application for insurance or an actual insurance policy
- Committing an unfair trade practice
- The producer demonstrates incompetence in their licensed line of authority
- Another state denies, revokes, or revokes the insurance producer's license
- Forging a name or signature on an insurance application or document

3. Appointments

When a producer is appointed, the insurer must pay the appointment fee. An appointment is the power granted to an agent by an insurance company to do business on their behalf.

More on Appointments:

- The insurance Commissioner has **10 DAYS** to verify an agent's appointment eligibility
- The insurer must file a notice WITHIN **30** days from the date that
    - The agent submits their first application or
    - The agency contract goes into effect
- When the Commissioner concludes that the producer is not qualified for an appointment, the insurer must be notified within FIVE DAYS.
- Insurers must notify The Commissioner WITHIN **30** days after terminating a producer's appointment.

4. Commissions

Most insurance producers usually receive compensation with commissions. A commission is a percentage of the client's premium the insurer pays the producer for selling an insurance policy. Note: Some producers, who are employees of an insurance company instead of independent agents, are paid a salary instead of a commission.

5. Reporting of actions

If an insurance producer's residence or business address changes, they must notify the Commissioner within a 30-day period.

Other Important Timelines for Producers:

- After establishing legal residency, a producer moving to this state is required to apply to become a resident producer within 90 days.
- If an insurer chooses to terminate a producer's appointment, contract, or employment, it must provide the Commissioner notice 30 days before the termination takes effect.
    - The insurance company must mail a copy of the notification to the insurance producer at their last known address within **15** days of notifying the commissioner.

- Insurers must also notify the Commissioner within **30** days when they appoint producers. After receiving the notification, the commissioner must verify within **ten** days that the insurance producer is eligible for an appointment.

6. License Renewal

Within the license period, a producer wanting to renew their license must complete at least 24 credit hours of continuing education, and at least three credit hours of the 24 hours must be in ethics.

Continuing Education (CE) Requirements

- A producer who wishes to renew their licence throughout the licence period must finish 24 credit hours of continuing education.
- If a producer wants to renew their life & health insurance license, they must take at least **six (6)** CE credit hours in life and health insurance.
- The agent may renew their license within 30 days of its expiration date by presenting proof of completing the required continuing education credits and paying the necessary late fee.
- After receiving a request from the producer 90 days before the end of the license period, the commissioner may waive continuing education requirements for up to 30 days.
- Unlike other states, *additional CE credit hours in Washington, DC, do not carry over to the following year*.

Termination

- A producer's insurance licence usually expires on the last day of his birth month, which is at least 18 months and not more than 29 months after the license's effective date, if it was originally issued or renewed on May 13, 2010, or later.
- The appointment of a producer ends when the producer's license expires.

Requirements for renewing a license

- Evidence of earning the necessary continuing education credits
- Evidence of excellent standing in one's home state if renewing a nonresident license
- Pay license renewal fees
- Be trustworthy and qualified

Note: If a producer lets their license lapse, they can reapply for it ***within one year*** of the expiration date without having to complete a written exam. The producer must, nevertheless, pay a penalty equal to twice the unpaid renewal cost.

D. Unfair Trade Practices

Unfair trade practices are illegal in this state.
The unfair trade practices are:

- Rebating
- Twisting
- Defamation
- False advertising
- Misrepresentation
- Discrimination
- False claims
- Boycott, Coercion, & Intimidation '

1. False Advertising

False advertising is advertising that is false and meant to mislead potential customers. It is illegal. An insurer exaggerating its dividends in an online advertisement is an example of false advertising. Examples of false advertising include:

- Misrepresenting the terms of the policy
- Persuading an insured to cancel an existing policy with incorrect details of the new policy
- Selling off an insurance policy as a stock share
- Advertiser telling prospective clients that the Insurance Guaranty Association's existence guarantees their policies

When advertising, an insurer must use its *true corporate* name.

2. Rebating

Rebating is the illegal act of offering "something of value" that is not specified in the insurance policy as an inducement to buy insurance. In The District, something of value is considered worth more than $10(ten dollars). Rebating does not include brochures, educational, or promotional materials that cost less than $10. An example of rebating would be a producer sharing their commission with an applicant as an incentive to purchase insurance.

No one may donate, sell, buy, or offer as an inducement to purchase a policy or contract, either directly or indirectly:

- An insurance company's stock, bonds, or other securities, as well as those of other corporations, associations, or partnerships
- Dividends or profits that have accumulated or will accrue
- Anything of value that is not stated in the contract

3. Misrepresentation

Misrepresentation means a false statement. The false statement could be a statement on an application made by an applicant or a statement made by a producer. Remember that a producer telling a client that an insurance policy is like a stock share is false and considered a misrepresentation. Insurance policies can never and should never be regarded as shares of a stock.

4. Defamation

Defamation is any false written or oral statement(s) intended to harm anyone (including a producer or insurance company) involved in the insurance business.
Defamation is also any malicious, false information or statement about the financial condition of any company or person.

5. Discrimination

Unfair discrimination occurs when two people of the same risk class are charged different rates solely due to differences in race, ethnicity, religion, sexual orientation, national origin, or where they live. Insurance companies can discriminate against people with high risks (ex, poor physical health). They reject them or charge a higher premium, particularly for poor health conditions.

6. Twisting

Twisting is inducing or attempting to influence a policy owner to cancel an existing life insurance policy for another similar or worse policy by misrepresentations or incomplete comparisons of the pros and cons of the two policies.

7. Penalties

A fine of $5,000, one year of imprisonment, or both are the maximum penalties for obtaining consumer reports under pretenses.
Information gathered by consumer reporting organizations, including credit bureaus, companies that provide medical information, and tenant screening services, is protected by the Fair Credit Reporting Act (FCRA). Credit reporting agencies MUST only provide information in a consumer report to people who have a purpose specified in the FCRA.
Engaging in an unfair trade practice is illegal in The District of Columbia.
The penalties for engaging in unfair trade practices are:

- A cease-and-desist order could be issued by the commissioner.
- The commissioner may issue a fine of up to $1,000 for each violation if the producer does not comply with the *cease-and-desist* order.
- The commissioner may suspend, revoke, or decline to renew the producer's license.
- The attorney general may prosecute the violator in the Superior Court of The District.

The commissioner has the authority to suspend, revoke, or decline to renew a producer's licence in addition to or instead of imposing a civil penalty of no more than $5,000.

8. Unfair Claims

Below are some examples of unfair claims settlement practices:

- Providing false information about coverages or important details in insurance policies
- Not establishing and enforcing appropriate guidelines for the timely examination of claims
- Attempting to resolve claims using an application that was modified without the insured's knowledge or approval
- Refusing to pay claims without carrying out a rational inquiry utilizing all of the information at hand
- Refusing to provide a reason for denial of a claim
- Inability to settle claims in a timely manner
- Misrepresenting insurance policy provisions that affect a loss
- Failing to effectuate a fair, equitable, and prompt settlement of a claim

E. Fiduciary Capacity of Licensee

A fiduciary is a person who acts in an ethical or legal capacity and receives or manages money for another person. *Producers are considered fiduciaries*. Premiums collected by producers must be kept separate from other money in a trust account and forwarded to the insurer as soon as possible. Misappropriation of premiums, commingling premiums with personal funds, improperly withholding premiums, and not transmitting premiums to the insurer in a timely manner are all breaches of an agent's fiduciary responsibility.

Related Term:

- Commingling
  - Commingling is mixing the premiums intended for the insurer with the producer's money. An example of this could be depositing premium checks the client gave the producer into the producer's personal bank account.
  - Commingling premiums with personal funds are illegal.

F. AIDS Law

The District's AIDS Laws:

- Insurers are ONLY permitted to disclose AIDS test results to:
  - The proposed insured or their legal guardian
  - Anyone designated by the proposed insured or their legal guardian
    - Proposed insureds usually designate their primary care doctors
  - A court
- Insurers are permitted to contest a policy for ***three*** years after it has been issued, renewed, or amended if the insured intentionally did not disclose that they had AIDS at the time of application AND the insurer was not permitted to test for AIDs at the time of application, renewal or amendment.

- Washington, DC, prohibits insurers from asking about the sexual identity, sexual orientation, or sexual expression of an applicant.
    - Note: Insurers cannot use them to make underwriting decisions
- Insurance companies cannot decide to test a proposed insured for HIV/AIDs based on
    - Gender
    - Occupation
    - Beneficiary designations
    - Sexual orientation
    - Sexual expression
    - Sexual identity
    - Lifestyle
    - Living arrangements

G. Insurance Guaranty Associations

Policyholders and beneficiaries are protected from insurer insolvency (bankruptcy) by the Life and Health Insurance Guaranty Association. The Association requires all insurers doing business in The District to be members. It is not a choice but a requirement.

The association's responsibility will not go above the following:

- In no case will the association be responsible for more than $300,000 in total for any single individual
- The cost of health insurance is $100,000 in addition to any net cash surrender and withdrawal amounts.
- Annuity benefits of $300,000, including $100,000 in net cash surrender and withdrawal values
- $300,000 in life insurance death payouts and $100,000 in net cash surrender and withdrawal values

The following are NOT covered:

- A policy that the insurer does not guarantee and the policyholder, contract holder, or certificate holder assumes the risk
- Unless assumption certificates have been issued and delivered, any reinsurance policy or contract

District Of Columbia Laws, Rules, And Regulations Pertinent To LIFE Insurance Only.

A. Required Provisions

1. Grace Period

The amount of time after the premium is due before the policy lapses due to nonpayment is known as the grace period. The grace period varies depending on the frequency or mode of premium payment. **Test Alert: The grace period in this state is 30 days.**

Note: In The District, the maximum interest an insurer may charge on past-due premiums is 6% per year.

2. Reinstatement

Policyowners may reinstate their lapsed policy ***within three years*** after it expires by paying any outstanding premiums with interest, proving insurability, submitting a new application, and repaying any outstanding loans and interest.

*Remember this difference: Policyowners may reinstate their variable life insurance policy within **two years** of the policy lapse date.*

B. Other Provisions

1. Policy Loans

An insurance company may lend an amount equal to a policy's cash surrender value if the policy has been in force for at least three years.

Test Alert: An insurer's interest rate on a loan may not exceed 8% per year.

2. Benefits Protected from Creditors

The Spendthrift Clause forbids a beneficiary's creditors from claiming benefits before they are received. The spendthrift clause protects the beneficiary only when the insurer pays the benefits under a settlement option, and the proceeds are kept by the insurance company, not in the case of lump sum payment.

The spendthrift clause limits beneficiaries' right to assign(transfer) their stake in the policy.

C. Group Life

1. Termination Rights

When a group life insurance policy member leaves the group, they can convert their policy to a whole life policy without having to provide proof of insurability. For every five years under the

group plan, employees can easily convert to an individual insurance with the same coverage when the insurer cancels the master plan, fires the employee, or resigns.
Test Alert: ***An employee or group member who leaves their job has 31 days to convert their group life insurance to an individual policy.*** However, if the group sponsor terminates a group policy (the master plan), the participants/employees can ONLY convert it if they have been on the group plan for *at least five years*.

D. Annuities

Variable Annuities
Insurers measure the value of variable annuities in units rather than dollars. The more money you pay, the more units you'll get. Annuitization converts accumulation units to annuity units, and the income given depends on the annuity unit value. Pre-tax dollars fund a qualified annuity. After-tax dollars fund a non-qualified annuity.

More on Variable Annuity

- A life insurance license and a securities license (FINRA) are required to sell it. Producers licensed to sell variable annuities must follow both SEC and state insurance regulations because variable annuities are securities products.
- The insurer must put all variable annuity contract premiums and considerations into one or more separate accounts.
- No company can offer variable contracts until the commissioner certifies that its techniques are safe for the public, and the commissioner can revoke an insurer's license to do so
- The insurer must report any change in management to the Commissioner within **5 days.**
- There is no guaranteed benefit.
- Annuity payouts and cash values vary based on the investment performance of the separate account established by the contract owner
- The contract owner is the one who bears the investment risk and reaps the benefits of the assets they invest in
- While serving as a director of a firm, no one may get commissions on the company's business transactions
- DC requires the regular transfer of all deposited funds under the company's general accounting procedure
- The insurer must keep track of each net annuity consideration applied, as well as the increment and accumulated balance on a unit or dollar value basis, for each variable annuity contract

E. Variable Life Insurance

Variable life is a whole life policy with certain benefits (cash value, death benefits) that will vary based on the market performance of its underlying account (aka separate account). Variable Whole Life is the same as Variable Life.

Variable Life provides life-long protection with death benefits and fixed premiums. In addition, it builds up cash value. Unless it expires or is cancelled, this policy is in effect for the insured person's entire lifetime.

Because the policy owner assumes all investment risk and the policy's cash value is dependent on the performance of a designated equity index, such as the S&P 500, the cash value is not guaranteed.

F. Credit Life

Credit life insurance is a *decreasing term* life insurance owned by a creditor and exclusively benefits a creditor upon a borrower's death. The maximum death benefit is the amount remaining on the debt. The policy automatically expires the moment the borrower repays the debt.

More on Credit Insurance:

- Can be issued on a group or individual basis
- Two types
  - Credit Life and Credit accident and health
- Credit life
  - life insurance on the debtor
- Credit accident and health
  - disability insurance on the debtor
- The policy's owner and beneficiary is the creditor.
- The debtor(borrower) pays the premium
- Policies for 5 YEARS or longer are NOT subject to credit insurance regulations.
- The policy term can only continue for up to 15 days beyond the scheduled maturity(payoff) date.

G. Standard Nonforfeiture Law

The insured will be eligible for nonforfeiture benefits and cash surrender values after *three years* if they default on paying premiums.

Mandatory Provisions

- If the policy owner pays premiums for a full year and the insurer receives a petition no later than 60 days after the premium due date, it will only provide a paid-up nonforfeiture benefit if the insured defaults on a premium payment.
- If the policy owner pays premiums for a full year and the firm receives a petition no later than 60 days after the premium due date, it will only provide a paid-up nonforfeiture benefit if the insured defaults on a premium payment.
- If the insured for traditional insurance misses a premium payment after paying policy premiums for at least three years and if requested no later than sixty days after the premium due date, the business will pay a cash surrender value rather than a paid-up nonforfeiture value.
- If the policy owner surrenders the policy within 30 days of any policy anniversary, the insurer will pay the cash surrender value. If the policy is continued by the insurance company under a paid-up nonforfeiture benefit that became applicable after the policy has been in force for three years, the insurer will not pay the cash surrender value.
- The mortality table, interest rate, and method used to determine cash surrender values and paid-up nonforfeiture options must be described or shown in guaranteed policies allowing unscheduled benefits or premiums changes.

Helpful Resources

11. Email us at MinzoPass@MinzoPass.com.

12. Subscribe to our email list

13. Join our private Facebook group
https://www.facebook.com/groups/1513896509443066/

14. Visit our website www.MinzoPass.com

15. Our Instagram https://www.instagram.com/minzopass/

16. Become an affiliate and earn up to $3,000 every month
    https://www.minzopass.com/affiliate_users/sign_up

17. Listen to our Pass Your Life and Health Insurance Exam Podcast
    https://minzopass.podbean.com/

18. Our Youtube Channel https://www.youtube.com/@minzopass3325

19. Our TikTok Page https://www.tiktok.com/@minzopass_lifeinsurance

20. Washington DC Life Insurance Exam Content Outline
    https://tinyurl.com/DCExamOutline

Acknowledgements

All things work together for good to them that love God," says Romans 8:28. I have come this far only by the grace of God. First, I thank God for his unending grace and favor. Ultimately, it all worked together for my good only because of HIM.

Next, I would like to express my gratitude to my mother, Mrs. Edith Gongloe-Weh, for introducing me to the insurance industry during my teenage years. Back then, you would take me to your insurance meetings in Philadelphia, sometimes on snowy Saturdays. Although I was often bored at most of those meetings, I learned about the benefits of cash value life insurance and how the wealthy use it to create tax-free income for life at a very young age. I also witnessed individuals from different professional, ethnic, and educational backgrounds earn life-changing income as licensed insurance producers.

You always wanted to prepare me financially for the future, so despite never buying me a name brand (but why Payless and thrift stores? lol), you made a financially savvy decision by opening a permanent life insurance policy for me. Little did either of us know at the time that your actions would, years later, ignite a passion within me for the financial industry and lead to the publication of books. Mom, detailing your sacrifices for me would require an entire book. I couldn't have asked for a better mother.

I also want to thank Mr. Carl Logan, my first trainer and mentor in the insurance industry. Thanks for your excellent field training and showing me the right way to do this business. I owe most of my insurance knowledge and expertise to you.

Next, I want to thank the Minzo Pass Family for helping to make this training manual possible. We did it!!!

To my editor, Mr. Roland Dweh, thank you for your meticulous and helpful critiques and feedback. Your input helped to make this book worth reading.

Last but certainly not least, I thank my family for their patience and support. I acknowledge that I deliberately isolated myself for almost two years to focus on writing this book and that you felt ignored, so I want to say I am sorry. Cheers, there's no more book writing, at least for now.

About The Author

Dr. Beko Saye Mantein was born and raised in Liberia during the Liberian Civil War. Like most Liberian youth his age, he experienced the worst of the civil war. He spent a portion of his childhood in refugee camps in West Africa. Luckily for him, he immigrated to The United States of America at the age of sixteen. He graduated from Upper Darby High School and obtained his doctoral degree in pharmacy from Temple University.

Although he received his doctoral degree in pharmacy, Dr. Beko Mantein has always been an entrepreneur at heart. Therefore, shortly after graduating from pharmacy school, Dr. Mantein, in addition to working his regular pharmacist job, decided to pursue his passion by becoming a licensed Life and Health insurance agent with one of the largest insurance agencies in the country. After working for several years in the insurance industry on a part-time basis, Dr. Mantein finally decided to pursue his passion on a full-time basis a few years ago.

He is passionate about all things business and personal finance. For example, before immigrating to America, he started his first business at the tender age of ten and his first business partnership at age fourteen. He is also passionate about using the free-market system to help lift his fellow Liberians out of poverty by creating jobs. He feels that you must look back down when you reach the top and help pull as many people up as possible. For example, during the ebola crisis in Liberia in 2014, he organized and raised about $50,000 worth of medical equipment and supplies for rural healthcare facilities in Nimba County, Liberia.

Dr. Beko Saye Mantein is a serial entrepreneur, podcaster, pharmacist, author, and philanthropist. He is a licensed life and health insurance agent in many states and has dozens of agents working with him in several states. In addition to doing his insurance business, he is also the founder of Minzo, a company whose express goal is to create at least 150,000 well-paying jobs for Liberian youth by the year 2034.

www.ingramcontent.com/pod-product-compliance
Lightning Source LLC
LaVergne TN
LVHW080023210926
848481LV00011B/3095